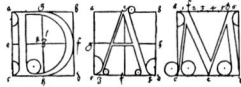

D.A.M Jahrbuch 2004

Architektur in Deutschland
Architecture in Germany

Thematischer Schwerpunkt: Rekonstruktion – alles bleibt anders
Key Topic: Reconstruction – plus ça change …

Herausgegeben von Edited by
Deutsches Architektur Museum, Frankfurt am Main
Ingeborg Flagge, Annina Götz

Mit Beiträgen von With contributions from
Harald Bodenschatz, Paul Kahlfeldt, Wolfgang Pehnt, Inge Wolf

Mit Baukritiken von And reviews by
Hubertus Adam, Olaf Bartels, Dieter Bartetzko, Christof Bodenbach,
Hans-Jürgen Breuning, Martina Düttmann, Kaye Geipel, Oliver G. Hamm,
Falk Jaeger, Gert Kähler, Ursula Kleefisch-Jobst, Niklas Maak,
Andreas Ruby, Ilka Ruby, Enrico Santifaller, Axel Simon, Rudolf Stegers,
Wolfgang Jean Stock, Christian Thomas

Prestel
München ▪ Berlin ▪ London ▪ New York

D.A.M **Deutsches Architektur Museum**
Frankfurt am Main

Inhalt
Contents

Vorwort
Foreword

■ Die Rekonstruktion geht um in Deutschland. Je weiter wir uns zeitlich von den Zerstörungen des Zweiten Weltkriegs und den ideologisch bedingten Sprengungen einiger Kriegsruinen entfernen, umso heftiger scheint die Sehnsucht nach einer Wiederherstellung des ehemaligen ›heilen‹ Zustands. Wo eine Rekonstruktion in Gänze nicht möglich ist, da soll wenigstens die Fassade die alten Verhältnisse spiegeln.

Solchen Rückgriff auf Vergangenes beobachtet man nicht nur in der Architektur. Auch in anderen Kulturbereichen wie zum Beispiel in der bildenden Kunst, Literatur, Musik sowie in Film und Theater spricht man von einem Neokonservatismus. Ermüden uns die ständigen Innovationen? Trauen wir der Zukunft so wenig, dass wir sie in der Vergangenheit suchen?

Unmittelbar vor der Fertigstellung der Frauenkirche in Dresden widmet sich das *DAM Jahrbuch 2004* dem Thema der Rekonstruktion und den damit verbundenen Fragen. Es möchte angesichts hitziger Debatten in den Fachkreisen und der Öffentlichkeit einen kleinen Beitrag zur Versachlichung der einem Glaubenskrieg ähnelnden Diskussion leisten.

Die überwältigende Spendenbereitschaft für den Wiederaufbau der Frauenkirche zeigt einmal mehr die Sehnsucht nach intakten Stadtbildern, zumindest jedoch das Bedürfnis nach einer Architektur der Erinnerung, die anders als die moderne Architektur nicht abstrakt, sondern in der Lage ist, positive Gefühle zu wecken. Dergleichen ist nicht neu, sondern reicht von der Rekonstruktion zerstörter Stadtbilder in den frühen fünfziger Jahren bis zu den postmodernen Bauten der siebziger, die die Vergangenheit allerdings eher zitierten als neu schufen. Wem ist eigentlich bewusst, dass auch der Barcelona Pavillon von Ludwig Mies van der Rohe eine Rekonstruktion ist – allerdings wohl die einzige eines modernen Baus. Aber gab es da nicht auch Bestrebungen, das Denkmal für Rosa Luxemburg wieder auferstehen zu lassen oder Mies' gläsernen Wolkenkratzer, der nie gebaut wurde, endlich zu realisieren?

Es gibt Architekten, für die die Geschichte keine Belastung darstellt und ihr Rückgriff auf die Vergangenheit ist entspannt und selbstverständlich. Andere allerdings sehen eine Marktlücke und stoßen hinein. Wieder andere sagen den neuerlichen Untergang der Moderne voraus, die selten so vielfältig war wie heute. Ein wenig Gelassenheit tut Not …

Auch die Verschiedenartigkeit der deutschen Rekonstruktionsprojekte zeigt, dass man der Frage nach dem angemessenen

■ Reconstruction is rife in Germany. With the passing years, wartime destruction and the subsequent ideologically motivated demolition of some bombed-out ruins recede ever further into the distance. At the same time, there is a growing nostalgia for the "good old days". If total reconstruction is not possible, then at the very least the facade should reflect the idyll of the past.

This return to the past is a phenomenon that is not restricted to architecture alone. In other cultural spheres, too, such as the fine arts, literature, music, film and theatre, there is talk of neo-conservatism. Are we tired of constant innovation? Do we have so little faith in the future that we now seek it in the past?

With the Frauenkirche in Dresden nearing completion, the *DAM Annual 2004* addresses the subject of reconstruction and the issues related to it. Given the heated debate that is now raging with the zealotry of a war of faith among professionals and specialists in the field, we hope to make a modest contribution towards bringing some objectivity into the discussion.

The overwhelming generosity with which donations have poured in for the reconstruction of the Frauenkirche indicates once again the yearning for an intact urban landscape. At the very least it shows the need for an architecture of remembrance that, unlike modern architecture, is not abstract, but capable of arousing positive feelings. This is not a new phenomenon, but one that can be traced from the reconstruction of ruined cityscapes in the early 1950s to the post-modernist buildings of the 1970s which tended to cite the past, however, rather than recreate it. How many people are actually aware of the fact that even Ludwig Mies van der Rohe's Barcelona Pavilion is a reconstruction – albeit probably the only reconstruction of a modern building? But was there not some talk of resurrecting the Memorial for Rosa Luxemburg, or of finally constructing Mies van der Rohe's unbuilt glass skyscraper?

There are architects who do not regard history as a burden and who take a relaxed, self-evident approach to the past. Others see it in terms of a market niche to be exploited. Still others predict the demise of modernism, which has rarely been as many-facetted as it is today. A more casual approach is needed....

The sheer variety of German reconstruction projects is in itself an indication that there is no simple solution to the question of how to handle ruined or demolished architecture. The case of the Berlin palace cannot be directly compared with that of the Brunswick Palace. The same is true of the Frauenkirche in Dresden, the Hotel

Umgang mit zerstörter oder abgerissener Architektur mit einer pauschalen Antwort nicht gerecht wird. Der Fall des Berliner Stadtschlosses ist sicherlich nicht mit dem des Braunschweiger Schlosses zu vergleichen. Gleiches gilt für die Dresdner Frauenkirche, das Hotel Adlon und die Schinkel'sche Bauakademie in Berlin, das Stadtschloss und die Garnisonkirche in Potsdam, das Rathaus in Halle, die Stadtbibliothek und das Palais Thurn und Taxis in Frankfurt am Main sowie viele andere Projekte. Die Motivationen für ihren Wiederaufbau sind vielfältig und verlangen im Einzelfall eine kritische Abwägung.

Der Architekturhistoriker Wolfgang Pehnt und der Architekt Paul Kahlfeldt widmen sich dem Thema und seinem Für und Wider in ihren Beiträgen für dieses Jahrbuch. Ausgehend von ihren unterschiedlichen Perspektiven gelangen sie zu divergenten Einschätzungen. Harald Bodenschatz beschäftigt sich als Stadtsoziologe in seinen Ausführungen mit dem Phänomen des Retro-Trends und bezieht neben der Rekonstruktion auch andere rückwärts gewandte architektonische und städtebauliche Bewegungen mit ein. Er wirft den Blick dabei auch über die deutschen Grenzen hinweg.

In ihrem Beitrag aus dem Archiv des DAM geht Inge Wolf auf die Stadtreparatur am Frankfurter Römerberg ein, die in den achtziger Jahren mit drei eigenständigen Elementen – der Rekonstruktion der Fachwerkbauten zum Römer, der postmodernen Schirn Kunsthalle und der Wohnbebauung an der Saalgasse – auf die Zerstörung im Stadtbild antwortete. Besondere Beachtung findet in ihren Darlegungen das Saalgassen-Projekt von Adolfo Natalini/Superstudio, dessen Entwurfsprozess in wunderbaren Zeichnungen aus dem Archivbestand des DAM dokumentiert ist.

Im Projektteil des Jahrbuchs werden drei kürzlich fertig gestellte Gebäude präsentiert, deren Fassaden (teil-)rekonstruiert wurden. Die gewählten Beispiele zeigen abweichende architektonische Ansätze bei der Bearbeitung dieser Bauaufgabe. So werden Unterschiede in der Form der baulichen Integration der rekonstruierten Gebäudeteile und im Grad der Abstraktion der historischen Vorbilder offensichtlich.

In 15 weiteren Projekten spiegelt sich das hohe Niveau des aktuellen deutschen Baugeschehens wider. Am Schluss steht mit der Erweiterung der Nikolaischule in Leipzig von schulz & schulz, ein Entwurf, der sich gegen die originalgetreue Rekonstruktion eines zerstörten Gebäudeteils entschieden hat und exemplarisch eine alternative Auseinandersetzung mit verlorener Baumasse aufzeigt.

Bei der Neuplanung und im Wiederaufbau – alles bleibt anders.

Ingeborg Flagge & Annina Götz

Adlon and Schinkel's Bauakademie in Berlin, the palace and the Garnisonkirche in Potsdam, the town hall in Halle, the municipal library and the Palais Thurn & Taxis in Frankfurt/Main, to name but a few. The motivating factors behind their reconstruction are many and varied. Each case deserves to be considered on its own merits.

Architectural historian Wolfgang Pehnt and architect Paul Kahlfeldt have taken this issue on board and present the pros and cons in their essays for this publication. From their own very different points of view, they arrive at different conclusions. Urban sociologist Harald Bodenschatz looks at the phenomenon of the retro trend and includes not only reconstruction in his contribution, but also other retrospective architectural and urban movements. In doing so, he also casts a glance beyond the borders of Germany.

In her essay based on the DAM archives, Inge Wolf takes a look at the post-war urban development of Frankfurt's Römerberg, which in the 1980s saw the reconstruction of the mediaeval half-timbered houses facing the Römer city hall, the post-modernist Schirn Kunsthalle and the new apartment buildings on Saalgasse as three discrete responses to the destruction of the old town. She focuses especially on the Saalgasse project by Adolfo Natalini/Superstudio, whose design process is documented in a wonderful collection of drawings held by the DAM archives.

The projects section of the Annual presents three recently completed buildings whose facades have been (partly) reconstructed. The examples selected show the divergent approaches taken in the realisation of each project, highlighting different ways of architecturally integrating the reconstructed parts of each building and the degree of abstraction that can be applied to historic models.

Fifteen further projects are also showcased that reflect the high standards of current German architecture. Finally, with the extension of the Nikolaischule in Leipzig by schulz & schulz, we present a design that goes against the grain of faithfully reconstructing what has been destroyed and shows an exemplary alternative approach to lost architecture.

In new planning and in reconstruction – plus ça change....

Ingeborg Flagge & Annina Götz

Amnesie statt Anamnese
Amnesia in Place of Anamnesis

Wolfgang Pehnt

Über Rekonstruktion, Reproduktion, Remakes und Retro-Kultur

On Reconstruction, Reproduction, Remakes and Retro

■ Auf vielen Gebieten ist Rekonstruktion eine hilfreiche Technik. Sie hilft die Vergangenheit aufzuklären und die Gegenwart zu bewältigen. Die Kriminalistik rekonstruiert den Hergang von Verbrechen, um Tätern auf die Spur zu kommen und neue Delikte zu verhüten. Die Rekonstruktion von Krankengeschichten, die Anamnese, soll zur angemessenen Therapie führen. In der Psychoanalyse ist die Rekonstruktion früherer Traumata und Konflikte schon die Therapie selbst. Nur in der Architektur scheint Rekonstruktion zumindest heute eher mit Amnesie, Gedächtnisstörung, als mit Anamnese, Erinnerung, zu tun zu haben.

Rekonstruiert wird vorwiegend in Krisensituationen: im Verbrechensfall, bei schwer therapierbarer Krankheit, bei psychischer Störung. Die Krise, die zu einer Vielzahl architektonischer Rekon-

In many areas, reconstruction is a useful technique. It helps to clarify the past and come to terms with the present. Forensic science reconstructs the way a crime was committed in order to track down criminals and prevent further crimes. Medical science reconstructs case histories (anamnesis) in order to determine the appropriate course of treatment. Psychoanalysis reconstructs past trauma and conflict as an integral part of the therapy itself. Only architecture appears to have more in common with amnesia than anamnesis, with loss of memory than with its recovery.

Reconstruction is primarily applied in crisis situations: in the case of a crime, a serious illness, a psychological problem. The crisis that led to many of Germany's architectural reconstructions was the catastrophe of the Second World War. The entire country lay in ruins, and the population was struggling to eke out a living. One of the most remarkable achievements of that post-war period was the bid to save historic buildings at a time when people were still sheltering in cellars and shanties. As early as 1945, there was an attempt to save the Zwinger in Dresden, and work on Semper's Opera began just one year later. There was a profoundly therapeutic message in the reconstruction of these buildings. It was this: there is still something that is even older than your survivors, something that will stand and last even if everything changes. It was the greatest comfort that architecture could possibly have provided in such a situation.

The post-war reconstructions that are now etched in the collective memory were not literal copies. The present left its traces. In the reconstruction of churches, especially, poverty and necessity were the mothers of some highly original inventions. Cologne's Romanesque churches were re-erected with pared-down, almost abstract interiors, creating spaces that have yet to find the deserved degree of recognition as being worthy of conservation in their own right. In the case of the Paulskirche in Frankfurt, the municipal authorities and the state created a place of assembly whose sober, sacred atmosphere has sustained the memory of the burned-out shell of its round walls.

In recent years, too, there have been examples where simply restoring the old building has not been the sole aim. While there are those who may dismiss Josef Paul Kleihues' twin villas on Berlin's Pariser Platz as bloodless and ghostlike, they do uphold the memory of their predecessors without allowing them to be confused with the lost originals. Nicola Fortmann-Drühes dou-

St. Gereon während des Wiederaufbaus, Köln, Deutschland, errichtet im 4.–13. Jahrhundert, Wiederaufbau bis 1979 durch Leo Hugot
St. Gereon under reconstruction, Cologne, Germany. Built in the fourth to thirteenth centuries, reconstruction by Leo Hugot completed in 1979

Kronentor im Zwinger, Dresden, Deutschland, errichtet 1711–1728 durch Matthäus Daniel Pöppelmann, Wiederaufbau 1945–1964
The Kronentor ("Crown Gate") of the Zwinger in Dresden, Germany, 1711–1728, by Matthäus Daniel Pöppelmann, reconstruction 1945–1964

struktionen in Deutschland führte, war die Katastrophe des Zweiten Weltkriegs: das ganze Land eine Trümmerwüste, die Bevölkerung mit den Anstrengungen des Überlebens ausgelastet. Dass die ersten Sicherungsmaßnahmen an historischer Bausubstanz unternommen wurden, während die Menschen ihr Dasein noch in Kellern und Behelfsheimen fristeten, gehört zu den erstaunlichen Leistungen jener Jahre. Rettungsversuche am Dresdner Zwinger wurden schon 1945 eingeleitet, an Sempers Opernhaus ein Jahr später. Die wiederhergestellten Bauten hatten eine durchaus therapeutische Botschaft. Sie besagte: Es ist noch etwas da, das älter ist als ihr Überlebenden, das weiterdauern und euch zur Seite stehen wird, auch wenn sich alles verändert. Es war der beste Trost, den Architektur in dieser Lage spenden konnte.

Die Wiederaufbauten aus der Nachkriegszeit, die sich dem Gedächtnis eingeprägt haben, waren keine buchstabengetreuen

bled-leafed paraphrase of the Palladian Kahle'sches Haus on Potsdam's Neuer Markt (see also pp. 36–41) provides an intelligent solution to the problem of reconstructing something while at the same time clearly indicating that it is not the original.

Generally speaking, however, reconstruction took a new direction in the late 1970s. The euphoria of seemingly boundless progress had come to end, but the pace of change did not slow. The pressure to modernise continued, and globalisation suppressed individuality. The fact that everything, everywhere, looks the same, became one of the inadequacies caused by modernism. Old fears were fuelled again.

After the frugality of the 1950s, the brutality of the 1960s and the urban blight that continued well into the 1970s, a new architecture of simulation was welcomed from the West German Römerberg square in Frankfurt to the East German Nikolaiviertel in Berlin.

Häuser Liebermann und Sommer, Berlin, Deutschland, errichtet 1845 durch Friedrich August Stüler, freie Rekonstruktion 1995–1999 durch Josef Paul Kleihues
Liebermann and Sommer Houses, Berlin, Germany, 1845, by Friedrich August Stüler, free reconstruction 1995–1999 by Josef Paul Kleihues

Kopien. Die Gegenwart hinterließ ihre Spuren. Vor allem bei der Rekonstruktion von Kirchen gelangen in Not und Armut originelle Leistungen. Die romanischen Kirchen Kölns wurden mit purgierten, fast abstrakten Interieurs errichtet. Raumschöpfungen, die von den Denkmalpflegern bis heute nicht hinreichend als schützenswerte Zustände eigenen Ranges erkannt worden sind. Mit der Frankfurter Paulskirche schufen Stadt und Staat ein Versammlungshaus, dessen heilige Nüchternheit die Erinnerung an das ausgebrannte Mauerrund bewahrte.

Auch in unseren Jahren sind Beispiele realisiert worden, bei denen die Rückgewinnung des Alten nicht das einzige Ziel war. Man mag Josef Paul Kleihues' Palais-Zwillinge am Pariser Platz in Berlin blutleer und geisterhaft schelten. Immerhin halten sie die Erinnerung an ihre Vorgänger wach, ohne eine Verwechslung mit den verlorenen Originalen zu riskieren. Nicola Fortmann-Drühes doppelschalige Paraphrase des palladianischen Kahle'schen Hauses am Potsdamer Neuen Markt (siehe auch S. 36–41) ist eine intelligente Lösung des Problems, etwas wiederherzustellen und gleichzeitig zu verdeutlichen, dass es nicht die Sache selbst ist.

Aber generell nahm das Rekonstruktionswesen in den späten siebziger Jahren eine andere Wendung. Die Euphorie unbegrenzten Fortschritts hatte ein Ende gefunden, doch das Tempo der Veränderungen hielt an. Die Modernisierungszwänge ließen nicht nach, die

It is interesting to note which buildings are reconstructed and which are earmarked for reconstruction: it is always the prestigious structures, widely regarded as beautiful, the decorative outward signs of a now defunct power, such as the churches and palaces, patrician villas and city gates, the palaces of Brunswick and Potsdam. The Berlin Palace, yes – but not the Berlin Wall; and when it comes to the Berlin Palace, then it is a question of restoring the magnificent baroque facades at the Lustgarten, the Kupfergraben and the former Schlossplatz – but not the huddle of gloomy mediaeval and renaissance remains that straggled along the bank of the Spree until Walter Ulbricht had them demolished.

Notions of reconstruction are influenced by the images in the mind's eye. Eduard Gaertner's panorama of Biedermeier Berlin from the roof of the Friedrichswerder Church; Canaletto's magical view of the River Elbe and baroque Dresden: that is how things should be again. One might think that the nostalgia of the reconstructors would call for caution in dealing with what actually remained. But the opposite was true. Wherever memorials are readily available, there is an increasing willingness to do whatever we want with them: get rid of them or highlight them. There is no longer any sense of loss. After all, what is lost need not be lost for ever. We can always bring it back again if we want.

Some sites have already come full circle: demolition, replacement, reconstruction. In Hildesheim, on the spot where the mediaeval Knochenhaueramt (Guild of Butchers) stood until 1945, and where Dieter Oesterlen built the Hotel Rose after the war (admittedly, he did build better things), the magnificent half-timbered building now stands again as though nothing had ever happened. In

Kahle'sches Haus, Potsdam, Deutschland, errichtet 1755 durch Johann Gottfried Büring, freie Rekonstruktion 2001/02 durch Nicola Fortmann-Drühe
Kahle'sches Haus, Potsdam, Germany, 1755, by Johann Gottfried Büring, free reconstruction 2001– 02 by Nicola Fortmann-Drühe

Globalisierung unterdrückte das Partikulare. Dass alles überall gleich aussieht, gehörte zum Ungenügen, das die Moderne verursacht hatte. Jetzt erhielten die alten Ängste neue Nahrung.

Nach der Frugalität der fünfziger Jahre, der Brutalität der sechziger und den Stadtzerstörungen bis in die siebziger Jahre kam eine neue Simulationsarchitektur gerade recht, vom Frankfurter Römerberg (BRD; siehe S. 176–183) bis zum Berliner Nikolaiviertel (DDR).

Aufschlussreich ist, was rekonstruiert wird und werden soll: immer das Repräsentative, landläufig Schöne, die ungefährlich gewordenen Dekorationen der Macht, die Kirchen und Paläste, Patrizierhäuser und Stadttore, die Schlösser in Braunschweig und Potsdam. Das Berliner Schloss, aber nicht die Berliner Mauer. Und wenn das Berliner Schloss: dann die prächtigen Barockfassaden an Lustgarten, Kupfergraben und ehemaligem Schlossplatz, aber nicht die unordentlich-finsteren Reste aus Mittelalter und Renaissance, die sich bis zu Walter Ulbrichts Sprengaktion entlang der Spree reihten.

Gesteuert werden die Wiederherstellungswünsche von den Veduten im Kopf. Eduard Gaertners Panoramablick vom Dach der Friedrichswerderschen Kirche über das biedermeierliche Berlin oder Canalettos zauberhafter Elbeblick auf das barocke Dresden: genauso sollte es wieder sein. Man hätte denken können, dass die Nostalgie der Rekonstrukteure zur Vorsicht im Umgang mit dem, was tatsächlich noch erhalten war, nötigte. Das Gegenteil war der Fall. Wo Denkmäler beliebig verfügbar werden, wächst auch die Bereitschaft, mit ihnen nach Belieben umzuspringen, sie je nach Opportunität abzuräumen oder hervorzuholen. Eine Empfindung von Verlust stellt sich nicht mehr ein. Was verloren geht, muss ja nicht für immer verloren sein. Falls gewünscht, zaubern wir es wieder herbei.

Manche Grundstücke durchliefen bereits den ganzen Zyklus von Abbruch, Ersatz und Wiedergewinnung. Wo das Hildesheimer Knochenhaueramtshaus bis 1945 stand und Dieter Oesterlen nach dem Krieg das Hotel Rose errichtete (zugegeben, er hat Besseres gebaut), prangt wieder, als wäre nichts geschehen, der gewaltige Fachwerkbau. In Moskau wurde die Christi-Erlöser-Kathedrale zugunsten des projektierten Sowjetpalasts gesprengt. An dem Ort entstand dann ein Schwimmbad, das nach dem Ende der UdSSR wieder einer Replik der Erlöserkirche wich. Kleinere Unterbrechungen der materiellen Existenz zählen da schon nicht mehr. Dass in Berlin das ausgebrannte Kronprinzenpalais Unter den Linden niedergelegt wurde, damit Baufreiheit für das Gebäude des DDR-Außenministeriums entstand, das nun auch schon wieder verschwunden ist, während das kleine Palais wiedererstand, wen schert es noch?

Mit der Fähigkeit und dem Kapital, ansprechende Faksimiles zu erzeugen, verwandelte sich das gesamte historische Erbe in Verfügungsmasse. Abbruch und Retrospektion gingen zusammen. Bei den großen Freiluft-Ausstellungen des 19. und 20. Jahrhunderts bis hin zu den Weltausstellungen von 1958 und 1967 stellten die Nostalgie-Abteilungen stets besondere Attraktionen dar. Vieux Paris, Alt-Berlin, Oud-Antwerpen, Old Chicago, La Belgique Joyeuse oder Vieux Québec bildeten ab, was ein paar Kilometer entfernt, in den alten Stadtkernen, eben noch existierte oder gerade der Modernisierung zum Opfer fiel. Oft wurden ein paar aus dem Abbruchmaterial gerettete Spolien dem Schwindel aus Stuck und Leinwand einmontiert.

Nikolaiviertel, Berlin, Deutschland, freie Rekonstruktion 1979–1987 durch das VEB BMK Ingenieurhochbau Berlin/Günter Stahn
Nikolaiviertel, Berlin, Germany, free reconstruction 1979–1987 by VEB BMK Ingenieurhochbau Berlin/Günter Stahn

Moscow, the Cathedral of Christ the Redeemer was initially demolished to build the planned Palace of the Soviets. Then a swimming pool was built there. Finally, after the end of the Soviet Union, a replica of the Church of the Redeemer was constructed on the site. Temporary interruptions in the material existence of a building no longer seem to count for much. Who cares that the burned-out shell of the Kronprinzenpalais on Berlin's boulevard of Unter den Linden was razed to make room for the East German Foreign Office, which no longer exists, and that the little palace has now been built again?

The technical and financial capacity to create pleasing facsimiles completely transformed attitudes to architectural heritage, making historical buildings readily available. Demolition and retrospection went hand in hand. In the huge open-air exhibitions of the nineteenth and twentieth centuries, up to and including the World Expos of 1958 and 1967, displays of architectural nostalgia were always real crowd-pullers. Vieux Paris, Alt-Berlin, Oud-Antwerpen, Old Chicago, La Belgique Joyeuse or Vieux Québec reproduced what still existed – or was already in the throes of modernisation – in the historic centres just a few miles away. As often as not, a few spoils salvaged from the demolition sites were even included in the plaster and canvas remakes.

Elsewhere, demolished and reconstructed districts coexist. "Islands of tradition" was the treacherous phrase used as an alibi for urban destruction. In Berlin during the GDR era, the remains of the historic Cölln on the Fischerinsel were razed and replaced by six high-rises. But on the opposite bank, the Märkisches Ufer, a row of typical Biedermeier Berlin buildings offers some small consolation. Division of labour is the name of the game: on the one hand a demolition crew, and on the other a building contractor creating a surrogate of what has been lost. It is a perfect example of the "schizophrenia of cultural memory".[1]

Such invocations of times past are by no means restricted to buildings that actually existed. Charles Rennie Mackintosh's House

Anderswo koexistieren zerstörte und rekonstruierte Quartiere dauerhaft nebeneinander. Traditionsinseln, wie der verräterische Ausdruck lautete, gaben das Alibi für Stadtzerstörungen ab. In Berlin wurden zu DDR-Zeiten die Reste des historischen Cölln auf der Fischerinsel niedergelegt und durch sechs Punkthochhäuser ersetzt. Aber gegenüber, am Märkischen Ufer, bietet sich eine Zeile biedermeierlichen Berlins als versöhnliche Kompensation dar. Die Arbeitsteilung hat sich eingespielt. Hier reißen die einen ab, dort stellen die anderen das Surrogat des Verlorenen wieder her. Die »erinnerungskulturelle Schizophrenie«[1] ist perfekt.

Wiederbeschwörungen beschränken sich keineswegs auf das, was einmal war. Imitiert wird auch, was noch gar nicht bestanden hat. Das Haus eines Kunstfreundes von Charles Rennie Mackintosh fristete neunzig Jahre lang sein Dasein auf elf Lithografien. Jetzt steht es lebensgroß in Glasgow. Die Angebote aus dem ungebauten Vorrat der Historie sind unbegrenzt und reichen von Palladios *Quattro Libri*, aus denen sich schon Friedrich der Große bediente, bis zu Frank Lloyd Wrights *Unbuilt Designs.* In Xanten ist über ausgegrabenen Fundamenten der Colonia Ulpia Traiana ein komplettes Römerlager zu besichtigen. Das Stichwort heißt experimentelle Archäologie. Rekonstruiert wird nicht aus gesichertem Wissen, sondern als Probe, ob es so gewesen sein könnte. In Dortmund wurde der mittelalterliche Adlerturm aus einem Stich des 17. Jahrhunderts vergrößert, auf dem er zwei Zentimeter maß. Und so geht es fort.

Da ein entscheidendes Merkmal authentischen Bestands, die Identität des Standorts, kaum noch eine Rolle spielt, ist der Übergang zu ortlosem Retro-Design fließend. Die ›klassizistischen‹ Stadtvillen, die Hans Kollhoff sowie Paul und Petra Kahlfeldt in Berlin-Dahlem beziehungsweise an der Hamburger Elbchaussee errichten, komplett mit Zahnschnittfries, Thermenfenster oder Pfeilergang, unterscheiden sich auf der Skala der Fiktionalität nur um wenige Grad von den vorgeblichen Wiederherstellungen. Solches Wiedergängertum erhält nicht Denkmäler der Geschichte, sondern erzeugt Dokumente der Geschichtslosigkeit. Allenfalls illustrieren sie, wie etwas ausgesehen hat oder haben könnte. Aber sie vermitteln nicht die Gewissheit der Kontinuität, die von der Wiederherstellung realer Ruinen nach dem Krieg ausging. Stattdessen verbreiten sie Ungewissheit und Zweifel auch über alles, was in materiell überlieferter Gestalt aus alten Zeiten auf uns gekommen ist. Wo vieles geschwindelt ist, kann alles geschwindelt sein.

Zur Rechtfertigung solcher Schattenbeschwörungen wird der Plan des Baumeisters gern mit der Partitur des Komponisten verglichen. Die Partitur enthält das Kunstwerk, die jeweilige Aufführung ist seine zufällige und vorübergehende Aktualisierung. Am Realitätscharakter von Architektur geht dieser Vergleich völlig vorbei. Nicht Pläne machen die Wirklichkeit des Bauwerks aus, sondern seine dreidimensionale Realität, die Mühe der Umsetzung, die Wunden, Reparaturen, Ergänzungen, Veränderungen, Erweiterungen, die der Bau im Laufe seiner Existenz erfahren hat. Die Metamorphosen seiner Nachbarschaft. Die alltäglichen Lebensgeschichten und die historischen Ereignisse, die sich an ihn banden. Kann man die Oberfläche eines Plans erleben wie die gekörnte Oberfläche des Steins, die gemaserte des Holzes, die Kühle des Stahls? Es bedarf der ganzen Gedanken-

for an Art Lover spent ninety years on the drawing board in the form of eleven lithographs. Now it is a life-size building in Glasgow. There is a rich and unlimited supply of historical designs, from Palladio's *Quattro Libri* – which Frederick the Great used – to Frank Lloyd Wright's *Unbuilt Designs.* In Xanten, a complete Roman camp can be seen over the excavated foundations of Colonia Ulpia Traiana. This goes by the name of experimental archaeology. Reconstruction is not undertaken on the basis of proven evidence, but as an experiment to see whether it might have been like this. In Dortmund, the mediaeval Adlerturm ("Eagle Tower") was magnified from a seventeenth-century engraving on which it measured just two centimetres. The list is endless.

Since one crucial characteristic of authenticity – the identity of the site – no longer plays an important role, there is a smooth transition to placeless retro-design. The neo-classical town houses built by Hans Kollhoff and by Paul and Petra Kahlfeldt in Berlin-Dahlem and on the Elbchaussee in Hamburg – complete with dentils, Diocletian windows and pillared hall – differ only marginally on the scale of fictionality from supposed reconstructions. Such recourse does not conserve the monuments of history, but generates documents of non-history. At best, they illustrate how something looked

Colonia Ulpia Traiana, Xanten, Deutschland, errichtet im 1.– 4. Jahrhundert n. Chr., Ausgrabungen und Teilrekonstruktionen seit 1972 durch den Landschaftsverband Rheinland/Gundolf Precht. Herberge und Badehaus
Colonia Ulpia Traiana, Xanten, Germany, first to fourth centuries AD, excavation and partial reconstruction since 1972 by Landschaftsverband Rheinland/Gundolf Precht. Hostelry and bath-house

or might have looked. But they do not convey the certainty of continuity that emanated from the reconstruction of real ruins after the war. Instead, they disseminate uncertainty and doubt about everything that has been handed down to us from past times. Where so many things are fake, anything and everything could be fake.

In defence of such dubiety, the architect's plan is often compared to the composer's score. The score contains the work of art, and the performance is its arbitrary and temporary execution in the present. Such a comparison misses the point of the reality of architecture. It is not plans that constitute the reality of a building, but its three-dimensional reality, the effort of actually building it, the wounds, repairs and extensions made to it in the course of its existence, the metamorphoses of the neighbourhood, the everyday life stories and

Goethes Gartenhaus an der Ilm (rechts) und Duplikat (links), Weimar, Deutschland, 17. Jahrhundert und 1999
Goethe's garden house on the River Ilm (right) and duplicate (left), Weimar, Germany, seventeenth century and 1999

blässe unserer abstrahierenden Epoche, um einen Plan zum Eigentlichen der Architektur zu erklären.

Partituren kann man beliebig oft aufführen. Der missverständliche Vergleich mit den Plänen der Architektur hat zu absurden Folgen geführt. Das barocke Ephraim-Palais im Berliner Nikolaiviertel hätte es um ein Haar zweimal gegeben: in Westberlin, wo die ausgelagerten Bauteile verwahrt wurden und aufgebaut werden sollten, und in Ostberlin am Mühlendamm, wo das Palais einst gestanden hatte, wenn auch um ein paar Meter versetzt. Goethes Gartenhaus existierte während des Jahres 1999, als Weimar Kulturstadt Europas war, auf der Ilm-Wiese gleich zweimal. Das zweite Exemplar war dem Original in Sichtweite bis hin zur ausgetretenen Holzstufe getreulich nachgebildet.

Den Weimarer Kopisten kann man immerhin bescheinigen, das Verhältnis von Kopie und Original reflektiert zu haben. Auch das ursprüngliche Gartenhaus sah plötzlich so künstlich aus wie dessen Nachahmung schräg gegenüber. Vollends chimärisch wird es, wenn der Reisende auf einem Autobahnparkplatz im französischen Jura einer Umsetzung frei nach Claude-Nicolas Ledoux begegnet oder in China einem Double von Le Corbusiers Ronchamp. Von historischen Nachahmungen des Pantheon oder der Palladio-Villen in England und den USA unterscheiden sich solche Repliken durch den gänzlichen Mangel an intellektueller oder gestalterischer Auseinandersetzung mit dem Vorbild. Die Sache noch einmal im

the historic events that are linked with it. Is it possible to experience the surface of a plan the way we can experience the sandy surface of stone, the grain of wood, the coolness of steel? It takes all the insipid intellectualism of our era with its tendency towards abstraction to declare a plan the very essence of architecture.

A score can be performed any number of times. The misplaced comparison with architectural plans has spawned some absurd results. The baroque Ephraim-Palais in the Nikolaiviertel in Berlin was very nearly built twice: in West Berlin, where the structural components were stored and were meant to be erected, and in East Berlin at Mühlendamm, where the palace used to stand – albeit a few metres away. In 1999, when Weimar was the European City of Culture, there were two versions of Goethe's garden house on the Ilm-Wiese. The second one was faithfully reconstructed, right down to the worn wooden steps, within eyesight of the original.

If there is one thing that can be said for the Weimar copy-cats, it is this: that they gave some thought to the relation-ship between copy and original. Suddenly, even the original garden house looked every bit as artificial as the fake. Things get really spooky when travellers encounter a Claude-Nicolas Ledoux look-alike on a motorway car park in the French Jura, or a doppelgänger of Le Corbusier's Ronchamp in China. What distinguishes historic copies of the Pantheon or of Palladio's villas in England and the United States is their complete lack of intellectual or creative understanding of the

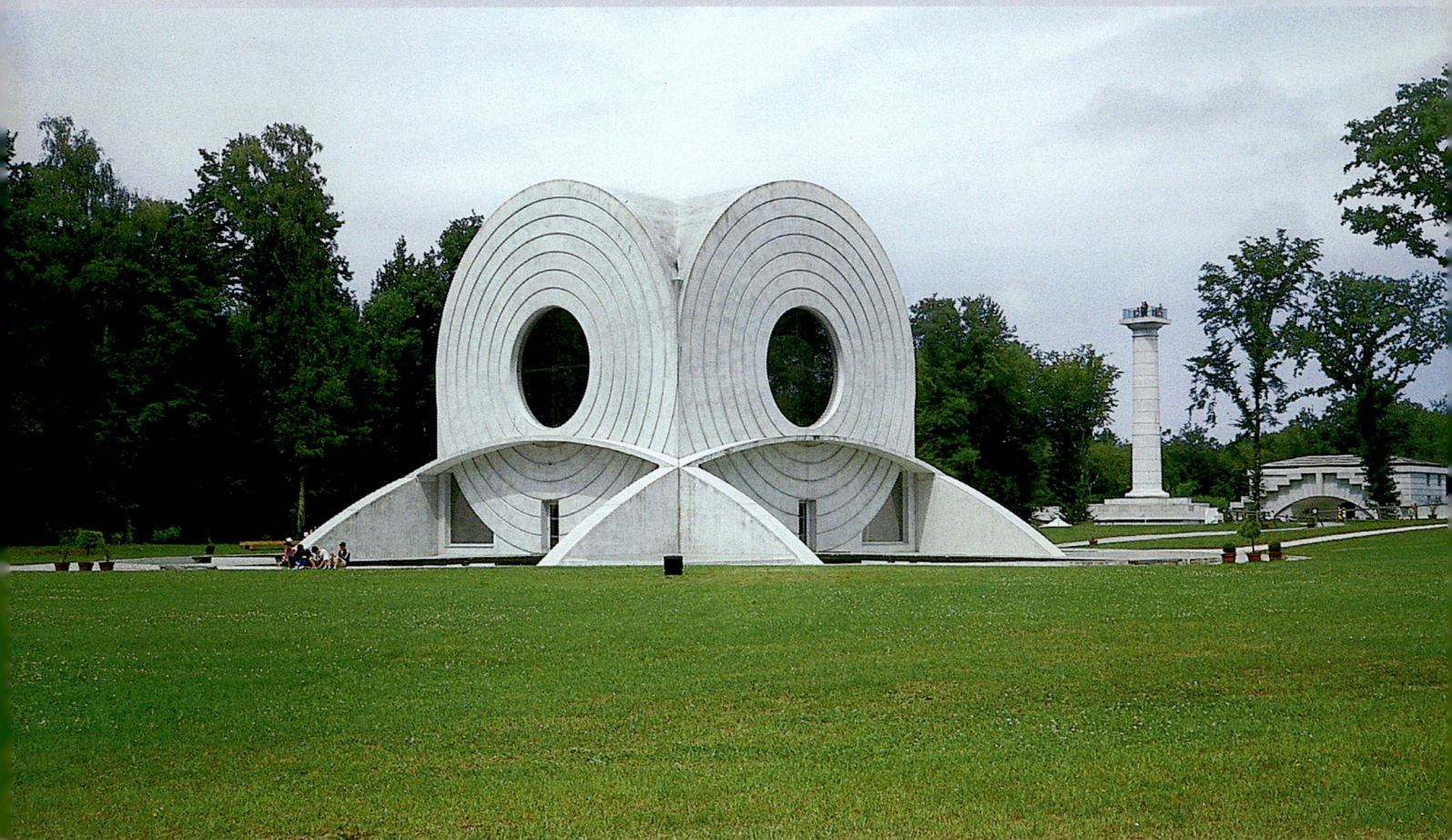

Atelier des Cercles von Claude-Nicolas Ledoux, publiziert 1804, freie Umsetzung in Aire du Jura, Frankreich, 2000 durch Jean Luc Grenard
Atelier des Cercles by Claude-Nicolas Ledoux, published 1804, free realisation in Aire du Jura, France, 2000 by Jean Luc Grenard

unvermuteten Kontext und zur unpassenden Zeit: Das ist der einzige Reiz.

Die heutigen Reanimateure in Deutschland beziehen sich auf die Praxis der Wiederaufbauzeit. Aber sie sollten nachlesen, welche Skrupel die Vätergeneration, auf die sie sich berufen, gekannt hat. Das Frankfurter Goethehaus wurde 1947–1951 am selben Ort wiedererrichtet, an dem es gestanden hatte. Vom Kellergewölbe bis zur Treppe wurden authentische Bestandteile verwendet. Die Datenlage war vorzüglich, noch vor dem großen Brand von 1944 war das Haus in allen Details aufgemessen worden. Die gesamte Inneneinrichtung war ausgelagert und erhalten. Niemand würde heute auch nur den Anflug eines Bedenkens äußern. Der Fall besaß alles, was eine Rekonstruktion rechtfertigt: derselbe Ort, die noch ganz und gar präsente Erinnerung der Zeitgenossen, die exzellente Datenüberlieferung, die wieder verwendeten Relikte, die dem Restrukt den Stempel der Glaubwürdigkeit geben. Aber wie ist über den Sinn dieser Wiederherstellung gestritten worden, in der Überzeugung auch der Befürworter, dass es sich hier nur um eine seltene Ausnahme handeln dürfe!

Noch vor der Einweihung des Goethehauses war die Neckarbrücke in Heidelberg ein Streitfall, der die Öffentlichkeit bewegte. Die Brücke über den Neckar, ein Meisterwerk des späten 18. Jahrhunderts, von Goethe und Hölderlin besungen, hatte das Kriegsschicksal ereilt. Drei ihrer neun Bögen waren von abrückenden deutschen

original. The only appeal that such copies have is their reiteration of the same architecture in an unexpected context and at an inappropriate time.

Today's revivalists in Germany look to the methods of the postwar reconstruction period. But they ought to read about the scruples of their fathers' generation of builders, to whom they refer. Goethe's house in Frankfurt was rebuilt in 1947–1951 on its original site. From the cellar vaulting to the stairs, the materials used were authentic components of the original house. The data available was impeccable, as the house had been surveyed and documented in minute detail before the great fire of 1944. The entire interior fittings had been put into storage and conserved. Nobody today would voice the slightest concern. It was a clear case of justified reconstruction: the same site, the reliable memory of contemporaries, the excellent data, the reusable relics – all of which gave the reconstruction the stamp of credibility. But what a debate it unleashed, with even those in favour of its reconstruction insisting that this should be and remain an exception!

Even before Goethe's house was completed, the Neckar Bridge in Heidelberg had become a bone of contention. A masterpiece of eighteenth-century engineering, the bridge that Goethe and Hölderlin had immortalised had been severely damaged in the war. Three of its nine arches had been blown up by the retreating German army. The reconstruction architect Rudolf Steinbach did not take his task

Alte Brücke, Heidelberg, Deutschland, errichtet 1786–1788, Wiederaufbau 1947 durch Rudolf Steinbach
Alte Brücke ("Old Bridge"), Heidelberg, Germany, 1786–1788, reconstruction 1947 by Rudolf Steinbach

Truppen gesprengt worden. Der Wiederaufbauarchitekt Rudolf Steinbach hat es sich nicht leicht gemacht. Rekonstruktion wollte er nur erlauben, wenn alle äußeren Bedingungen wie funktionale Notwendigkeit und genaueste Kenntnis des Baukunstwerks gegeben seien, wenn die alte handwerkliche Technik aufs Sorgfältigste angewendet werde und wesentliche originale Teile erhalten seien. »Nur was vom Bestande durchseelt werden kann, gewinnt den Geist und das Gesicht seiner Zeit.«[2] Der gewissenhafte Steinbach fürchtete, der Rekonstruktionsflut die Tore geöffnet zu haben. Nun drohe auch der Wiederaufbau des Goethehauses, des Stuttgarter Königsbaus, des Münchner Hofbräuhauses…

Von Steinbachs Skrupeln ist das heutige Rekonstruktionswesen weit entfernt. In der Medienwelt von heute erregt die Forderung nach Authentizität verständnislose Heiterkeit. Warnungen der Denkmalpfleger-Patriarchen, der Ruskin, Dehio, Riegl, Clemen, die sich über das Masken- und Gespensterwesen empörten, gelten als nicht mehr zitierfähig. Das Bauwerk, das nicht mehr lebendiges Zeugnis ist, sondern ein Produkt der Retro-Kultur, verschafft die Illusion, alles sei

lightly. He only wanted to allow a reconstruction if all the external conditions such as functional necessity and precise knowledge of the structure were assured, if the old techniques of craftsmanship were painstakingly applied and if the main original parts were still in existence. "Only that which can be brought alive by existing material can gain the spirit and face of its time".[2] The conscientious Rudolf Steinbach feared that the floodgates of reconstruction might be opened. Already, there was a threatened reconstruction of Goethe's house, the Stuttgart Königsbau, the Hofbräuhaus in Munich, and so on….

Reconstruction today is a far cry from such scruples. In the current media world, the call for authenticity tends to meet with bemusement. The warnings of such conservation patriarchs as Ruskin, Dehio, Riegl or Clemen, who disdained all that might smack of masquerade or ghosts, are quite unmentionable these days. A building that is no longer a living witness, but a product of retro culture, creates the illusion that everything has always remained as it has been and that sometimes it was even better. The majority

immer so gewesen, und manchmal sogar noch etwas schöner. Fraglos lauten so die Wünsche der Mehrheit. Am Ende steht die *Truman Show*, in der nur die fiktionale Welt existiert. Und niemand will sich mehr – wie am Schluss des gleichnamigen Films – den Kopf am Leinwandhorizont stoßen, der die ganze Fiktion umhüllte.

Doch sollte man wissen, was man tut, wenn man den Truman Shows von heute folgt. Reproduktionen dieser Art haben nichts mehr mit therapeutischer Rekonstruktion zu schaffen. Das, was die Zeit dem Denkmal angetan hat, bleibt ausgeklammert. Unsere eigenen Spuren, unsere eigene Patientengeschichten sind nicht mehr in diesen Fällen enthalten: Amnesie statt Anamnese. Solche Rekonstrukte haben mit Dekorationslust zu tun, mit dem Vergnügen an schönen Gegenständen, womöglich auch mit der Reparatur unbefriedigender Stadträume, mit dem Ungenügen der baulichen Manifestationen der Gegenwart, mit didaktischer Veranschaulichung durch das Modell im Maßstab 1:1. Nur mit dem, was Geschichte ist, mit ihrer Unwiederholbarkeit, ihrer Einmaligkeit, ihrer Fremdartigkeit, ihrer letztendlichen Unzugänglichkeit haben sie nichts zu tun.

undoubtedly wants it this way. What we end up with is the *Truman Show*, in which the fictional world is the only one that exists, and nobody wants to bump their head against the on-screen horizon surrounding the whole fiction, as happened at the end of the film.

But we ought to know what we are doing when we go down the path of today's *Truman Shows*. Reproductions of this kind have nothing whatsoever to do with therapeutic reconstruction. All that time has visited upon the historic structure is put aside. Our own traces, our own case histories, are no longer included in the equation: amnesia in place of anamnesis. Reconstructions of this kind have more to do with love of decoration, with pleasure in looking at beautiful objects, perhaps even with repairing unsatisfactory urban spaces, with making up for the shortcomings of contemporary architecture, with didactic presentations on a scale of 1:1. But they have nothing to do with what history is, nor with its irrevocability, its uniqueness, its otherness and ultimately, its inaccessibility.

1   Gottfried Korff, *Von der Leidenschaft des Bewahrens*, in: *Die Denkmalpflege*, 1994, 1, S. 39.
2   Rudolf Steinbach, *Die Alte Brücke in Heidelberg und die Problematik des Wiederaufbaus*, in: *Hefte für Baukunst und Werkform*, 1948, 2, S. 35.

1   Gottfried Korff, "Von der Leidenschaft des Bewahrens", in *Die Denkmalpflege*, 1994, 1, p. 39.
2   Rudolf Steinbach, "Die Alte Brücke in Heidelberg und die Problematik des Wiederaufbaus", in *Hefte für Baukunst und Werkform*, 1948, 2, p. 35.

Neue Schlösser
New Palaces

Paul Kahlfeldt

Nostalgische Nachahmungen oder erinnernde Neuschöpfungen

Nostalgic Reproductions or Evocative New Creations

■ Die gegenwärtig wieder intensiv und an vielen Orten in Deutschland geführte Diskussion und Prüfung, ob und wenn ja, wie nicht mehr vorhandene Bauwerke rekonstruiert werden sollen, ist eine nachvollziehbare Konsequenz aus dem aktuellen baulichen Zustand der Städte. Die Argumente sind ausgetauscht, Beispiele benannt, Positionen festgelegt, obwohl eine ernsthafte architektonische Betrachtung kaum vorgenommen wurde.

Anders als bei den vergleichbaren Auseinandersetzungen im 19. Jahrhundert um einen möglichen Wiederaufbau des Heidelberger Schlosses oder zur Fertigstellung des Kölner Doms, geht es heute nicht mehr um die stilgetreue Herstellung eines Idealzustands, sondern um die vollständige Rekonstruktion im Zweiten Weltkrieg zerstörter oder danach abgerissener Gebäude. Auch haben heute politische, insbesondere nationale Belange keinen bestimmenden Einfluss mehr auf die Argumentation. Fast immer beschränkt sich der Wunsch nur auf die Wiederherstellung eines Stadtbilds oder Ensembles und reflektiert selten darüber hinausgehende Fragen nach Authentizität, architektonischer Qualität, Konstruktion und innerem Gefüge. Deren Klärung bleibt so genannten Fachleuten vorbehalten, denen es ein Leichtes ist, das Ansinnen als nicht realisierbar, reaktionär und sentimental abzulehnen. Der durchweg zutiefst konservativ geprägte Diskurs verdrängt leider die notwendige Suche nach einer zeitgemäßen architektonischen Lösung der Aufgaben.

Ottheinrichsbau des Heidelberger Schlosses, Heidelberg, Deutschland, erster Rekonstruktionsvorschlag 1900 von Carl Schäfer, nicht ausgeführt
Ottheinrich Wing of Heidelberg Castle, Heidelberg, Germany, first proposed reconstruction 1900 by Carl Schäfer, not realised

▨ The current heated debate throughout Germany as to whether and, if so, how, lost buildings should be reconstructed, is an understandable result of the current architectural state of our cities. Arguments for and against have been exchanged, examples cited, positions staked out, but there has been no really serious architectural reflection.

Unlike comparable debates in the nineteenth century about the possible reconstruction of Heidelberg Castle or the completion of Cologne Cathedral, it is no longer a question of creating an ideal state faithful to the original style, but of completely reconstructing buildings that were destroyed in the Second World War or demolished in its wake. Nor do political and, in particular, national interests seem to have any real influence on the debate these days. The discussion is almost invariably limited to a wish to reconstruct an urban landscape or ensemble and rarely, if ever, involves any deeper issues concerning authenticity, architectural quality, construction and interior structure. These are left to the so-called specialists, who have no difficulty in rejecting such considerations as unfeasible, reactionary and sentimental. This profoundly conservative debate unfortunately leaves no room for the necessary quest for an appropriate architectural solution.

Pessimism and justified dissatisfaction with the banal mediocrity of purpose-built structures, together with an understandable suspicion of the redemption promised by an architectural elite that sees itself as being at the cutting edge of creativity have spawned a yearning for the romantic imagery of pre-industrial cities and landscapes whose permanent loss even the most cultured sophisticates refuse to accept. It is all too easy to be satisfied with the mask-like facade of merely average architecture, such as the Ratslaube in Halberstadt or House No. 5 at Neuer Markt in Potsdam (see pp. 36–41), or to be pawned off with such dubious new buildings as the Kommandantenhaus in Berlin (see also pp. 50–57) in which the use of traditional artisanally produced facade stucco is enough for it to pass as exemplary in the planned reconstruction of this city palace. These supposed reconstructions pander superficially to the desire for historical picture-postcard imagery, but they also provide cannon fodder for the proponents, resistant to criticism as they are, of an abstraction that adheres firmly to the notion of architectural history as a straight and uninterrupted line of development, and who regard the call for a rejection of historical references in architecture, voiced almost a hundred years ago in theoretical mani-

Ratslaube, Halberstadt, Deutschland, Rekonstruktion 1998 durch Hülsdell & Hallegger Architekten
Ratslaube (City Hall), Halberstadt, Germany, reconstruction 1998 by Hülsdell & Hallegger Architekten

Kommandantenhaus, Berlin, Deutschland, Rekonstruktion 2001–2003 durch van den Valentyn – Architektur
Kommandantenhaus, Berlin, Germany, reconstruction 2001–2003 by van den Valentyn – Architektur

Pessimistischer Zeitgeist und gerechtfertigte Verdrossenheit über die banale Mittelmäßigkeit zweckoptimierter Bauproduktionen, gepaart mit einer verständlichen Angst vor den Heilsversprechen einer sich als künstlerische Avantgarde verstehenden Architektenschaft lassen den Wunsch nach romantischen Bilderwelten vorindustrieller Städte und Landschaften entstehen, deren Unwiederbringlichkeit sich auch kulturbeflissene Großbürger nicht eingestehen wollen. Schnell gibt man sich mit maskenhafter Kaschierung architektonischen Durchschnitts wie bei der Ratslaube in Halberstadt und bei Haus Nr. 5 am Neuen Markt in Potsdam (siehe S. 36–41) zufrieden oder begnügt sich mit fragwürdigen Neubauten wie dem Kommandantenhaus in Berlin (siehe auch S. 50–57), bei dem die traditionelle handwerkliche Herstellung üblicher Stuckteile an der Fassade ausreicht, um als beispielhaft für den geplanten Aufbau des Stadtschlosses zu gelten. Diese vermeintlichen Rekonstruktionen bedienen oberflächlich die Sehnsucht nach historischen Postkartenmotiven,

festos, as an inviolable and eternal law. But this principle, first applied in post-war reconstruction, often in the form of banal reality, has itself become a historic factor and a tradition to which lip service is unthinkingly paid.

The intellectual leap of reducing form to the crucial elements of architecture was quickly achieved, and the subsequent quest for creative originality led to a primitive minimalism whose last compositional will and testament is manifested in printed glass panes anchored with stainless steel and minor variations on the theme of unfaced concrete. The world-wide spread of cultural sameness has been accelerated still further by the media cult of the star architect. Images generated arbitrarily in computer processes and stopped at random are electronically transposed into architectural sculptures for sensation-hungry mayors and marketing strategists, ensuring that any location boasting some explosive-convulsive structure or biological form blown up out of proportion can have its brief brush

liefern aber das Kanonenfutter für die kritikresistenten Vertreter einer Abstraktion, die unbeirrt an eine geradlinige Entwicklung in der Baugeschichte glauben und die vor fast hundert Jahren in theoretischen Manifesten geforderte Abkehr von geschichtlichen Bezugsebenen für die Architektur als ewig geltendes Gesetz ansehen. Das jedoch erst beim Wiederaufbau nach dem Zweiten Weltkrieg in oftmals banale Realität umgesetzte Prinzip ist selbst zu einer historischen Konstante und Tradition geworden, deren Bewahrung gebetsmühlenartig eingefordert wird.

Die intellektuelle Leistung einer Reduzierung der Formen auf das architektonisch Wesentliche war schnell vollbracht und die anschließende Suche nach künstlerischer Originalität hat zu einem primitiven Minimalismus geführt, dessen letzter Gestaltungswille sich in bedruckten Glasscheiben an Edelstahlankern und irgendwie bearbeiteten Sichtbetonflächen manifestiert. Die weltweite Ausbreitung kultureller Einfalt wurde durch die Einführung des medialen Starkults für Architekten noch beschleunigt. Willkürlich am Bildschirm durch zufällig gestoppte Rechenvorgänge entstandene Bilder werden vom Computer in beliebig konstruierte Bauplastiken umgerechnet, die das Sensationsbedürfnis von Bürgermeistern und Marketingstrategen bedienen und den Aufstellungsorten abwechselnd durch explosionsartige Zuckungen oder unendlich vergrößerte Formwelten aus biologischen Versuchsanordnungen kurzzeitige Aufmerksamkeit garantieren. Geradezu zynisch sind die Implantationen scheinbar poppiger Blechschachteln in die Innenstädte. Die vermeintliche Ästhetik öder Vorortstrukturen aus notdürftig zusammengefügten Baumarktutensilien bleibt nur den vermeintlich Eingeweihten vorbehalten und die Notwendigkeit einer Erklärung und huldvollen Würdigung der Banalitäten als vorbildlich kreativ übernimmt gerne ein Kulturkritiker des Feuilletons einer großen Zeitung.

Das Bild einer erkennbaren und Identität stiftenden Stadt als einer kulturellen Gemeinschaft von Häusern und Räumen entsteht so nicht. Konturen gewinnen die durch vielfältige Zerstörungen deformierten Städte nur als im Ganzen Gedachtes, das mehr ist als eine Summe von Einzelteilen. Wieder im Bewusstsein eines kulturellen Erbes und Bezug nehmend auf eine architektonische Tradition sind ohne ideologische Beschränkungen die tatsächlich überzeitlichen Elemente, Symbole und Typologien auf ihre Verwendbarkeit zu prüfen und in geändertem Kontext anzuwenden. Ziel sind keine nostalgischen Nachahmungen, sondern erinnernde Neuschöpfungen, die forschend Unbekanntes entdecken. So wird das Bedürfnis der Allgemeinheit nach Vertrautem und Bewährtem bedient und das intellektuelle Verlangen nach Ernsthaftigkeit und sinnhaftem Ausdruck akzeptiert. Orte von ausgewogener Harmonie, Räume von ausbalancierter Klarheit und Bauten von glaubwürdiger Materialität und Konstruktion bilden eine ästhetische Verbindlichkeit, deren Gleichheit nicht Uniformität und deren Komplexität nicht Gleichgültigkeit bedeutet. Architektonisches Bauen als ein von der Vernunft bestimmtes System im Geist einer neuen Renaissance, in der Gestalt eines neuen Humanismus. Rekonstruktionen, die einen erreichten Zustand rückgängig, ungeschehen machen wollen, werden dann überflüssig, unnötig und falsch. Rekonstruktionen als Reparatur, als Wiederherstellung oder als Vervollständigung bleiben

with fame. The implantation of luridly trendy metal boxes in our inner cities is nothing short of cynical. The purported aestheticism of dull suburban structures hammered together d-i-y style seems evident only to those supposedly in the know, and some art critic or other can always be found who is willing to pay sycophantic homage to such banalities by expounding on them and hailing them as exemplary creations in the review pages of the broadsheets.

This is not how a recognisable, identifiable city with a cultural community of buildings and spaces is created. A city deformed by major destruction can be given firm contours only if it is considered as a complete entity that is more than the sum of its parts. The existing timeless elements, symbols and typologies have to be examined in terms of their viability and applied in a changed context, with an awareness of the respective cultural heritage and with reference to architectural tradition, but without ideological constraints. It is not nostalgic reproduction that is the aim here, but evocative new creations that foster memory by exploring and revealing the unknown. This is an approach that serves a general need for familiarity and reliability, while accommodating the intellectual demand for earnestness and meaningful expression. Places of balanced harmony, spaces with clarity and equilibrium, buildings of credible material and construction – this is what creates an aesthetic bond that does not mistake homogeneity for uniformity and whose complexity is carefully considered: architecture as a rationally determined system in the spirit of a new renaissance, in the form of a new humanism. Reconstructions that seek to reverse and negate a state already achieved will then become superfluous, unnecessary and false. Reconstructions as repairs, as a reinstatement or completion will remain legitimate, but they will still require the application of clearly defined standards.

All reconstructions are, by definition, interpretations. Archaeological or art historical reconstructions reflect something that is absent, demanding individual decisions in order to materialise. In addition to technical, structural and historical considerations, this also requires a high degree of architectural and compositional competence if the concepts in question are to be viable at all.

Music, with its creative logic, has much in common with the requirements of architecture, and can provide some insights into the problem. The composition is design. Its content is conveyed by a two-dimensional documentation of drawings whose coding requires no further verbal explanation in order to be grasped. The musical score, like the architectural drawing, can be regarded from a purely artistic point of view, but that still does not represent the actual work itself. The realisation of the work – through the interpretation of the score or drawing – is up to someone else. An orchestra as a group of trained specialists performs a symphony under the direction of a conductor. Needless to say, a group of amateurs can also play Beethoven, but the interpretation comes into its own under the baton of, say, Sir Simon Rattle and the Berlin Philharmonic. A current performance is like the new build of a design. Even if the architect were already dead, all the necessary documents – the score – would still be available. Nobody would seriously maintain that only contemporary composers should have their works

Nicht rekonstruierbar, nicht wieder herstellbar sind künstlerisch gefertigte Einzelstücke. Es wäre anmaßend, von einem Bildhauer gefertigten Bauschmuck, von einem Maler ausgeführte Decken-gemälde oder von einem namhaften Kunsttischler gefertigte Tür-skulpturen nach deren Totalverlust wieder aufleben zu lassen. Dieses sind unwiederbringliche Produkte menschlicher Individualität. Auch außergewöhnliche, nur in ihrer ursprünglichen Entstehungszeit an-gewendete handwerkliche Herstellungsmethoden sind nicht mehr re-produzierbar. Nur für eine kunsthistorisch orientierte Denkmalpflege ist die Konservierung derartiger Praktiken sinnvoll und notwendig. Die Gestaltung einer ernsthaft relevanten neuen Baukunst kann nur mit den Mitteln unserer heutigen Zeit erfolgen. Statt wehmütiger Klagen über die sich seit der Renaissance kontinuierlich ändernden Bauzustände, muss das gestalterische Potenzial industrieller Ferti-gung angemessen ausgeschöpft werden. Der zunehmenden Kom-plexität der Technik steht eine Vereinfachung und Standardisierung des Bildhaften gegenüber. Aus dem freiwilligen Nicht-mehr-gestal-ten-wollen der frühen Moderne ist ein Nicht-mehr-gestalten-können der Neuzeit geworden.

Modellhaft und allgemeingültig hat Karl Friedrich Schinkel die Möglichkeiten architektonischen Ausdrucks und deren Wirkung in den Formen industrieller Reproduzierbarkeit bei der Bauakademie in Berlin verdeutlicht. Zur Schulung des Sehens, als Orientierung und Verpflichtung ist der Aufbau des Gebäudes in seiner inneren Struktur und kompletten Erscheinung notwendig. Die Schlossattrappen in Potsdam, Berlin oder Braunschweig braucht es nicht. An deren Stelle müssen Gebäude treten, die die Gegebenheiten reflektieren und die architektonische Tradition radikal fortsetzen: neue Schlösser.

Bauakademie, Berlin, Deutschland, errichtet 1831–1836 durch
Karl Friedrich Schinkel, Planungen zum Aufbau von Petra und
Paul Kahlfeldt. Grundriss Erdgeschoss, 1. und 2. Obergeschoss
**Bauakademie, Berlin, Germany, 1831–1836, by Karl Friedrich
Schinkel, reconstruction plans by Petra and Paul Kahlfeldt.
Floorplans of ground floor, first and second floors**

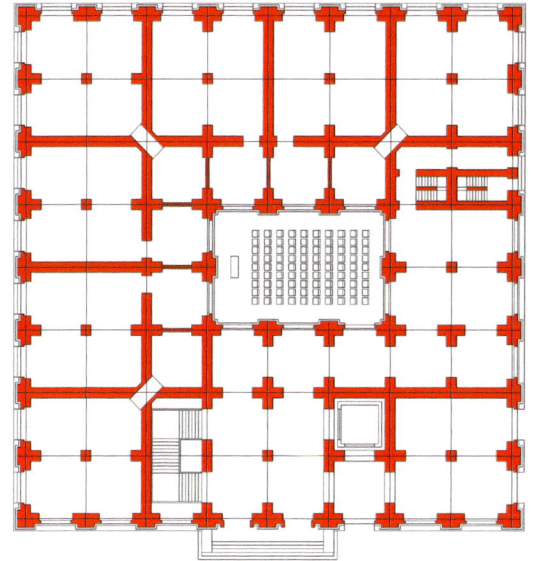

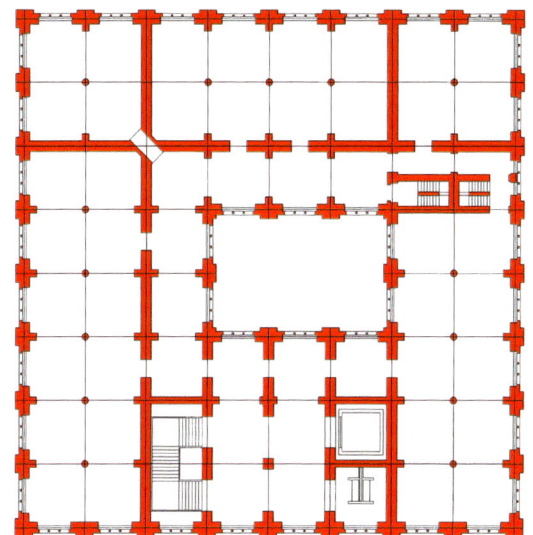

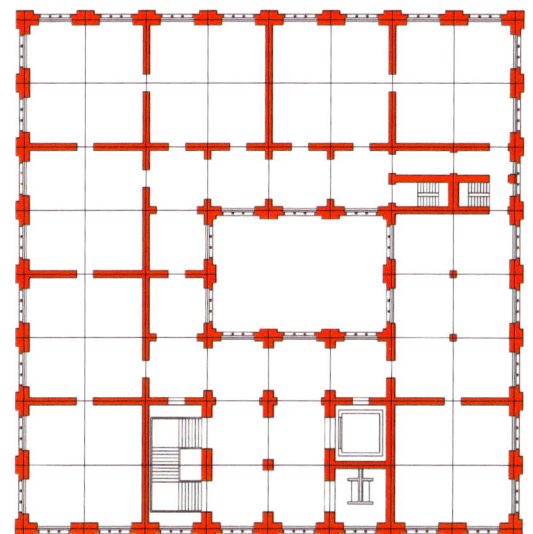

Turm des Geschäftshauses Kurfürstendamm 56, Berlin,
Deutschland, nach Brand Rekonstruktion 1997–2003
durch Petra und Paul Kahlfeldt
**Tower of commercial premises at Kurfürstendamm 56,
Berlin, Germany, destroyed by fire, reconstruction
1997–2003 by Petra and Paul Kahlfeldt**

»Es gibt einen anhaltenden Trend zum Nostalgischen …«[1]
"There is a strong trend towards the nostalgic…"[1]

Harald Bodenschatz

Ein Plädoyer für mehr Gelassenheit im Umgang
mit Traditionalismus in Architektur und Städtebau

A Plea for a More Relaxed Approach to Traditionalism
in Architecture and Urban Planning

■ Die Fachwelt ist sichtlich irritiert: Was ist los auf dem Markt der architektonischen und städtebaulichen Eitelkeiten? Gibt es einen Retro-Trend? Wenn ja, wie stark ist er? Wie lange kann er dauern? Und vor allem: Was sind seine Ursachen? Die Anlässe für diese Irritation sind vielfältig: In Deutschland werden zunehmend verschwundene historische Bauten rekonstruiert, Neubauten in traditioneller Form errichtet und die Bausteine der traditionellen Stadt beschworen. Die rekonstruierte Frauenkirche in Dresden und der traditionelle Neubau des Hotel Adlon in Berlin sind ja nur die Höhepunkte einer Entwicklung, die die Fachwelt überrollt hat. Dazu kommen viele Beispiele der ›kritischen Rekonstruktion des Stadtgrundrisses‹.[2] Selbst die Denkmalpflege, lange Zeit zuverlässige Lieferantin wissenschaftlicher Argumente gegen Rekonstruktionen und traditionelle Architektur, ist ins Wanken geraten.[3] Inzwischen gibt es eine ganze Palette von Begriffen, die den Retro-Trend fachlich untersetzen: etwa ›Europäische Stadt‹, ›New Urbanism‹, ›kompakte Stadt‹, ›klassische Architektur‹, ›traditionelle Architektur‹, ›regionale Architektur‹ und so weiter. Architekten und Planer, die mit diesen Begriffen jonglieren, sind durchaus erfolgreich – nicht zuletzt Rob Krier, und dies in den Niederlanden![4] Was aber am meisten irritiert, ist die Ausbreitung und Stärkung zivilgesellschaftlicher Organisationen, die diese Entwicklungen radikalisieren: die historischen Vereine in Berlin[5], Dresden[6] und anderswo, die sich für die historische Rekonstruktion der alten Stadt einsetzen und ihren Einfluss ausbauen. Die Macht, festzulegen, was der Stadt gut tut, droht der Fachwelt zu entgleiten.

Vor gut zwanzig Jahren schien die Welt noch in Ordnung.[7] In der Nachkriegszeit festigte sich eine professionelle Grundhaltung, die klar zwischen gut und schlecht unterscheiden konnte: Traditionelle oder gar rekonstruierte Architektur galt als rückwärts gewandt, rückschrittlich, politisch rechts, reaktionär, im Grunde sogar als ›faschistisch‹. Der unverbesserliche Konsument einer so entwerteten traditionellen Architektur war irgendwie nicht in Ordnung – politisch, sozial und kulturell. Er galt als unsicher, ungebildet, als Patient mit krankhafter Sehnsucht – eben als nostalgisch. Architekten, die solchen ›Sehnsüchten‹ entgegenkamen, waren selbst verdächtig, wurden ausgegrenzt und diskreditiert. Das Vokabular, das für die stigmatisierte Architektur geschaffen wurde, spiegelte diese Haltung wider: Begriffe wie Nostalgie, Historismus, Eklektizismus verdeutlichten, was wir von traditioneller Architektur hielten, sie erklärten aber weder etwas, noch waren sie in der Lage zu differenzieren. Sie eröffneten keine Debatte, sondern beendeten sie, bevor sie begonnen hatte. Sie ersetzten Kritik durch eine massive Mauer der Abwehr. Architekturzeitschriften, -bücher, -ausstellungen, -kritiken und vor allem auch die Architekturausbildung an den Hochschulen reproduzierten diese Haltung über Jahrzehnte.

The professionals are clearly perplexed. What is fuelling the bonfire of architectural and urban planning vanities? Is there a retro trend? If so, how strong is it? How long can it last? Above all, what sparked it? The reasons for all this confusion are many and varied. In Germany, more and more lost historical buildings are being reconstructed. Traditional-style new buildings are going up, and homage is being paid to the cornerstones of traditional urban development. The reconstructed Frauenkirche in Dresden and the traditional-style new Hotel Adlon in Berlin are just the crest of a wave that has engulfed the profession. There are many other examples of "critical reconstruction of the urban layout".[2] Even architectural heritage officials, for so long a reliable source of well-founded arguments against reconstruction and traditional architecture, are wavering.[3] In the meantime, a whole barrage of terms has emerged to lend gravitas to the retro trend, among them: "European City", "New Urbanism", "compact city", "classic architecture", "traditional architecture", "regional architecture", and so on. The architects and planners who juggle these concepts are distinctly successful – none more so than Rob Krier, and in the Netherlands of all places![4] But the most perplexing thing of all is the spread of public organisations that are radicalising this trend: the historic societies in Berlin, Dresden and elsewhere, lobbying for the historic reconstruction of their cities and becoming increasingly influential.[5] It looks as though the professionals are losing the power of determining what is good for a city.

Some twenty years ago, all seemed to be well with the world.[6] The post-war years had seen a consolidation of the professional approach that could clearly distinguish between what was good and what was bad. Traditional, let alone reconstructed, architecture was seen as backward-looking, politically right-wing, reactionary, even fundamentally "fascist". There was surely something politically, socially and culturally wrong with dyed-in-the-wool proponents of such a devalued traditional architecture. They were regarded as insecure, unenlightened, pathologically nostalgic. Architects willing to pander to such nostalgic fantasies were viewed with suspicion, shunned and discredited. The vocabulary coined for this stigmatised architecture reflects the prevailing attitudes: terms such as nostalgia, historicism or eclecticism clearly indicate what was thought of traditional architecture. But they offered neither an explanation nor a means of making distinctions. Rather than cultivating debate, they nipped it in the bud. These were terms that stonewalled constructive criticism. Architecture periodicals, books, exhibitions, reviews – and most especially architectural training at colleges and universities – reproduced this attitude for decades.

Port Grimaud, Frankreich, städtebauliches Konzept der neotraditionellen Lagunenstadt von François Spoerry, seit 1966
Port Grimaud, France, urban development concept for neo-traditional lagoon city by François Spoerry, since 1966

Diese Sichtweisen implizierten oft eine direkte Kopplung der nationalsozialistischen Herrschaft mit einer traditionellen architektonischen und städtebaulichen Form. Noch heute wird traditionelle Architektur nicht selten unter Faschismusverdacht gestellt. Mit dieser Sichtweise korrespondierte die unzureichende Rezeption der Verhältnisse im faschistischen Italien, wo die moderne Architektur eine andere politische Rolle als in Deutschland spielte.[8] Verstärkt wurde diese Konstellation durch den Kalten Krieg der frühen fünfziger Jahre, in dem es gelang, die Architektur und den Städtebau der Moderne als westliche und demokratische Alternative zur DDR-Entwicklung im Schatten Stalins zu inszenieren. Dagegen wurde die Tatsache, dass ausgerechnet ein politisch linker Architekt, François Spoerry, mit Port Grimaud ein frühes Schlüsselprojekt traditioneller Architektur

Such views often implied a direct connection between the National Socialist regime and traditional architecture and urban planning. Even today, there is still a tendency to associate traditional architecture with fascist thinking. But this fails to take into account the situation in fascist Italy, where modern architecture played a very different political role than in Germany.[7] The situation was further exacerbated by the Cold War of the early 1950s, when modern architecture and urban planning were seen as a democratic western alternative to developments in an East Germany under the shadow of Stalinism. But the fact that it was actually a politically left-wing architect, François Spoerry, who designed an early key project of traditional architecture and traditional urban planning in Port Grimaud, was conveniently ignored.[8] Nor did it quite fit the picture

Via San Leonardo im historischen Zentrum von Bologna, Italien, Ensemble mit typologisch rekonstruierten Bauten, seit 1973
Via San Leonardo in the historic centre of Bologna, Italy; ensemble with typologically reconstructed buildings, since 1973

und traditionellen Städtebaus entworfen hatte, schlicht ignoriert.[9] Ebenso wenig passte ins Bild, dass im eurokommunistisch regierten Bologna, der Modellstadt des Europäischen Denkmalschutzjahrs 1975, nicht nur die überkommenen Bauten des historischen Zentrums geschützt wurden, sondern auch zerstörte Gebäude »typologisch« rekonstruiert wurden.[10]

Die Sicherheiten der Vergangenheit setzten einen spezifischen, herrschenden Interessensblock im Bauwesen voraus, der heute nicht mehr existiert: ein Bündnis von Politikern auf Landes- und Kommunalebene, die durch moderne Architektur ihre Fortschrittlichkeit demonstrieren wollten und die über ihre Rolle als Bauherren oder über ihren Einfluss auf das private Bauen, ihre Perspektive durchsetzen konnten; von Bauherren, die von der öffentlichen Hand direkt oder indirekt abhängig waren wie etwa die gemeinnützige Wohnungswirtschaft; sowie von privaten Investoren, die sich sicher waren, ihr Image mit fortschrittlicher Architektur unter Beweis stellen zu können. Diesem Bündnis stand eine Kundschaft gegenüber, deren Wahlmöglichkeiten zwar begrenzt waren, denen aber im sozialstaatlichen Rahmen eine solide, soziale Unterschiede auch baulich

that Bologna, model city of the 1975 European Architectural Heritage Year, had not only preserved and refurbished the dilapidated buildings of its historic centre, but had even "typologically" reconstructed lost buildings – and had done so under a Eurocommunist government.[9]

The certainties of the past presupposed a specific set of given interests in the field of construction that no longer exists today. Politicians at the regional and local level who wanted to demonstrate their progressiveness through modern architecture and who could assert their views in their role as client or through their influence on private sector building were in league not only with clients who were directly or indirectly dependent on public sector funding (such as housing associations) but also with private investors who saw progressive architecture as a way of enhancing their image. On the other hand, there was a clientele whose choices were limited, but for whom the welfare state offered the solid prospect of an architecture that levelled out social differences. Today, the situation is radically different: a shrinking society offers new urban choices to those upwardly mobile beneficiaries of the weakening of the

nivellierende Perspektive angeboten wurde. Heute sind die Verhältnisse radikal anders: Eine schrumpfende Gesellschaft eröffnet den sich stärker differenzierenden sozialen Gewinnern des Abschieds von der sozialstaatlich vermittelten Industriegesellschaft neue Wahlmöglichkeiten in der Stadtregion, die Rolle der öffentlichen Hand ist geschwächt, die der privaten Investoren gestärkt. Die Kundschaft ist aufmüpfig geworden, sie lässt sich von der Haltung der Profession immer weniger beeindrucken.

Die Übergangszeit zwischen der Ära der Sicherheiten und der heutigen Irritation war in Deutschland durch eine besondere und merkwürdige Konfliktfront gekennzeichnet. Während auf der Ebene der Architektur der Retro-Trend bis vor kurzem erfolgreich aus jeder ernsthaften Diskussion herausgehalten werden konnte, entfaltete sich auf der städtebaulichen Ebene eine harte Auseinandersetzung zwischen Vertretern der traditionellen ›Europäischen Stadt‹ und der ›Zwischenstadt‹[11]. Beide Fronten übersahen in ihrem Eifer manchmal die realen Entwicklungen: Zum einen wurde oft ausgeblendet, dass wir heute bereits in einer durch und durch suburbanisierten Gesellschaft leben und die bauliche Form dieser Gesellschaft zwar nicht akzeptieren, aber uns ihr stellen müssen. Zum anderen wurde die sich verändernde Rolle der traditionellen ›Europäischen Stadt‹, vor allem der Stadtzentren, oft unterschätzt, wenn diese nur mehr als eine Facette der Netzstadt neben anderen wahrgenommen wurde.

Der neue Blick auf die ›Zwischenstadt‹ enthüllte der Fachwelt, dass die Retro-Form längst im alltäglichen Bauen angekommen war. Neu war nur, dass sie auch in der Sphäre des Besonderen, der Architektur, in den stärker beachteten Zentren einzudringen begann. In der Tat sind gerade die Zentren im Rahmen der Suburbanisierung einem zunehmenden Veränderungsdruck ausgesetzt. Sie sind in einem Prozess des Umbaus begriffen, und dieser Umbau führt dazu, dass sie mehr und mehr zum Zentrum einer suburbanen Landschaft werden. Die Zentren werden dabei nicht verschwinden, wie oft behauptet wird, sie werden aber neue Aufgaben übernehmen müssen. Sie werden zu einem symbolischen Zentrum, in dem sich die Suburbaniten, die Bewohner der zersiedelten Landschaft im Umkreis der kompakten Städte, zu Hause fühlen. Sie werden zu Standorten besonderer, zur Schau gestellter Gebäude, die eine wenig aufregende suburbane Landschaft dringend benötigt. Sie werden zu einem Ort besonderer, inszenierter Tradition, die eine ohne gestalterischen Bezug zur Geschichte beplante suburbane Landschaft braucht. Sie werden zum Ziel des Tourismus, und zwar nicht nur des weltweit wachsenden Ferntourismus, sondern vor allem auch des suburbanen Lokaltourismus.

All diese Aspekte verstärken den Druck auf die Städte, historische Besonderheiten zu präsentieren und diese – wo nötig – neu zu bauen. Allerdings besteht keineswegs die Gefahr, dass die Zentren der großen Städte zu Museen werden; sie müssen sich zugleich als Orte der symbolischen Demonstration von Zukunftsfähigkeit und Innovation präsentieren. Neue, spektakuläre, von so genannten Stararchitekten entworfene Bauten, in Großstadtzentren oft in der neuen Form von Hochhausskulpturen, übernehmen diese Aufgabe. Das Zentrum der Zukunft braucht beides: die Bekenntnis zur eigenen Tradition wie

nanny state that governed industrial society; the role of the public sector has declined while that of private investment has grown. The clients are rebelling: they are less likely to be influenced by the attitudes of the professionals.

In Germany, the transition from an era of certainties to the confusion of today was marked by a specific and rather strange conflict of interests. Whereas, in architecture, the retro trend has, until recently, been successfully excluded from all serious discussion, in urban planning there was heated debate between the proponents of the traditional "European City" and those in favour of the "In-between City".[10] Both sides sometimes lost sight of actual developments: on the one hand, there was a tendency to ignore the fact that we already live in a thoroughly suburbanised society whose architectural forms we may not condone, but must nevertheless acknowledge. On the other hand, the changing role of the traditional "European City", especially with regard to the inner cities, was often underestimated and simply regarded as just one aspect of the urban network among others.

A closer look at the "In-between City" revealed to the professionals that retro style had already become firmly established in everyday building. What was new, however, was that it had already begun to infiltrate the "special" aspects of life, such as architecture in the more high-profile centres. Indeed, it is the inner cities that have come under increasing pressure to change within the scope of suburbanisation. Inner cities are undergoing a process of redevelopment, and this redevelopment is increasingly turning them into the centres of a suburban landscape. The centres are not dying out, as is so often claimed, but they do have to take on a new role. They will become symbolic centres where the suburbanites living in the sprawling outskirts of the compact cities feel at home. They will become the locations of striking, high-profile buildings that add a

Poundbury, England, städtebauliches Konzept der traditionellen Stadterweiterung von Leon Krier, seit 1993
Poundbury, England, urban development concept for traditional city extension by Leon Krier, since 1993

auch die Demonstration der Kraft zum Neuen. Die rekonstruierte, mit Innovationssymbolen angereicherte ›Europäische Stadt‹ richtet sich vor allem an die neuen, postindustriellen Eliten, an Menschen, deren Elterngeneration die alte Stadt in Richtung Suburbia bereits verlassen hatte, an die Gewinner der Dienstleistungsgesellschaft, aber auch an die lernenden Generationen und natürlich an die älteren Generationen.

Die neuen Eliten der postindustriellen Gesellschaft bevorzugen aber auch im suburbanen Raum mehr und mehr Gebäude und Räume, die zu den monotonen Siedlungsteppichen der Nachkriegszeit auf Distanz gehen. Mit der Pluralisierung der Lebensstile wird auch der traditionelle Städtebau jenseits der Stadt salonfähig. Neue Siedlungen aus einem Guss im Gewand historischer Orte werden zunehmend populärer, insbesondere in Großbritannien und den Niederlanden. Poundbury und Brandevoort sind nur die Spitzen des Eis-

touch of much-needed excitement to an otherwise dull suburban landscape. They will become the showcase of a distinctive tradition that the suburban landscape developed without reference to historic needs. They will become tourist magnets – not just in the conventional sense of attracting visitors from afar, but, more importantly still, generating a local form of suburban tourism.

All these aspects increase the pressure on cities to present historic highlights – if necessary by building them. But there is no danger of the city centres being turned into museums; they also have to be seen as places that symbolise future potential and innovation. The new, spectacular buildings designed by so-called star architects, often in the new form of high-rise sculptures in major cities, take on this role. The centre of the future needs both an awareness of local tradition and a demonstration of innovative energy. The reconstructed "European City" with its symbols of innovation is

Brandevoort, Niederlande, städtebauliches Konzept für die neotraditionelle Ortschaft von Rob Krier, seit 1996
Brandevoort, Netherlands, urban development concept for neo-traditional settlement by Rob Krier, since 1996

»Es gibt einen anhaltenden Trend zum Nostalgischen ...«
"There is a strong trend towards the nostalgic..."

31

Neu errichtete ›Medina‹ in der Touristenstadt Yasmine Hammamet, Tunesien, 2003
Newly built ›Medina‹ in the tourist resort of Yasmine Hammamet, Tunisia, 2003

bergs. Schon vorher entstanden Shopping- und Entertainment-Welten im Retro-Look. Und gerade exklusive Urlaubswelten präsentieren sich zunehmend in traditioneller Form.[12] Aber auch hier ist keineswegs eine vereinheitlichte Welt zu erwarten, sondern eine bunte Palette konkurrierender Siedlungsformen, zu denen auch Retro-Bauhaussiedlungen[13] gehören.

Inzwischen ist auf der anderen Seite der Mauer, bei den Anhängern traditioneller Architektur und traditionellem Städtebaus, einiges in Bewegung geraten. Ihre Vertreter haben sich weltweit im International Network for Traditional Building, Architecture & Urbanism (INTBAU) organisiert.[14] Auf europäischer Ebene gibt es ein weiteres Netzwerk – A Vision of Europe.[15] Beide Netzwerke werden von der Prince's Foundation in London unterstützt.[16] Im Gegensatz zu diesen beiden Netzwerken, die eine direkte Verknüpfung von traditioneller Architektur mit traditionellem Städtebau propagieren, startete 2003 ein neues europäisches Netzwerk zum Thema Städtebaureform, das sich nicht auf architektonische Stile festlegt, aber die Vertreter traditioneller Architektur auch nicht ausgrenzt: der Council for European Urbanism (C.E.U.).[17] Dieses Netzwerk wurde im Frühjahr 2003 in Brüssel und Brügge vorbereitet und im Herbst in Stockholm begründet. Die deutsche Sektion tagt 2004 erstmals in Görlitz. C.E.U. ist auch eine Reaktion auf die US-amerikanische Bewegung des New Urbanism. Die Frage des architektonischen Stils wird dort – anders, als die deutsche Rezeption vermuten lässt – äußerst pragmatisch behandelt.

geared primarily towards the new post-industrial elite, towards people whose parents' generation had already left the old city for the suburbs, towards the people who have profited from society's shift of focus to the service sector, but also towards the learning generations and, of course, the older generations.

The new elites of post-industrial society, however, also increasingly favour buildings and spaces, even in the suburbs, that set them apart from the monotonous dormitories of the post-war era. The pluralisation of lifestyles has made traditional urban planning acceptable, even beyond the inner city boundaries. New towns created in the guise of historic places are gaining popularity, especially in the UK and the Netherlands. Poundbury and Brandevoort are just the tip of the iceberg. Even before that, there had already been retro-style shopping and entertainment worlds. Exclusive holiday resorts, in particular, are increasingly presented in traditional form.[11] Here again, there is no sign of uniformity, but a broad range of rival forms that even includes retro-Bauhaus estates.[12]

In the meantime, on the other side of the fence, things are changing too. The supporters of traditional architecture and urban planning have founded the International Network for Traditional Building, Architecture & Urbanism (INTBAU).[13] In Europe, there is another network – A Vision of Europe.[14] Both these networks are supported by the Prince's Foundation in London.[15] In contrast to these two networks propagating a direct link between traditional architecture and traditional urban planning, a new European network for urban

Quartier McNair, Berlin, Deutschland, städtebauliches Konzept von d-company/Anatole du Fresne sowie Baumschlager & Eberle, seit 2000
Quartier McNair, Berlin, Germany, urban development concept by d-company/Anatole du Fresne and Baumschlager & Eberle, since 2000

Angesichts der sich spürbar verändernden Verhältnisse werden die der deutschen Fachwelt lange selbstverständlichen Sicherheiten der Nachkriegszeit peu à peu in Frage gestellt. Die eiserne Grundhaltung gegen den Traditionalismus war solange stark, als sie unbesehen akzeptiert wurde, sie erweist sich aber zunehmend als hilflos, wenn diese Akzeptanz zu bröckeln beginnt. Sie hilft der Profession dann nicht mehr, sondern macht sie kritikunfähig und sprachlos. Sie kann nicht zwischen verschiedenen Facetten der traditionellen Architektur unterscheiden. Sie macht keinen Unterschied zwischen guter und schlechter traditioneller Architektur – eine Unterscheidung, für die Kriterien notwendig sind, die zu erarbeiten eine Abkehr von pauschaler Ausgrenzung voraussetzt.

Allerdings hat die Fachwelt längst begonnen, sich aus ihrer Starre zu lösen. Die Grundhaltung der Nachkriegszeit ist gebrochen, wenngleich noch keineswegs verschwunden. Der Blick in die Fachzeitschriften zeigt, dass die veränderten Verhältnisse nicht mehr ignoriert werden, aber auch, dass eine Neuorientierung mühsam ist.[18] Wir soll-

planning reform that does not insist on a particular architectural style, but does not exclude the traditionalists either, was launched in 2003: the Council for European Urbanism (C.E.U.).[16] Prepared in the spring of 2003 in Brussels and Bruges, it was officially founded in Stockholm in the autumn. The German section holds its first meeting in Görlitz in 2004. C.E.U. is also a response to the New Urbanism movement in the United States, where the question of architectural style is treated with a pragmatism that the German approach looks unlikely to deliver.

Given the obviously changing situation, the post-war certainties that went unquestioned for so long are starting to be called into question. The firm rejection of traditionalism remained strong as long as traditionalism was unthinkingly accepted, but it is looking increasingly fragile as this acceptance begins to crumble. Such a rejection no longer aids the profession, but makes it unable to criticise or speak out. It cannot distinguish between various facets of traditional architecture and it makes no distinction between good

»Es gibt einen anhaltenden Trend zum Nostalgischen ...«
"There is a strong trend towards the nostalgic..."

33

ten uns davon verabschieden, Baukultur und Bauqualität an einer Messlatte zu orientieren, die traditionelle Architektur per se als unzumutbar erklärt. Dies ist kein Plädoyer für traditionelle Architektur und gegen den Streit um architektonische Qualität, sondern für die Wiedergewinnung der Diskursfähigkeit. Architektur und Städtebau entwickeln sich nur in entkrampften Kontroversen weiter.

and bad traditional architecture – a distinction requiring the formulation of criteria that are not based on exclusion.

The professionals have long since begun to relax their attitudes. The fundamental views of the post-war era are changing, but they have by no means disappeared entirely. A glance at the specialist periodicals not only indicates that the changing situation can no longer be ignored, but also that reorientation is difficult.[17] We should stop measuring the quality of our buildings by a yardstick that deems traditional architecture unacceptable. This is a call neither for traditional architecture nor against the debate on architectural quality, but a call to reclaim the possibility of discourse. Architecture and urban planning can only develop in a climate of tolerant controversy.

1 So die Einschätzung des Marktforschers Stephan Grünewald anlässlich der zunehmenden Popularität von Klingeltönen alter Telefone. Vgl. den *Berliner Tagesspiegel* vom 22.04.2004. Für Anregungen und Kritik danke ich Ursula Bodenschatz, Harald Kegler, Frank Roost und Barbara Schönig.

2 Vgl. etwa Harald Bodenschatz, *Berlin – Potsdam – Brandenburg an der Havel. Annäherungen an den historischen Stadtgrundriß*, in: Architektenkammer Berlin (Hrsg.), *Architektur in Berlin. Jahrbuch 1998*, Hamburg 1998, S. 10–19.

3 Zur Haltung der Denkmalpflege vgl. *Rekonstruktion in der Denkmalpflege. Überlegungen – Definitionen – Erfahrungsberichte*, Schriftenreihe des Deutschen Nationalkomitees für Denkmalschutz, Band 57, Bonn 1998.

4 Zu den Projekten Rob Kriers in Holland vgl. Rob Krier, *Town Spaces. Contemporary Interpretations in Traditional Urbanism Krier Kohl Architects,* Basel, Berlin und Boston 2003.

5 Zur Gesellschaft Historisches Berlin vgl. www.ghb-online.de/de/index.php4.

6 Zur Gesellschaft Historischer Neumarkt Dresden vgl. www.neumarkt-dresden.de/ PDF-Dateien/satzung1.pdf.

7 Ein Paukenschlag war zweifellos die erste internationale Architekturausstellung *La presenza del passato (Die Gegenwart der Vergangenheit)* der Biennale in Venedig 1980.

8 Wie schwer sich die Fachwelt mit der Rezeption der italienischen Entwicklung bis heute tut, zeigt die Nichtbeachtung des Buchs *Albert Speer e Marcello Piacentini. L'architettura del totalitarismo negli anni trenta* (Mailand 1999), einer Forschung von Sandro Scarrocchia, die als Dissertation an der Universität Bonn angenommen wurde.

9 Vgl. François Spoerry, *L'architecture douce de Port-Grimaud à Port-Liberté*, Paris 1991.

10 Vgl. die Neubauten an der Via San Leonardo im historischen Zentrum von Bologna. Pier Luigi Cervellati, Roberto Scannavini und Carlo De Angelis, *La nuova cultura delle città*, Mailand 1977, S. 159–164.

11 Vgl. Thomas Sieverts, *Zwischenstadt zwischen Ort und Welt, Raum und Zeit, Stadt und Land,* Braunschweig und Wiesbaden 1997.

12 Ein herausragendes Beispiel in dieser Hinsicht ist die neue tunesische Urlaubsstadt Yasmine Hammamet, in deren Zentrum eine neue Altstadt (Medina) errichtet wurde, die zahlreiche historische Gebäude zwischen Marokko und Iran zitiert.

13 Ein Beispiel hierfür ist das Quartier McNair in Lichterfelde-West, Berlin.

14 www.intbau.org.

15 www.avoe.org.

16 www.princes-foundation.org. Zur gestalterischen Orientierung der Prince's Foundation vgl. Peter Neal (Hrsg.), *Urban Villages and the Making of Communities,* London 2003.

17 www.ceunet.org. Der Autor ist an dieser Initiative beteiligt.

18 Vgl. dazu unter anderen die Hefte zu den Themen »Rekonstruktivismus« (*archithese* 3/1998), »Alte Stadt – neu gebaut« (*Die alte Stadt* 4/1998), »New Urbanism« (*Stadt-Bauwelt* 145/2000), »Populismus« (*ARCH+* 162/2002), »Dirty Urbanism« (*StadtBauwelt* 156/2002), »Postmoderne« (*StadtBauwelt* 158/2003) sowie die Monografie Werner Sewing, *Bildregie. Architektur zwischen Retrodesign und Eventkultur*, Basel, Boston und Berlin 2003.

1 Market researcher Stephan Grünewald on the increasing popularity of old-style telephone ring tones. See *Berliner Tagesspiegel*, 22.04.2004. I wish to thank Ursula Bodenschatz, Harald Kegler, Frank Roost and Barbara Schönig for their constructive criticism and ideas.

2 See for instance Harald Bodenschatz, "Berlin – Potsdam – Brandenburg an der Havel. Annäherungen an den historischen Stadtgrundriß", in *Architektur in Berlin. Jahrbuch 1998*, edited by Architektenkammer Berlin, Hamburg 1998, pp. 10–19.

3 On attitudes in architectural conservation, see *Rekonstruktion in der Denkmalpflege. Überlegungen – Definitionen – Erfahrungsberichte*, Schriftenreihe des Deutschen Nationalkomitees für Denkmalschutz, vol. 57, Bonn 1998.

4 On Rob Krier's projects in the Netherlands, see Rob Krier, *Town Spaces. Contemporary Interpretations in Traditional Urbanism Krier Kohl Architects*, Basel, Berlin and Boston 2003.

5 Go to www.gbh-online.de/de/index.php4 for information on Gesellschaft Historisches Berlin and for information on Gesellschaft Historischer Neumarkt Dresden go to www.neumarkt-dresden.de/PDF-Dateien/satzung1.pdf.

6 A major impact was made by the first international architecture exhibition *La presenza del passato* at the 1980 Venice Biennale.

7 Just how reticent the professionals have been, right up to the present day, with regard to the reception of the Italian development, is evident from the way they have ignored the publication of *Albert Speer e Marcello Piacentini. L'architettura del totalitarismo negli anni trenta* (Mailand 1999), a doctoral thesis by Sandro Scarrocchia at the University of Bonn.

8 Cf. François Spoerry, *L'architecture douce de Port-Grimaud à Port-Liberté*, Paris 1991.

9 Cf. the new buildings on Via San Leonardo in the historic centre of Bologna. Pier Luigi Cervellati, Roberto Scannavini and Carlo De Angelis, *La nuova cultura delle città*, Milano 1977, pp. 159–164.

10 Cf. Thomas Sieverts, *Zwischenstadt zwischen Ort und Welt, Raum und Zeit, Stadt und Land*, Braunschweig and Wiesbaden 1997.

11 An outstanding example in this respect is the new Tunisian resort of Yasmine Hammamet, where a new Medina was built citing many historic buildings from Morocco to Iran.

12 An example of this is the Quartier McNair in Lichterfelde-West, Berlin.

13 www.intbau.org.

14 www.avoe.org.

15 www.princes-foundation.org. On the design principles of the Prince's Foundation see Peter Neal (ed.), *Urban Villages and the Making of Communities*, London 2003.

16 www.ceunet.org. The author is involved in this initiative.

17 See for example such publications as "Rekonstruktivismus" (*archithese* 3/1998), "Alte Stadt – neu gebaut" (*Die alte Stadt* 4/1998), "New Urbanism" (*StadtBauwelt* 145/2000), "Populismus" (*ARCH+* 162/2002), "Dirty Urbanism" (*StadtBauwelt* 156/2002), "Postmoderne" (*StadtBauwelt* 158/2003) and the monographic study by Werner Sewing, *Bildregie. Architektur zwischen Retrodesign und Eventkultur*, Basel, Boston and Berlin 2003.

Rekonstruktion in Deutschland
Reconstruction in Germany

Wohn- und Geschäftshaus Am Neuen Markt 5, Potsdam
Apartment and office building, Am Neuen Markt 5, Potsdam

Nicola Fortmann-Drühe

■ Im allgemeinen Bewusstsein ist Potsdam die Stadt, die mehr als jede andere unserer Republik sich müht, verschwundene Denkmäler nachzubauen: Seit der populäre Fernsehmoderator Günther Jauch die Kopie des so genannten Fortunaportals aus eigener Tasche bezahlte, ist Potsdams 1959/60 gesprengtes Stadtschloss bundesweit ein Begriff. Das Gleiche gilt für die ebenfalls gesprengte barocke Garnisonkirche, für deren Kopie derzeit ein Stifterverein nach Spolien fahndet und nie daran zweifelt, Spenden in Millionenhöhe sammeln zu können.

Ein Besuch in Potsdam macht die Kulissensucht verständlich: Geschunden von Bomben und vom Wiederaufbau stellt sich das Zentrum rund um die Kuppelherrlichkeit der Hauptkirche St. Nikolai dar. Wie eine Fata Morgana muten deshalb das sanierte Holländische Viertel oder das barocke Quartier zwischen Marstall und Neuem Markt an, deren Schönheit die Rekonstruktionslust der Potsdamer Bürger anfacht. Damit muss die Stadt für Architekten, die nicht dem Lager der Retro-Bauer angehören, ein Albtraum sein. Nicola Fortmann-Drühe hat ihm mit ihrem 2002 vollendeten Ergänzungsbau am Neuen Markt widerstanden. Nichts wäre einfacher gewesen, als in die einzige Bombenlücke des 1752 einheitlich bebauten Platzes eine Fassadenreplik samt rückwärtigem Neubau zu stellen. Zwei wichtige Vorgaben haben es ihr erleichtert, stattdessen eine subtil aufklärende dreidimensionale Kulisse aufzurichten: Eine stammt von Friedrich dem Großen, der anordnete, den Neuen Markt mit »angenehmen Prospekten« (Heinrich Ludewig Manger, 1789/90) zu rahmen. Die zweite lieferte Andrea Palladio. Das Kahle'sche Haus, der Vorgängerbau von 1755, war Palladios Palazzo Thiene in Vicenza nachempfunden worden. Auch das italienische Baugenie war so vernarrt in schöne Fassaden, dass es ihnen sogar das Innere unterwarf.

In Potsdam, wo 1755 statt der zwei Geschosse des Palazzo Thiene vier entstanden, konnte man, so hieß es 1789 »nur auf dem Fußboden liegend schreiben« (Heinrich Ludewig Manger). Fortmann-Drühes Entwurf, der sich 1998 gegen Wettbewerbsbeiträge so namhafter Konkurrenten wie Kleihues + Kleihues, Gerhard Spangenberg, Franco Stella und Léon Krier/Helmut Peucker durchsetzte, zwingt im ersten Geschoss dazu, mit Rundbogenfenstern knapp über dem Fußboden zu leben; im zweiten beengen frei gestellte Fensterlaibungen vor den Panoramascheiben die Weitsicht, im dritten ragen Segmentbögen und Dreiecke ins Blickfeld, im obersten nimmt eine kahle, von Quadraten perforierte Betonattika die Sicht. Sechs Geschosse sind im Neubau, einem Kubus in Betonrahmenkonstruktion, untergebracht – zwei Läden im Erdgeschoss, darüber eine Büroetage, über dieser fünf Maisonettewohnungen. Das Innere ist sachlich und elegant: die Büroetage ein offener, nur von Pfeilern gegliederter Raum mit separaten Nebenflächen; die Wohnungen nach dem Muster der ›gestapelten Räume‹ holländischer Stadthäuser bestechen durch kubistische Helldunkeleffekte.

Erschlossen wird das Haus über rückseitige Laubengänge und Treppen. Zwischen einer Rückwand von jenem intensiven Rot, das im

▫ Potsdam is widely regarded in Germany as the city that tries harder than any other to reconstruct its lost monuments. Ever since the popular television presenter Günther Jauch paid for the copy of the so-called Fortunaportal out of his own pocket, everyone in the country has been aware of Potsdam's palace, demolished in 1959/60. The same is true of the baroque Garnisonkirche, also demolished; a foundation set up with the aim of faithfully reconstructing it is constantly on the lookout for remnants of the church and is determined to collect the necessary millions in the form of donations.

A visit to Potsdam easily explains this obsession: ravaged by war-time bombing and blighted by post-war development, the focal point of the city centre is the magnificent cupola of St. Nikolai. The refurbished district of the Holländisches Viertel and the baroque quarter between Marstall and Neuer Markt must seem like a fata morgana whose beauty fuels the locals' desire for reconstruction. On the other hand, this city must be a nightmare for any architect who lacks sympathy for such retro tendencies. Nicola Fortmann-Drühe has challenged the status quo with her development of a gap site at Neuer Markt. Nothing could have been simpler than constructing a new building behind a replica historic facade to fill the bombed site on this city square with its homogenous architecture of 1752. But two important factors facilitated her decision to create a subtle and enlightened three-dimensional backdrop instead. One of these was Frederick the Great's own insistence that the Neuer Markt should be framed by "pleasant views" (Heinrich Ludewig Manger, 1789/90). The second came from Andrea Palladio. The building that previously occupied the site was the Kahle'sche Haus (1755) based on the design of Palladio's Palazzo Thiene in Vicenza. The Italian architectural genius was so enthralled by beautiful facades that he was even prepared to make the interior fit the facade, rather than vice versa.

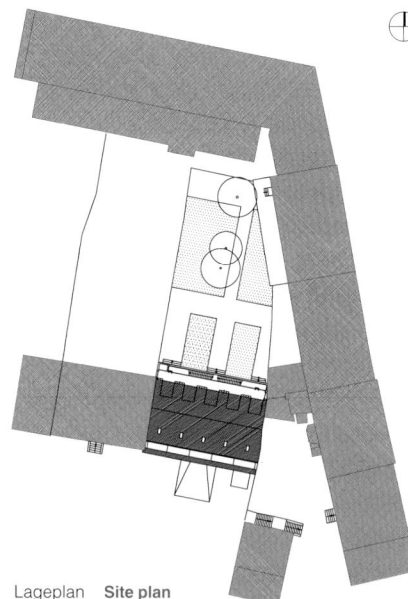

Lageplan **Site plan**

Architekten Architects Nicola Fortmann-Drühe, Potsdam, www.fortmann-druehe.de; Team: Horst Brockmann, Birgit Hübner, Karsten Kajo, Ulrich Klaphecke, Martin Scholz **Bauherr Client** Gertrud Fortmann, Witten **Bauleitung Construction Management** Ingenieurbüro Kraft, Berlin, Astrid Kneib **Tragwerk Structural** GSE Ingenieur-Gesellschaft mbH, Berlin; Fassade Facade Ingenieurbüro Dr. Stich, Potsdam; Innentreppen Stairwell Ingenieurbüro Dr. Zauft, Potsdam **Wettbewerb Competition** 1998 **Ausführung Construction** 2001/02 **Standort Location** Am Neuen Markt 5, Potsdam

barocken Rom beliebt war, und einem vorgestellten Betonstützenraster angeordnet, akzentuieren sie eine Zweitfassade. Diese Hoffassade, die an die besseren Berliner Bauten Max Dudlers gemahnt, würde andernorts als vorbildliche, den örtlichen Klassizismus modern modulierende Schaufront anerkannt. Die überragende Qualität aber beruht auf der palladianischen Fassadenkulisse am Neuen Markt. Nur durch schlanke metallene Loggienstege mit dem eigentlichen Bau verbunden, steht sie unabhängig vor dessen neutraler Glasfassade. Unverkennbar Palladio, spiegelt sie dennoch den Minimalismus des Kernbaus, so wie umgekehrt die Rückfront Palladios bis zur Sturheit meisterhafte Harmonie verarbeitet – die Frage nach dem Prae wäre die nach Henne und Ei. Eigenständigkeit und Gegenwärtigkeit sind die Schlüsselformeln dieses Prospekts: Fortmann-Drühe hat das palladianische Vorbild gleichsam skelettiert, hat die Wand von Beletage und Mezzanin aufgelöst und auf die querrechteckigen Mezzaninfenster verzichtet. Damit sind die einstigen korinthischen Pilaster zu freien Pfeilern geworden, und aus den prunkvollen Laibungen der Hauptfenster isolierte Ädikulen. Als folgenreichster Verzicht fehlen die skulptierten Rosengirlanden und weiblichen Büsten der Oberzone. Da also, wo sich ehemals Schöpfertum zur individuellen Kunst verdichtete, hat die Architektin sich vor der Unwiederholbarkeit des Baukunstwerks verbeugt. In diesem Sinne wirkt auch das Baumaterial – Betonwerkstein, der die Wand irreal flirren lässt wie eine Computersimulation. Die Architektin hört es nicht gerne, aber sie hat damit ein Prinzip geliefert, wie bei den wohl unvermeidlichen künftigen Großprojekten – dem Nachbau des Berliner oder des Potsdamer Stadtschlosses, des Dresdner Neumarkts oder der Garnisonkirche – verfahren werden könnte, wenn leblose Klone vermieden werden sollen.

Dieter Bartetzko

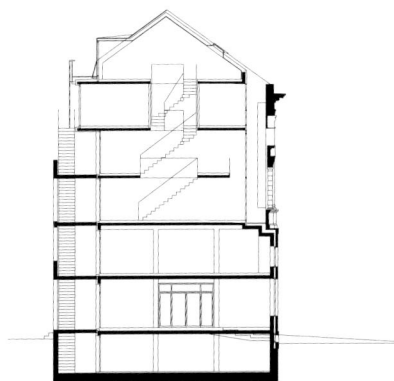

Schnitt **Section**

In Potsdam, where the 1755 building had four storeys instead of the two storeys of Palazzo Thiene, Heinrich Ludewig Manger complained in 1789 that one had to "lie on the floor to write". Fortmann-Drühe's design, which, in 1998, won against such renowned competitors as Kleihues + Kleihues, Gerhard Spangenberg, Franco Stella and Léon Krier/Helmut Peucker, forces the building's users to live with round-arched windows just above floor level on the first floor, while on the second floor freestanding window embrasures in front of the panorama glazing narrow the view. On the third floor segment arches and triangles jut into the field of vision and on the upper floor a spartan concrete attica perforated by rectangles blocks the view. There are six floors in all in this new building, which takes the form of a cube in a concrete frame structure – two shops on the ground floor, offices on the first floor, and five maisonette apartments on the upper levels. The interior is sober and elegant. The office floor is an open-plan space divided only by pillars, with separate ancillary spaces. The apartments above are designed along the lines of Dutch town houses with "stacked rooms" and cubist light-and-shade effects.

The house is accessed from the rear by covered walkways and stairs. Between a rear wall of the same intense red popular in baroque Rome, and a protruding concrete grid of supports, these accentuate a secondary facade. Constructed elsewhere, this courtyard facade, reminiscent of Max Dudler's finest Berlin buildings, could have been recognised as an exemplary main facade that takes a modern approach to modulating the neo-classicism of the region. The outstanding quality of this architecture, however, is based primarily on the Palladian facade towards Neuer Markt. Linked to the building itself only by slender metal loggia bridges, it is independent of the neutral glass facade. Unmistakably Palladian in character, it nevertheless mirrors the minimalism of the core building, just as the rear facade recalls Palladio's almost stubborn magisterial harmony – to ask which came first would be like asking the age-old question of the chicken and the egg. Independence and presence are the key concepts behind this. Fortmann-Drühe has pared Palladian architecture down to its very skeleton, dissolving the wall of belle étage and mezzanine and doing away with the rectangular mezzanine windows. Where once there were Corinthian pilasters, she has created freestanding columns, and she has turned the ostentatious embrasures of the main windows into isolated aedicules. The most striking omission is that of the sculpted garlands of roses and female busts on the upper level. In other words, where creativity was once concentrated into individual art, the architect has paid homage to the impossibility of repeating a work of architecture. This is also reflected in the materials she has chosen to use – the rough concrete makes the wall shimmer unreally like a computer simulation. Although the architect does not like to hear this said, what she has done is to provide a benchmark for ways of approaching future major projects, inevitable as they are, such as the reconstruction of the Berlin Palace or the Potsdam Palace, the Dresdner Neumarkt or the Garnisonkirche, without falling into the trap of creating lifeless clones.

Dieter Bartetzko

Ansicht von Süden **View from the south**

Ansicht von Norden
View from the north

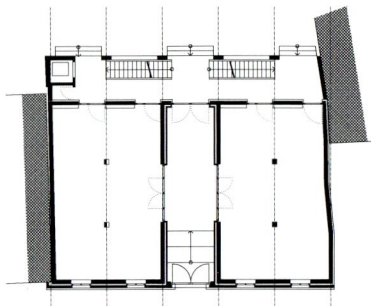

Grundriss Erdgeschoss   **Ground-floor plan**

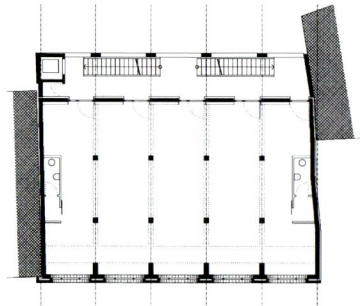

Grundriss 1. Obergeschoss   **First-floor plan**

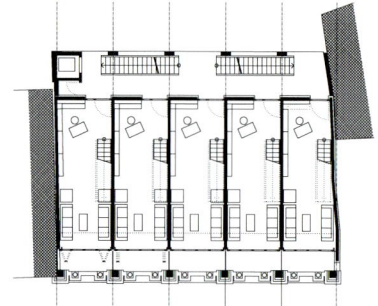

Grundriss 2. Obergeschoss   **Second-floor plan**

Büro 1. Obergeschoss   **Office, first floor**

Wohnraum 2. Obergeschoss   **Living area, second floor**

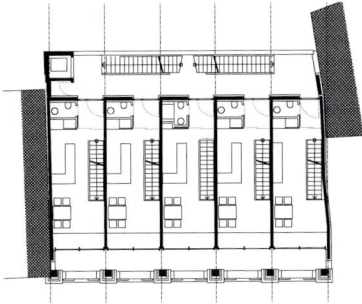

Grundriss 3. Obergeschoss **Third-floor plan**

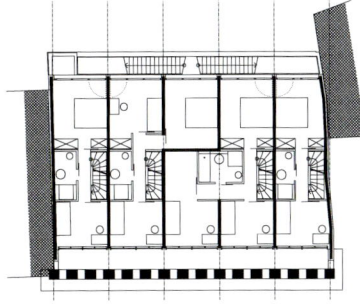

Grundriss 4. Obergeschoss **Fourth-floor plan**

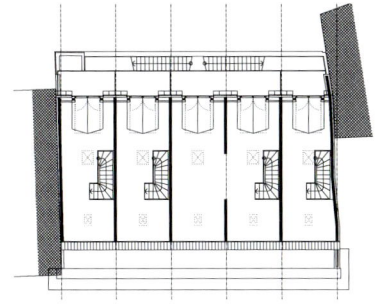

Grundriss Dachgeschoss **Top-floor plan**

Küche 3. Obergeschoss **Kitchen, third floor**

Maximilianhöfe, Neubebauung am Marstallplatz, München
Maximilianhöfe, new development at Marstallplatz, Munich

Gewers Kühn und Kühn

■ München hat einen Ruf zu verlieren. Vor fünf Jahren noch konnte die Stadtbaurätin Christiane Thalgott in einem Gespräch mit der Zeitschrift *Der Architekt* (Heft 2/1999) die örtliche Planungskultur loben, und mit Verweis auf die von Herzog & de Meuron überarbeiteten Fünf Höfe sogar behaupten: »In München werden Entscheidungen mit den großen Investoren getroffen, nicht von ihnen.« Doch seither hat sich auch hier der Wind gedreht. Jüngere Beispiele dafür sind der vom Investor scheinheilig betriebene Wettbewerb für das Gelände der Alten Chemie und die wundersame, durch eine nachträgliche Änderung des Bebauungsplans bewilligte Aufstockung der Twin Towers aus dem Büro Murphy/Jahn an der Einfahrt zur Nordautobahn, die eine wichtige historische Blickachse aus der Altstadt zerstört.

Von dieser schleichenden Entwicklung ist auch das Gebiet um den Marstallplatz im Münchner Zentrum leider nicht verschont geblieben – besonders betrüblich angesichts der Wettbewerbe, die für alle Projekte durchgeführt wurden. Dabei handelt es sich um ein Gelände, das trotz seiner prominenten Lage zwischen Maximilianstraße und Hofgarten bis vor 15 Jahren noch die Wunden des Bombenkriegs zeigte: Ruinenreste auf verwilderten Grundstücken, Brandmauern, behelfsmäßige Werkstätten der benachbarten Staatsoper und barackenähnliche Flachbauten. Inmitten dieser riesigen Brachfläche erhob sich der mächtige Baublock des Marstalls von Leo von Klenze – Anlass genug für eine groß angelegte Stadtreparatur, die eine ausbalancierte Mischung von Rekonstruktion und Neubau hervorbringen sollte. Heute jedoch lässt sich nur noch von versäumten Chancen sprechen.

Das Unglück begann schon früh, nämlich um 1990, als am Ostrand des Hofgartens der postmodern aufgeputzte Bürotempel der Bayerischen Staatskanzlei beidseits der rekonstruierten Armeemuseumskuppel errichtet wurde. Gegenüber entstand dann zwar der neue Hauptsitz der Max-Planck-Gesellschaft der Architekten Graf, Popp und Streib als eine städtebaulich fulminante Lösung, doch danach fiel man wieder in die übliche Münchner Beliebigkeit zurück. So wird der Altstadtring, der östlich des Marstalls verläuft, seit 2002 von zwei typischen Beispielen flankiert: von einem insgesamt banalen Glasriegelbau aus dem Büro Lanz und von einem Bürohausensemble, das Hilmer & Sattler in steife Terrakotta-Kleider gesteckt haben. Umso größer waren die Hoffnungen, dass wenigstens die Maximilianhöfe gelingen mögen.

Für dieses große Bauvorhaben gab es sogar zwei Wettbewerbe. Im ersten Verfahren wurde ein Investor ermittelt, dem der Freistaat Bayern das Gelände im Erbbaurecht überließ mit der Gegenleistung, dass dieser auf seine Kosten ein Probengebäude für die Staatsoper errichten musste. Im darauf folgenden eingeladenen Architektenwettbewerb kam es zu keiner eindeutigen Entscheidung: Jeweils ein zweiter Preis ging an die Berliner Architekten Gewers, Kühn und Kühn (GKK) und an das Münchner Büro Kiessler und Partner. Danach wurde das Verfahren undurchsichtig. Während nämlich die Jury noch den dritten Preisträger zur Überarbeitung empfohlen hatte, ging der

Munich has a reputation to lose. Just five years ago, chief municipal architect Christiane Thalgott had occasion to praise local planning policy in an interview with *Der Architekt* magazine (2/1999). She even singled out the Herzog & de Meuron redevelopment of Fünf Höfe with the claim that, "In Munich decisions are taken with, not by, major investors". But times have changed since then. More recent examples include the competition, piously launched by the investor, for the redevelopment of the Alte Chemie, the former site of the university's chemistry faculty, and the miraculous approval, thanks to a last-minute planning amendment, of Murphy/Jahn's extension to the Twin Towers at the entrance to the Nordautobahn, which blocks an important vista from the historic Old Town.

This stealthy change of direction, unfortunately, has not spared the district around Marstallplatz in the centre of Munich either – which is particularly galling given that competitions were held for all the projects. This is a site which, in spite of its prominent position between Maximilianstrasse and Hofgarten, still displayed the wounds of Second World War bombing until 15 years ago: ruins on overgrown sites, firewalls, temporary workshops for the nearby Staatsoper and shed-like flat-roofed low-rises. In the midst of this huge wilderness stood the magnificent block of the Marstall – the former royal riding school designed by Leo von Klenze. Surely this was a rare opportunity for urban repair on a grand scale, calling for a balanced mix of reconstruction and new building. Today, we can only talk of an opportunity missed.

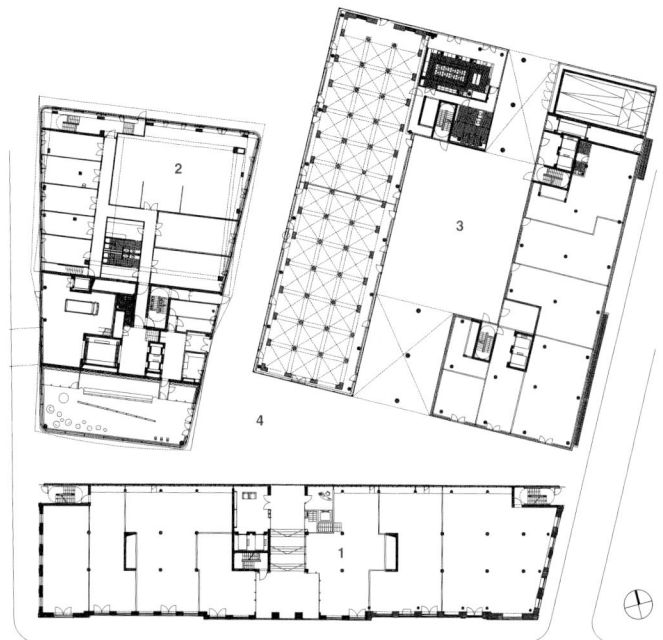

Lageplan **Site plan**

1 Bürkleinbau **Bürklein Building**
2 Probebühnengebäude **Rehearsal studio building**
3 Maximilianhof **Maximilianhof**
4 Salpeterhof **Salpeterhof**

Architekten Architects Gewers Kühn und Kühn, Gesellschaft von Architekten mbH, Berlin, www.gkk-architekten.de; Georg Gewers, Prof. Swantje Kühn, Oliver Kühn; Team: Oliver Kühn & Markus Funke, Tilman Richter von Senfft, Uwe Karl & Oliver Bormann, Ulrike Franke, Don Lee, Michael Leone, Myoung-Ju Lee, Arnd Manzewski, Kristin Neise, Jan Papenhagen, Barbara Schlungbaum, Vlatka Seremet, Lennaart Sirag, Frank Weber **Bauherr** Client Palos Immobilien- und Projektentwicklungs GmbH & Co. München KG/Dreyer, Brettel und Kollegen Management GmbH, München **Tragwerk** Structural Hartwich/Mertens/Ingenieure Planungsgesellschaft für Bauwesen mbH, Berlin **HL-Technik** Technical HL-Technik AG, München **Freianlagen** Landscape ST raum a. Landschaftsarchitektur, Berlin **Wettbewerb** Competition 2000 **Ausführung** Construction 2000–2003 **Standort** Location Maximilianstraße 10, München

Investor seinen eigenen Weg und teilte schließlich mit, dass er GKK beauftragen werde. Noch erstaunlicher war die Tatsache, dass der nicht ordnungsgemäß abgeschlossene Wettbewerb vom federführenden Finanzministerium hingenommen wurde.

GKK hatten für ihre Maximilianhöfe viel versprochen. Und was hat München bekommen? Das einzig Positive ist eine angenehme städtische Dichte mit zwei Höfen und wechselnden Wegbreiten. Die Architektur aber ist unbedeutend bis abstoßend. Dies beginnt bei der Rekonstruktion des Bürkleinbaus aus dem 19. Jahrhundert an der noblen Maximilianstraße, der durch den Weltkrieg zu zwei Dritteln verloren gegangen war. Entgegen dem ersten Anschein handelt es sich nämlich nicht um die Rekonstruktion eines Bauwerks, sondern lediglich um die Nachäffung einer historischen Fassade, die als nichttragende Kulisse mit einem neuen Stahlbetonbau rückverdübelt ist – purer »Fassadismus« (Dieter Bartetzko). Besonders grotesk ist die Rückseite dieses neuen ›Altbaus‹ als durchgehend dunkle Glasfassade, die sich an den Ecken irgendwie in grob gestaltete Treppenhäuser auflöst: Hier ist Täuschung in Unvermögen umgeschlagen.

Ebenso marktgängig wie uninspiriert sind die Glas-Aluminium-Fassaden der Geschäfts- und Bürohäuser. Im Bereich der dreischiffigen Säulenhalle, die als Denkmal zu integrieren war, haben GKK freilich das Kunststück fertig gebracht, die Glashaut wie ein Präservativ über die Bogenreihen zu ziehen. In der Säulenhalle residiert das Restaurant Brenner, der bislang einzige lebendige Ort in den Höfen. Dessen große Freifläche ist zum Treffpunkt für Shopping- und Business-People geworden, die es nicht zu stören scheint, dass gegenüber der metallisch harte Klotz des neuen Probengebäudes aufragt. Gäbe es denn eine Prämie für den derzeit hässlichsten Münchner Neubau – das Probengebäude mit seinen unsinnig gefalteten Fassaden hätte ihn verdient.

Nach der apodiktischen Entscheidung des Investors für GKK hatte die Kritikerin Dorothea Parker zu Recht geunkt, die Qualität werde der Rentabilität zum Opfer fallen. Wäre jedoch der zweite Preisträger Kiessler und Partner zum Zuge gekommen, hätte München eine konzeptionell und architektonisch herausragende Lösung bekommen. Ein Jammer!

Wolfgang Jean Stock

Things began to go wrong quite some time ago, in 1990, in fact, with the erection of a pompous postmodernist office temple for the Bayerische Staatskanzlei (Bavarian State Chancellery) flanking either side of the domed Army Museum building at the eastern edge of the Hofgarten. At the time, the new headquarters of the Max Planck Society was built opposite it by architects Graf, Popp and Streib – in itself a grandiose piece of urban planning, but one that was not followed up. Instead, Munich sank back into its customary hit-and-miss approach to urban planning, with the result that the Altstadtring running to the east of the Marstall has been flanked since 2002 by two typical examples: a thoroughly banal glass block by Lanz and an office ensemble clad in unbecoming terracotta by Hilmer & Sattler.

Hopes were high that the Maximilianhöfe, at least, might fare better. There were even two competitions for this major project. In the first phase, an investor was found to whom the state of Bavaria would grant hereditary rights to the site in exchange for funding and building a rehearsal studio complex for the Staatsoper. In the subsequent architectural design competition, held by invitation, there was no clear-cut decision. A joint second prize was awarded to Berlin-based architects Gewers, Kühn and Kühn (GKK) and to the Munich firm of Kiessler and Partner. Then the whole process became vague. Whereas the jury had recommended that the design of the third prize winner should be reworked, the investor announced that GKK had been awarded the contract. More remarkable still was the fact that the competition, which had not been concluded according to regulations, had been accepted by the Ministry of Finance in charge.

GKK had promised a great deal in their version of the Maximilianhöfe. But what did Munich get? The only positive aspect is a pleasing urban density with two courtyards and alternating pathway widths. The architecture is mediocre, verging on unacceptable. This starts with the reconstruction of the nineteenth-century Bürklein building on prestigious Maximilianstrasse, two thirds of which had been destroyed in the war. Though the first impression may be one of a reconstruction, this is merely a poor imitation of a historic facade – a non-loadbearing backdrop pinned onto a new reinforced concrete building, a prime example of what Dieter Bartetzko has dubbed Facadism. Most grotesque of all is the back of this new "old building": a dark glass facade that somehow dissolves into roughly formed stairwells at the corner. Here, illusion has given way to incompetence.

The glass and aluminium facades of the commercial and office buildings are as commonplace as they are uninspired. In the area of the three-naved columned hall that was supposed to be integrated as a historic monument, GKK have even gone so far as to pull the glass skin over the row of arches like a condom. The columned hall now houses the Restaurant Brenner – the only place in the complex that has any life in it so far. The huge open space has become a meeting point for shoppers and business people who do not seem to take umbrage at the soaring lump of hard metal opposite that is the new rehearsal studio complex. If a prize for the ugliest new building in Munich were given out, the rehearsal studio

Bürkleinbau, teilrekonstruierte Fassade an der Maximilianstraße   **Bürklein Building, partially reconstructed facade on Maximilianstrasse**

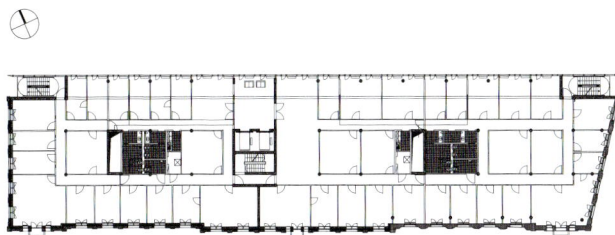

0   5 m

Bürkleinbau, Grundriss 3. Obergeschoss
Bürklein Building, third-floor plan

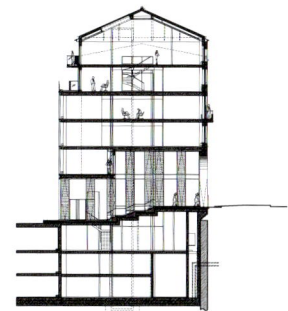

Bürkleinbau, Schnitt
Bürklein Building, section

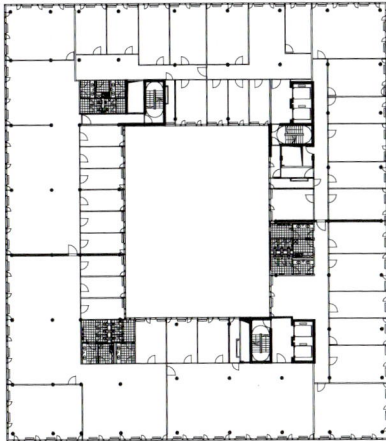

Maximilianhof, Grundriss 3. Obergeschoss
Maximilianhof, third-floor plan

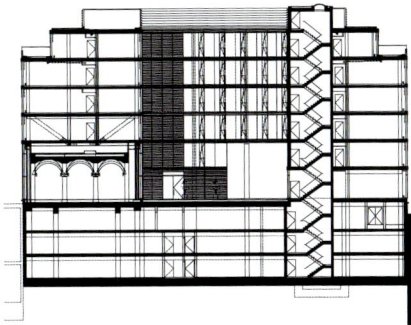

Maximilianhof, Innenhof   **Maximilianhof, courtyard**

Maximilianhof, Schnitt   **Maximilianhof, section**

building with its nonsensically folded facade would surely be one of the hottest contenders.

Following the investor's apodictic decision to commission GKK, critic Dorothea Parker quite rightly quipped that quality would be a victim of profitability. Had second prize winners Kiessler and Partner been given a chance, Munich would have been graced with a conceptually and architecturally outstanding solution. Shame, really.

Wolfgang Jean Stock

Maximilianhof, Blick auf die umbaute historische Säulenhalle
Maximilianhof, view towards converted historic pillared hall

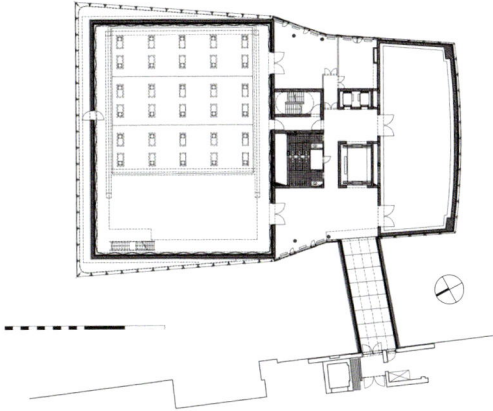

Probebühnengebäude, Grundriss 1. Obergeschoss
Rehearsal studio building, first-floor plan

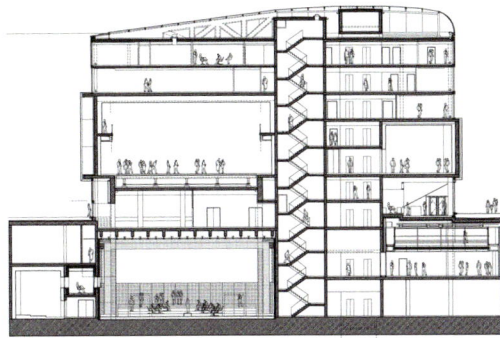

Probebühnengebäude, Schnitt
Rehearsal studio building, section

Probebühnengebäude, Eingang Kassenhalle   **Rehearsal studio building, entrance with box office**

Probebühnengebäude
Rehearsal studio building

Große Probebühne   **Main rehearsal studio**

Firmenrepräsentanz Unter den Linden 1, Berlin
Company representation, Unter den Linden 1, Berlin

van den Valentyn

■ Rekonstruktionen sind objektive Realitäten, die auf irrealen Vorstellungen von Wirklichkeit fußen. Ihnen ist kein Entwurf gewachsen. Bei Menschen spricht man von Identitätskrisen, in manchen Fällen von Schizophrenie.

Fünf Büros hatte die Bertelsmann AG zur Erstellung eines Konzeptes für die prominente Adresse Unter den Linden 1 eingeladen, bevor feststand, dass die Rekonstruktion des Kommandantenhauses beschlossene Sache ist. Das Büro Baumschlager & Eberle zog sich daraufhin zurück. Keiner sonst schien Zweifel zu hegen, ob an dieser Stelle, gegenüber vom Zeughaus und am Beginn des Schlossplatzes, genau das Gebäude wieder errichtet werden sollte, das die Geschichte irgendwann einmal dorthin gepflanzt hatte und das dreimal umgebaut wurde, bevor es von der Bildfläche verschwand. Krieg und Abriss hatten sein natürliches Schicksal besiegelt. Die Stadt Berlin gewährt ihm nun ein Schicksal danach.

Dieses Schicksal ist das eines Zwitters, so sieht es schon die Aufgabenverteilung vor. Das Büro Stuhlemmer & Stuhlemmer sorgte für die historische Fassade, das Büro van den Valentyn war zwar verantwortlich für das Ganze, konnte aber doch nur das Innere eines ›entkernten historischen Gebäudes‹ gestalten und folgte dabei der Vorstellung, dass hier zwei Realitäten nebeneinander entstehen und erlebbar gemacht werden könnten.

Wir betreten das Haus so, wie es einst betreten wurde. Sein Eingang liegt unter einem sich über drei Fensterachsen erstreckenden Balkon. In gleicher Breite folgt innen eine Treppe, sieben Stufen hoch. Von hier an ein breiter stützenfreier leerer Raum, zumindest im vorderen Teil des Hauses. Die Betondecken spannen über zwei Erschließungskerne in der Mittelzone. Der Reiz dieser Halle liegt in der ›historischen‹ Fassade, die innen genauso sichtbar ist wie außen und weiß gestrichen eine befremdlich vertraute Kulisse bildet, sich in den großen Saal auf der Ostseite erweitert und eigentlich bis in den kleinen Saal gegenüber sichtbar bleiben müsste. Dort ist sie zurzeit durch provisorische Ausstellungstafeln verstellt, was die Wirkung erheblich beeinträchtigt. Vorausschauend hätte der Architekt die Möglichkeit, dass in diesem Saal immer wieder Präsentationen gezeigt werden, einberechnen und mit einer gestalterischen Lösung darauf reagieren müssen. Haben es sich die Architekten mit dem Nebeneinander der beiden Welten zu leicht gemacht? Haben sie geglaubt, durch die Eigenständigkeit der Vokabulare stelle sich Spannung wie von selbst ein? Sie waren vor allem darum besorgt, welche zeitgemäßen Lösungen das Image des Hauses Bertelsmann am besten widerspiegeln. Im Eingangsbereich gibt es eine blau gestrichene Wand um einen der Kerne, die unterbrochen wird von Linien in Orange mit kleinen Stecklichtern, auf die eine Bildwand zu montieren ist, ein sehr eigenes Element in den Kennfarben des Hausherrn. Zudem gibt es herrlich schwere Glastüren, die den durchgehenden Raum in drei Teile zerlegen können oder zusammengefaltet in ihrer Ruheposition warten. Über dem großen Saal hängt eine helle Ahorndecke, aus der das Licht durch handwerkliche, in Tschechien

Reconstructions are objective realities rooted in unreal notions of reality. No design can measure up to them. A person in this situation is said to have an identity crisis – or even schizophrenia.

Bertelsmann AG invited five architectural firms to draw up a concept for their prestigious address at Unter den Linden 1 before it became clear that the reconstruction of the Kommandantenhaus was definitely in the cards. At that point, architects Baumschlager & Eberle withdrew from the competition. Nobody else seems to have had any scruples about whether it was really a good idea for this site opposite the Zeughaus, at the entrance to Schlossplatz, to be given the exact same building that history had once planted there and which had been altered three times before it disappeared. War and demolition had sealed its fate in the natural course of history. Now the city of Berlin has decided to grant it an afterlife.

Its fate is that of a hermaphrodite. Even the division of labour involved points in that direction. The firm of Stuhlemmer & Stuhlemmer was in charge of the historic facade, while the firm of van den Valentyn was responsible for the overall building, but ended up designing only the interior of a "completely gutted historic building", pursuing the notion that two realities could be created and perceived side by side here.

We enter the building just as it was entered in the past. The entrance is situated under a balcony that stretches across three window axes. A seven-tread stairway of the same width follows on the inside. From here, there is a broad, empty space without supports, at least in the front part of the building. The concrete ceilings span two access cores in the central zone. The appeal of this hall lies in the "historic" facade, which is visible both inside and outside. Painted white to create a strangely alienated yet familiar backdrop, it extends into the large room on the east side and ought to be visible as far as the little room opposite. At the moment, however, it is concealed by temporary display panels, to the detriment of the

Lageplan **Site plan**

Architekten Architects van den Valentyn – Architektur, Köln, www.vandenvalentyn.de; Thomas van den Valentyn; Team: Matthias Dittmann, Johannes van Linn & Beate Borghoff, Susanne Falke, Franziska Lüke, Liane Wilke, Armin Tillmann **Bauherr Client** Bertelsmann AG, Gütersloh **Rekonstruktion der historischen Fassade Reconstruction of historic facade** Stuhlemmer & Stuhlemmer, Berlin **Projektsteuerung Project Management** Ingenieurbüro Löffler & Kuscher, Berlin **Tragwerk Structural** Hartwich/Mertens/Ingenieure Planungsgesellschaft für Bauwesen mbH, Berlin **Innenausstattung Interior furnishing** SPS-Projekt, Stuttgart **Wettbewerb Competition** 2000 **Ausführung Construction** 2001–2003 **Standort Location** Unter den Linden 1, Berlin

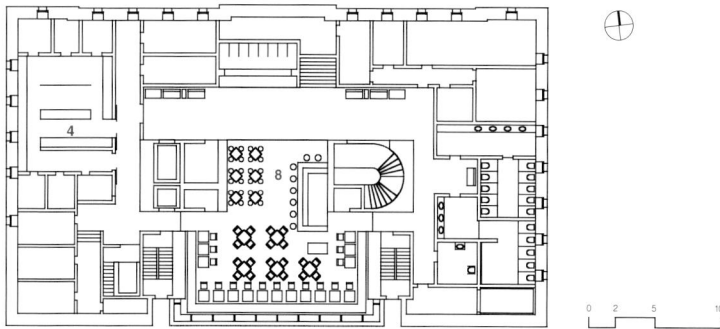

Grundriss 1. Untergeschoss   **Floorplan of basement level 1**

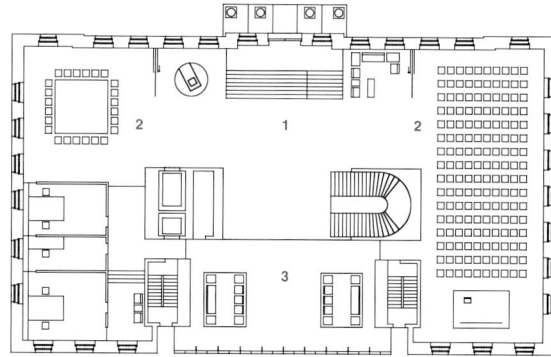

Grundriss Erdgeschoss   **Ground-floor plan**

gefertigte Glasplatten geschickt wird, die es auch einfärben können. Es ist wie in einem Einrichtungshaus, wo teure Einzelstücke angeboten werden. Die alte Innenfassade mischt sich überall ein und isoliert die Teile voneinander.

Gen Süden, jenseits der Kerne, liegt der Wintergarten. Der wurde dem rekonstruierten Haus als einziges fremdes Element zugestanden. Er überdeckt die Fläche, um die das Haus einst zurücksprang und einen Hof übrig ließ, der aber auch den Rekonstruktionsarchitekten wenig bemerkenswert schien. Der Wintergarten, ursprünglich als dreigeschossige gebogene Glasfläche über den Hof gezogen, ist jetzt nur noch eine am oberen Ende gebogene Glaswand, weil die Architekten, eine zu starke Sonneneinstrahlung befürchtend, eine raumhohe u-förmige Manschette eingestellt haben, die mit einem Bildschirmhimmel ausgestattet ist, weil sie den wirklichen Himmel verdeckt. Auch hier zerfällt das Haus in unverbundene Teile, die durch das helle Ahornholz und den portugiesischen Kalkstein, der sich auch durch alle Treppenhäuser zieht, zusammengehalten werden sollen. Im Lindensaal in der Beletage mit anschließendem Restaurant und Mediathek könnten die ›historischen‹ Fensterreihen wieder zu ihrem Recht kommen. Sie erhielten ein ornamentales Gegenüber durch Vertäfelungen aus stark gemustertem Makassarholz. Doch dem tiefdunklen Makassar ist ein Lichtkasten aus Alabaster zugeordnet, wodurch das Spiel mit Gegensätzen in die neue Ausstattung gebannt wird und die ›historische‹ Wand wieder außen vor bleibt. Im zweiten Obergeschoss, wo die einzigen ständigen Arbeitsräume liegen, bilden die ›historischen‹ Fenster nur noch schmale senkrechte Streifen über viel zu hohen Brüstungen. Diesen wenig erhellten Arbeitsluken haben die Architekten raumhohe flexible Trennwände zugeordnet, die in großen Schränken verschwinden und einem Loftausbau gut anstehen würden. Ganz oben, auf dem gepflasterten Dach mit einem herrlichen Rundblick, übernimmt erstmals die Historie den dominanten Part: Man steht oder geht hinter nachgegossenen Adlern.

Martina Düttmann

overall effect. The architect should have had the foresight to take into account that this room would be used from time to time for presentations, and should have acted accordingly in finding a design solution. Have the architects taken the easy way out by juxtaposing these two worlds? Did they believe that these two distinct architectural vocabularies would create an impact all by themselves? They were primarily concerned with finding contemporary solutions that would best mirror the image of the Bertelsmann concern. In the entrance area, there is a blue wall around one of the core areas, interrupted by orange lines with little plug-and-play sockets for wall-mounted monitors – a distinctive element in the client's familiar corporate colours. There are wonderfully heavy glass doors that can partition the room into three zones or be folded back on standby. Above this large space is a pale ceiling of maple, with light channelled in changing colours through glass panels produced by artisans in the Czech Republic. It is a little like a furniture store selling expensive one-offs. The old interior facade intrudes on everything, isolating the individual parts from one another.

To the south, beyond the core areas, is the winter garden. This is the only concession to change in the form of a foreign body added to the reconstructed building. It covers the area where there was previously a recess forming a courtyard, though the reconstruction architects seem to have deemed it too unremarkable to retain. The winter garden, originally in the form of a three-storey bowed glass structure drawn over the courtyard, is now merely a glass wall curved at the upper end, because the architects, fearing that the sunlight would be too strong, have inserted a ceiling-high U-shaped cuff complete with a video-screen sky to make up for concealing the real sky. Here again, the design disintegrates into unconnected parts which the pale maple and Portuguese limestone running throughout all the stairwells are expected to hold together. In the Lindensaal room on the first floor, with its adjacent restaurant and media library, the "historic" windows come into their own again. They have been given an ornamental counterpoint in the form of strongly patterned macassar wood panelling. However, the dark macassar wood has been fitted with an alabaster light-box, with the result that any attempt to play with opposites has been limited to the new interior, leaving the "historic" wall out on a limb yet again.

1 Foyer
Foyer
2 Konferenzraum
Conference room
3 Wintergarten
Winter garden
4 Küche
Kitchen
5 Club
Club
6 Mediathek
Mediathek
7 Lindensaal
Lindensaal
8 Brasserie
Brasserie

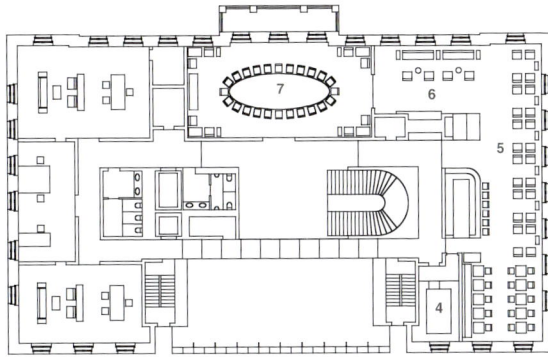

Grundriss 1. Obergeschoss **First-floor plan**

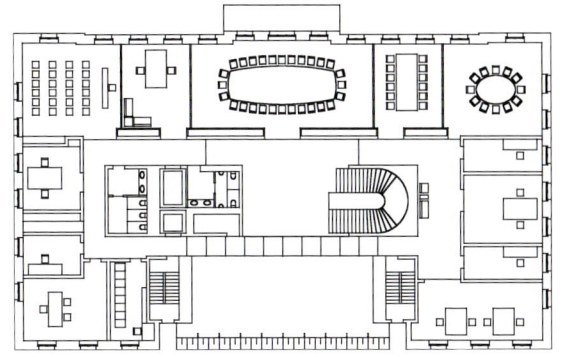

Grundriss 2. Obergeschoss **Second-floor plan**

Ansicht von Nordosten **View from the north-east**

Ansicht von Südosten   **View from the south-east**

On the second floor, where the only permanent office spaces are situated, the "historic" windows are merely narrow vertical strips set above parapets that are far too high. These small workplace windows receive little light, and the architects have provided flexible ceiling-height partition walls that can disappear into large cupboards and would not be out of place in a loft conversion. Right at the top on the stone-paved roof with its magnificent panoramic views, history takes centre stage for the first time as we stand or walk behind the cast copies of eagles.

Martina Düttmann

Wintergarten **Winter garden**

Foyer **Foyer**

Lindensaal **Lindensaal**

Club **Club**

Treppe **Staircase**

Architektur in | aus Deutschland
Architecture in | from Germany

Institut für Physik der Humboldt-Universität, Berlin
Institute of Physics at Humboldt University, Berlin

Augustin und Frank

■ Mit einem Mal, da geht es aufs freie Feld zu, scheint sich das allgemein herrschende Bauklima geändert zu haben. Sicher, das Straßenschema darf man orthogonal nennen, hier, zwischen ehemaligen Kasernen und historischem Flugfeld. In Sonderlaboren und bizarren Bauwerken hat das deutsche Flugwesen seine Wiege hinterlassen. Sie birgt Windkanal, Motorenprüfstand und Trudelturm, alles denkmalgeschützt. Und doch, auf diesem Raster wirkt Berlin geradezu zurückgelassen – nicht geografisch, aber bauideologisch deutlich distanziert. Denn hier, in Berlin-Adlershof, ballen sich Wissenschaftsbauten heterogen und unhierarchisch zu einem Technologiepark – darunter auch der Neubau des Instituts für Physik der Humboldt-Universität.

Dass mit dem Institut die Grundstückskanten besetzt sind, mag zunächst als klassische Lösung betrachtet werden. Doch dass mit dem Gebäudekomplex mehr als nur Anleihen bei den bekannten Berlintypologien genommen wurden, ist den Architekten Georg Augustin und Ute Frank zu verdanken. Wo Kollegen auf manchem Berliner Baugrund angesichts der Trinität der ›Kritischen Rekonstruktion‹ (Traufhöhe, Tektonik, Tradition) resignierend oder gläubig die Hände falten, haben Augustin und Frank selbstbewusst unorthodox gehandelt. Nach Nordwesten, in Richtung des historischen Flugfelds, fasst eine Industrieglasfassade den viergeschossigen Baukörper meergrün. Ihr offener Charakter wird aus der Transparenz des Profilbauglases und den dahinter liegenden Betonfertigteilen entwickelt, die die Haut genauso beleben wie das zweigeschossige ›Fensterband‹. Das Ergebnis besteht in einer aquamarinen Fassade, die das Bild einer Festplatte aufscheinen lässt, je nach Lichtverhältnissen einmal matt, einmal suggestiv.

Nach Nordosten und Südwesten hin sind die sich überlagernden Raumschichten deutlich erkennbar, auf der Eingangsseite der auch öffentlich zugängliche Hörsaal und ein Seminarraum, der in das Foyer schwebend eingehängt ist. Er bildet einen angeschwollenen Körper aus Glasbausteinen in einem ansonsten streng orthogonalen Bauwerk. Das Institut bietet auf seinen immerhin 150 Meter langen Erschließungsachsen rein funktionale Routen. Auf ihnen, über den Estrich und entlang der Sichtbetonwände sind die Labore, die Büros und Lehrräume zu erreichen, insgesamt nicht mehr als drei Raumtypen. Obendrein, neben aller zweckgerichteten Lauferei, erlaubt das Institut gezielte Abschweifungen – mit seinen fünf Innenhöfen als Orientierungspunkten, um die sich ökologische Interessen oder Entspannungssuchende bewegen können. Mit seinem ebenerdigen ›Wald‹ aus schrägen Betonstützen und einem Steg, der einen der Gärten überspannt, erlaubt das Gebäude eine Architekturpromenade, auf der man sich für sehr unterschiedliche Dinge interessieren kann. Ob für die mikadoartig angeordneten Leuchtkörper unter den Decken der langen Flure oder die Pinnwände aus geleimtem Pressspan. Ob für die manuell zu bedienenden Züge und die Klappen für eine natürliche Belüftung oder die Stadionbestuhlung im Hörsaal. Tüfteleien sind Details in einem Gesamtkonzept, dessen Systematik

Suddenly, there are open fields; the generally prevailing built environment seems to have changed. Admittedly, the street layout can still be described as orthogonal here between the former barracks and the historic airfield, where the cradle of German aviation has left its traces in the form of special laboratories and bizarre buildings that house the wind-tunnel, the engine test bench, and the rotary balance test tower – all of them now on the list of protected historical monuments. And yet, Berlin seems to have been left behind in this pattern – clearly distanced, if not geographically, then in terms of building ideology. Here in Berlin-Adlershof, the heterogeneous and non-hierarchical concentration of science and technology buildings includes the new building of the Institute of Physics of the city's Humboldt University.

The fact that the Institute of Physics occupies the edges of the site may appear at first glance to be a classical solution. Thanks to architects Georg Augustin and Ute Frank, however, the complex has achieved far more than merely citing familiar Berlin typologies. Whereas many a colleague, faced with the sacred urban planning trinity of "critical reconstruction" (eave height, tectonics, tradition), would have shrugged their shoulders in resignation or conformist piety, Augustin and Frank have acted with a healthy disdain for orthodoxy. To the north-west, in the direction of the historic airfield, an industrial glass facade immerses the four-storey building in ocean green. Its open character has been developed from the transparency of the glass and the prefabricated concrete components

Lageplan **Site plan**

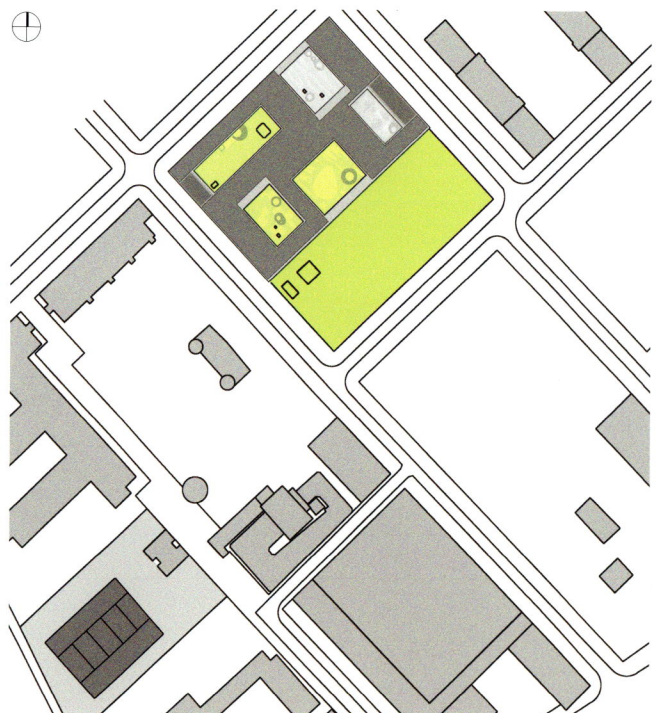

Architekten Architects Augustin und Frank Architekten, Berlin, www.augustinundfrank.de; Georg Augustin, Ute Frank; Team: Anja Hoffmann, Daniel Rozynski, Karine Stight, Lukas Weder **Bauherr Client** Land Berlin vertreten durch die represented by Senatsverwaltung für Wissenschaft, Forschung und Kultur **Tragwerk Structural** Pichler Ingenieure GmbH, Berlin/Potsdam **Freianlagen Landscape** Burger + Tischer Landschaftsarchitekten, Berlin **Wettbewerb Competition** 1997/98 **Ausführung Construction** 2000–2003 **Standort Location** Newtonstraße 15, Berlin-Adlershof

auf Sinnfälligkeit basiert – und das mag der Grund sein, warum man die Fensterprofile prüfend betastet.

Man darf das Gebäude als ein Betätigungsfeld der Neugier auffassen, hier, in Adlershof, einem Ortsteil im Berliner Stadtbezirk Treptow-Köpenick, wo mit den Technologiezentren von Sauerbruch Hutton, Ortner & Ortner oder ef+ seit den neunziger Jahren ein kleiner Ortsteil entstanden ist, der das Verblüffende bereitstellt. Auch der Neubau des Instituts für Physik aus dem Büro von Augustin und Frank liefert an diesem Standort Anregungen. Beispielhaft erfährt dies das Interesse, das sich der Südostfassade zuwendet. Mit ihr fügen sich gestalterische Finesse und ökologische Besonnenheit zu einer verhalten-vibrierenden Gesamtansicht: einer aus Bambusstäben, schrägen Stahlprofilen und Betonstützen. Einer, an der Ranken aus Betontrögen klettern, an Bootsleinen empor, der Fassade einen grünen Saum vorhängend. Dass der in einem Wasserschutzgebiet liegende Bau obendrein mit einem wissenschaftlich kontrollierten Konzept zur Regenwasserbewirtschaftung und zum Gebäudeklima aufwartet, unterstreicht den experimentellen Anspruch.

Der Baukörper spricht eine Einladung an die Aufmerksamkeit aus. Prinzip Offenheit. Bereits in den Treppenhäusern gelingt das allein dadurch, dass die Setzstufen fehlen und somit ein schweifender Blick durch ein Bauwerk möglich wird, das auf dem entspannten Zusammenspiel heterogener Einzelelemente basiert. Dass darunter das eine oder andere Detail dennoch massiv geerdet werden musste, versteht sich von selbst: angefangen von gewaltigen, erschütterungsfreien Fundamenten (für ein Elektronenmikroskop), über Hochfrequenzabschirmungen bis hin zu weiteren Sicherheitsstandards, die all die physikalischen Experimente und intellektuellen Grenzüberschreitungen vor ihrer Berliner Umgebung schützen.

Christian Thomas

Schnitt **Section**

behind it, which lend vitality to the skin of the building, as does the two-storey "ribbon of windows". The result is an evocative, matte aquamarine facade that changes with the light, reminiscent of the image of a hard disk.

To the north-east and south-west the layered levels are clearly visible, while the main entrance facade leads to a publicly accessible auditorium and has a seminar room suspended into the foyer, its swathe of glass bricks contrasting with the otherwise strictly orthogonal structure. The institute has no less than 150 metres of purely functional concrete and plaster traffic routes leading to the three room types: laboratories, offices and classrooms. Moreover, for all the functionality of these passageways, the institute still has room for detours thanks to its five internal courtyards which not only act as points of orientation but also offer scope for relaxation and ecological interest. The ground-floor "forest" of tilted concrete pillars and a footbridge over one of the gardens lend the building a many-facetted architectural promenade on which to appreciate the Mikado-style ceiling strip-lighting in the long corridors, the chipboard notice boards, the manually operated air vents and the stadium-style auditorium seating. These are carefully considered details within an overall concept whose system is based on a sensory awareness so keen that visitors are tempted to touch and feel the window profiles.

The building might be seen as a place of discovery. Here, in Adlershof in Berlin's Treptow-Köpenick district, where the technology centres of Sauerbruch Hutton, Ortner & Ortner and ef+ have burgeoned since the 1990s to form a small urban district in its own right, the effect is remarkable. The new Institute of Physics by Augustin & Frank adds much to the area. The south-east facade, for instance, is exemplary in melding compositional finesse with ecological awareness to create a subtle yet vibrant overall effect using bamboo stalks, angled steel profiles and concrete pillars. The facade is hemmed with green, as climbing plants in concrete troughs cling to heavy-duty ropes. The experimental nature of the project is further underlined by the fact that this building, on an ecologically protected site, even has a scientifically controlled concept for rainwater recycling and climate control.

With its basic principle of openness, the building itself positively invites closer scrutiny. This is achieved in the stairwells by the simple device of open-backed steps, allowing the eye to wander throughout the building which itself is based on the casual interaction of heterogeneous individual elements. Needless to say, these details also include some massive security features – among them shock-proof foundations (for the electron microscope), high frequency screening and further cutting-edge protective measures that guard the scientific experiments and intellectual quantum leaps against their Berlin surroundings.

Christian Thomas

Ansicht von Westen **View from the west**

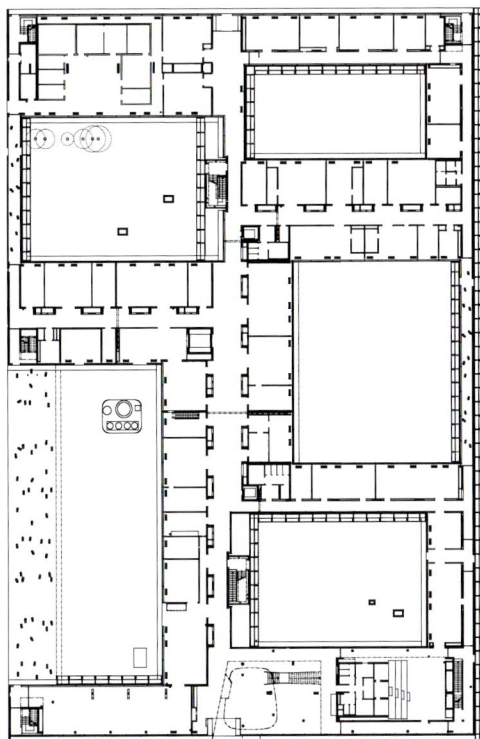

Grundriss Erdgeschoss **Ground-floor plan**

10 m

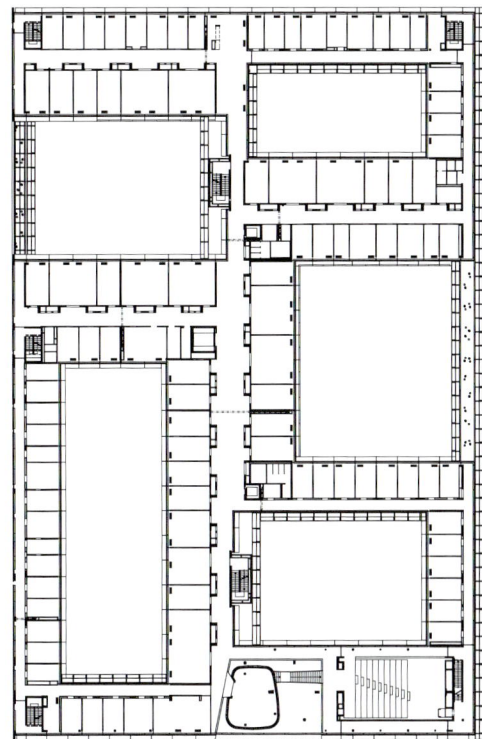

Grundriss 1. Obergeschoss **First-floor plan**

Ansicht von Südosten   **View from the south-east**

Fassadenausschnitt   **Detail of the facade**

Innenhof   **Courtyard**

Brücke   **Bridge**

Foyer   **Foyer**

Hörsaal Lecture hall

Vertriebs- und Servicezentrum, Ditzingen
Customer and administration building, Ditzingen

Barkow Leibinger

■ »Die Straße, die zur Fabrik führt, ist glatt, eben; sie ist so hell und sauber wie ein Tanzboden. Die klaren Fassaden des Gebäudes, lichtes Glas und graues Metall, erheben sich gegen den Himmel. Der Ort strahlt absolute Heiterkeit aus.«[1] So schwärmte Le Corbusier über den Neubau der Tabakfabrik Van Nelle in Rotterdam von 1929. Diese »Schöpfung des modernen Zeitalters«[2] hatte durch ihre Offenheit und gläserne Transparenz der Arbeitswelt eine neue, bis dahin kaum gekannte Qualität verliehen. Nun ist in Ditzingen zwar keine Fabrik, sondern ein Vertriebszentrum entstanden, doch Parallelen sind erwünscht. Immerhin sollten nach dem Willen der Architekten, Frank Barkow und Regine Leibinger, auch hier ›neue Arbeitswelten‹ entstehen, in denen die Angestellten gerne die besten Stunden des Tags verbringen. Doch wie kann das gehen, wenn das Grundstück neben der lärmenden Autobahn liegt und die Zufahrtsstraße ganz und gar nicht nach Tanzboden aussieht?

Schon beim Betreten des kleinen Vorplatzes, der durch eklatant spitzwinklige Niveausprünge gegliedert wird, fällt die große Transparenz des Neubaus auf. Über dem Sockelbereich, der von robusten Betonscheiben und schmalen Wandöffnungen geprägt wird, erhebt sich ein schlanker rechtwinkliger Baukörper mit einer vollkommen verglasten Schauseite. Während sich die eher geschlossenen Kubaturen im Sockel plastisch nach vorne heraus schieben und den Weg zum Eingang flankieren, verbleibt bei dem fast schwebenden Büroriegel alles in der Fläche. Bündig stoßen die Glasflächen mit ihren schwarzen Metallprofilen aneinander und legen sich schützend vor eine zweite innere Glashaut, die die Büroetagen umgibt. Innenwände scheint es dort nicht zu geben. Keine Spur von stereotypen Bürozellen, die das Rastermaß der Fassade aufgreifen könnten und sich brav aneinander reihen! Das lässt den Besucher neugierig weiter nach oben gehen – vorbei an der Lobby, dem Auditorium und den Ausstellungsflächen im Erdgeschoss. Ist hier tatsächlich alles offen? Dunkelgraue Steinplatten empfangen die Besucher im Foyer, Wände aus Sichtbeton und schräg angeschnittene Treppenläufe begleiten den Weg in die neuen Arbeitswelten.

Plötzlich wird spürbar, dass die Architekten hier zwei gegeneinander verschobene Baukörper durch ein offenes Treppenhaus miteinander in Beziehung gesetzt haben – alles ohne Trennwände oder Türen. Selbst die Ebenen spielen miteinander. Als Splitlevel-System sorgen sie für ständig wechselnde Raumeindrücke, für ein Hin und Her zwischen den Ausblicken der beiden Baukörper. Das Arbeiten im gläsernen Haus gewinnt schnell an Gestalt. Man spürt etwas von jener Heiterkeit und Offenheit, die schon Le Corbusier in Rotterdam empfunden hatte. Das Haus beflügelt.

Bevor man den dunkelgrauen Nadelfilz des Bürobereichs betritt, läuft man über Holzparkett aus geräucherter Eiche. Große Wollfilzplatten bedecken die Innenwände aus Sichtbeton und dämpfen die Akustik im Großraum. Die Tischreihen sind nur durch filigrane, stoffbespannte Stellwände in unterschiedlichen Grüntönen voneinander getrennt – klein genug, um den Raum immer noch in seiner vollen

"The road that runs into the factory is smooth, flat…. It is as clean and bright as a dance floor. The sheer facades of the building, bright glass and grey metal, rise up … against the sky…. The serenity of the place is total."[1] This was how Le Corbusier described the new Van Nelle tobacco factory in Rotterdam, built in 1929. This "creation of the modern age" had an openness and transparency that imbued the world of work with a new and hitherto almost unknown quality.[2] Although the building in Ditzingen is not a factory, but a customer and administration building, there are certain deliberate parallels. Architects Frank Barkow and Regine Leibinger are eager to create "new worlds of work" here, too – places where employees are happy to spend the best part of their day. But how are they to achieve this on a site adjacent to a busy motorway, with an approach road that looks nothing like a dance floor?

As soon as we enter the little forecourt with its sharp angularity and staggered planes, we are struck by the transparency of the new structure. Rising above the basecourse, with its stark concrete panels and narrow apertures, is a slender rectangular building with a fully glazed facade. Whereas the closed cuboid forms of the basecourse protrude to flank the approach to the entrance, the office tract is sheer and planar and seems almost to hover. Swathes of glass, flush with black metal profiles, protectively clad the second, inner glass skin that surrounds the office floors. There seem to be no internal walls. There is no trace of the tidy rows of stereotypical office cells that might echo the grid structure of the facade. This draws the visitors further into the building, inexorably upwards past the lobby, the auditorium and the exhibition spaces on the ground floor. Is it really as open as it looks? In the foyer, visitors are

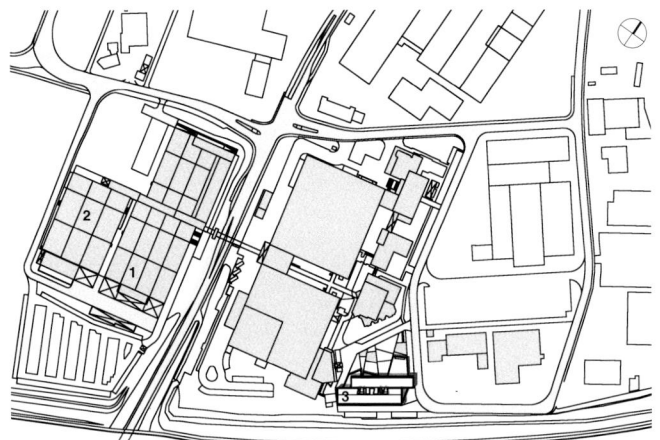

Lageplan **Site plan**

1 Laserfabrik und Logistikzentrum 1997/98
   Laser factory and logistics centre 1997/98
2 Halle für Systemtechnik 1999–2000
   Systems technology hall 1999–2000
3 Vertriebs- und Servicezentrum 2001–2003
   Customer and administration building 2001–2003

Architekten Architects Barkow Leibinger Architekten, Berlin, www.barkowleibinger.com; Frank Barkow, Regine Leibinger; Team: Josephine von Hasselbach, Martina Bauer & Larissa Böhler, Gian-Marco Jenatsch, Christina Möller, Jason Sandy, Jakob Schemel Bauherr Client TRUMPF GmbH + Co. KG, Ditzingen Bauleitung Construction Management Gassmann + Grossmann Baumanagement GmbH, Stuttgart Tragwerk Structural Konzeption Conception Conzett, Bronzini, Gartmann AG, Chur; Realisierung Realisation Boll und Partner GmbH, Stuttgart Energie Energy Transsolar Energietechnik GmbH, Stuttgart Freianlagen Landscape Büro Kiefer Landschaftsarchitektur, Berlin Ausführung Construction 2001–2003 Standort Location Johann-Maus-Straße 2, Ditzingen

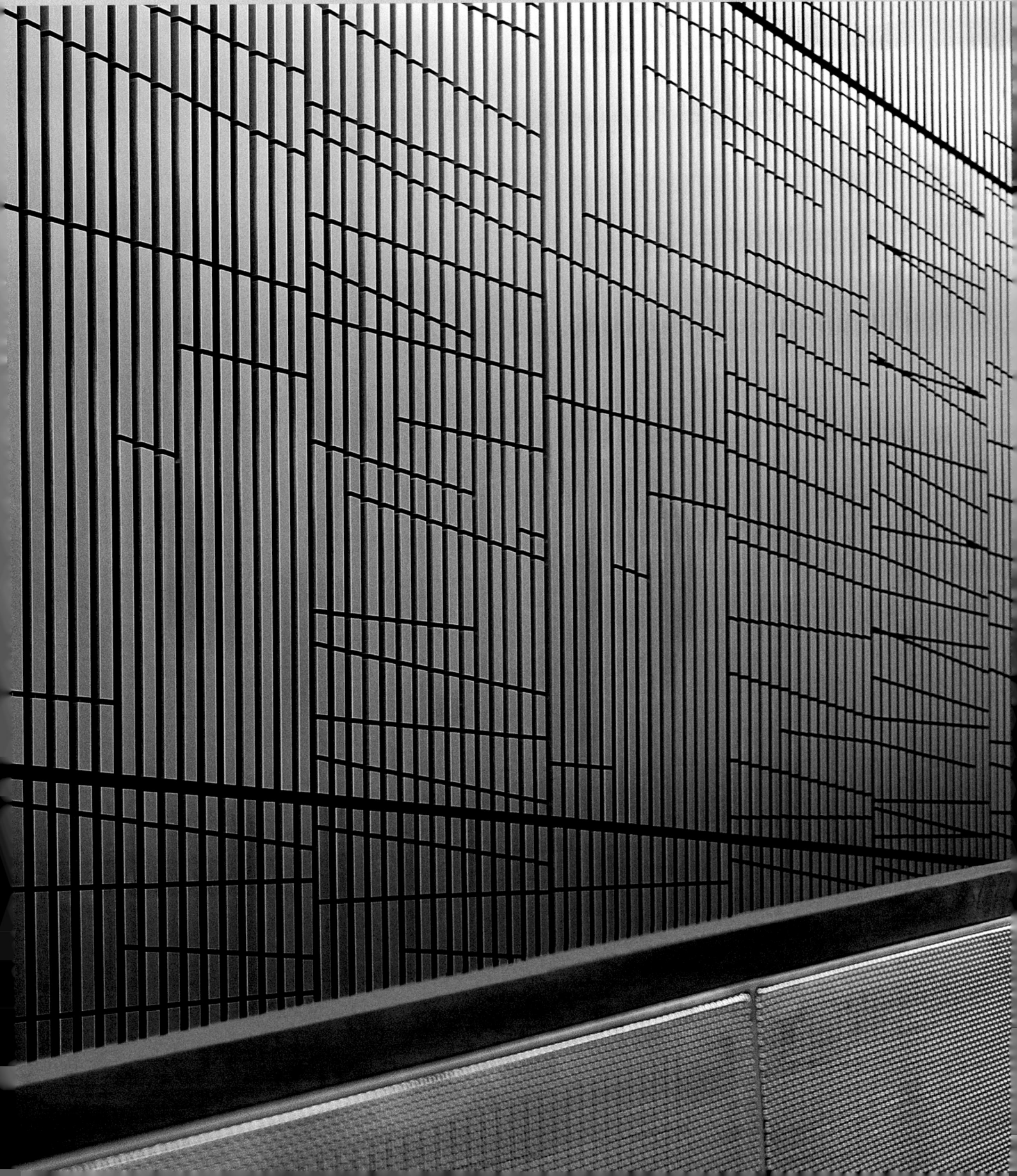

Größe wahrzunehmen. Überhaupt ist alles einsehbar, für die persönliche Gestaltung des Arbeitsplatzes bleibt bewusst kein Raum. Manchem mag daher diese große Freiheit des Bürogebäudes, das möglichst ohne Kommunikationsbarrieren auskommen möchte, ein wenig zu verordnet erscheinen, denn die spürbare räumliche Offenheit setzt eine Offenheit der Mitarbeiter voraus.

Das Büroloft wirkt jedoch mehr als nur überzeugend: erfrischend anders, und mit der Doppelfassade aus Glas und den beiden offenen Treppenhäusern findet das Thema der Offenheit und Transparenz sein passendes architektonisches Pendant. Die spannungsreiche Interpretation des Themas Büroräume, die zu einer offenen Teamarbeit anregt, ist motivierend für die Mitarbeiter.

Auch wenn der Sockelbereich kompositorisch etwas ungelenk wirkt, weil er mit seinen Betonfertigteilen nicht so richtig zur schwebenden Eleganz der beiden Büroriegel passen will, ist hier – direkt neben der Autobahn – ein echtes Juwel entstanden. Nach der Laserfabrik und dem Logistikzentrum, die Barkow Leibinger bereits in den neunziger Jahren in Ditzingen realisierten, ist das neue Vertriebs- und Servicezentrum ein dritter wichtiger Baustein des Stammsitzes der Maschinenfabrik Trumpf. Ein Neubau für 300 Mitarbeiter, der seinen eher gesichtslosen Nachbarn aus den siebziger und achtziger Jahren vor allem eins deutlich macht: Gute Architektur ist in der Lage, Identität stiftend zu wirken und damit entscheidend zum Selbstverständnis, zur Corporate Identity eines Unternehmens beizutragen, gerade auch im bunten Durcheinander eines Industriegebiets neben der Autobahn.

»Es war immer meine Überzeugung, dass erstklassige Arbeit nur in erstklassiger Umgebung entstehen kann«, betont der Firmenchef und Vater der Architektin, Berthold Leibinger. Die 19 Millionen Euro, die in den beflügelnden Verwaltungsbau investiert wurden, hätte man indes auch ganz anders verbauen können. Geld allein war noch lange kein Garant für diese qualitätvolle und stimulierende Architektur. Doch hier steckt das Verständnis für eine Baukultur des Unternehmens im Kopf – nicht im Portemonnaie. Das war auch in Rotterdam so.

Hans-Jürgen Breuning

1 Zitiert in: Kenneth Frampton, *Die Architektur der Moderne. Eine kritische Baugeschichte*, 5. Auflage, Stuttgart 1995, S. 117.
2 Ebenda.

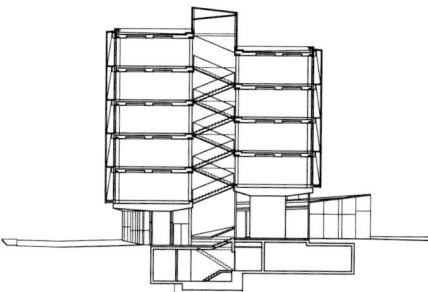

Schnitt **Section**

greeted by dark grey stone panels; walls of unfaced concrete and angled stairways lead them into the "new worlds of work".

All at once, it becomes evident that here the architects have linked two tracts by means of an open stairwell – all without partitions or doors. Even the different levels correspond and interact, thanks to a split-level system that creates constantly changing spaces and alternating views. The notion of working in a glass house becomes tangible. There is a palpable sense of the serenity and openness that Le Corbusier noted in Rotterdam. The building is inspirational.

Before stepping onto the dark grey carpeting of the office area, we walk across smoked oak parquet. The unfaced concrete interior walls are clad in huge panels of sound-insulating wool felt. The rows of desks are separated only by delicate, fabric-clad partition walls in varying shades of green – small enough not to detract from the overall size of the space. Indeed, everything is visible here, and there is deliberately no room for any personal adaptation of the workspace. Some people may find the vast openness of the office building, which seeks to do without any barriers to communication, dauntingly ordered. After all, the obvious spatial openness also presupposes a certain openness on the part of the staff.

The loft-style office space, however, is not only persuasive but refreshingly different, with the double facade of glass and the two open stairwells providing an appropriate architectural counterpart to the theme of openness and transparency. This exciting take on the theme of office layouts aimed at stimulating teamwork does motivate the people who work here.

Even if the basecourse appears compositionally awkward with its prefabricated concrete components that do not seem to harmonise fully with the weightless elegance of the two office tracts, this building right beside the autobahn is a real jewel. Following the laser factory and logistics centre built in Ditzingen by Barkow Leibinger in the 1990s, the new customer and administration building forms an important third module in the Maschinenfabrik Trumpf headquarters complex. This new building designed to accommodate a 300-strong workforce stands out from the anodyne surrounding architecture of the 1970s and 1980s and is a clear illustration of the fact that good architecture can indeed create a sense of identity. As such, it makes an essential contribution to the company's corporate identity, particularly in the chaos of an industrial estate beside the autobahn.

"I have always believed that you can only do first-class work in first-class surroundings," points out CEO Berthold Leibinger, the architect's father. The 19 million Euro invested in this inspiring office building could quite easily have bought a very different building indeed. Money alone was no guarantee for such a stimulating and high-quality piece of architecture. Understanding the company's architectural needs was a matter of attitude, rather than money. Just as it was in Rotterdam.

Hans-Jürgen Breuning

1 Kenneth Frampton, Yulio Futagawa, *Modern Architecture 1920–1945*, New York, 1983, p. 299.
2 Ibid.

Ansicht von Norden   **View from the north**

Ansicht von Süden   **View from the south**

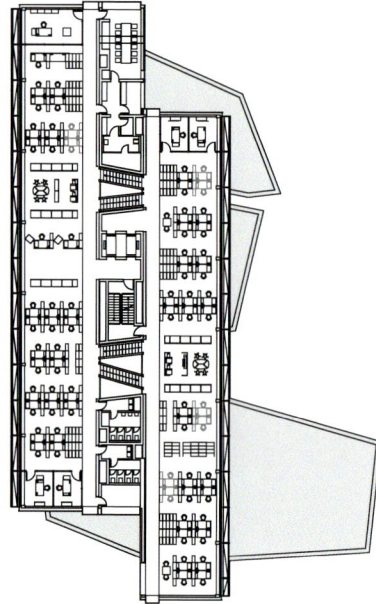

Grundriss Obergeschosse   **Floorplan, upper floors**

Lobby Saal   **Lobby hall**

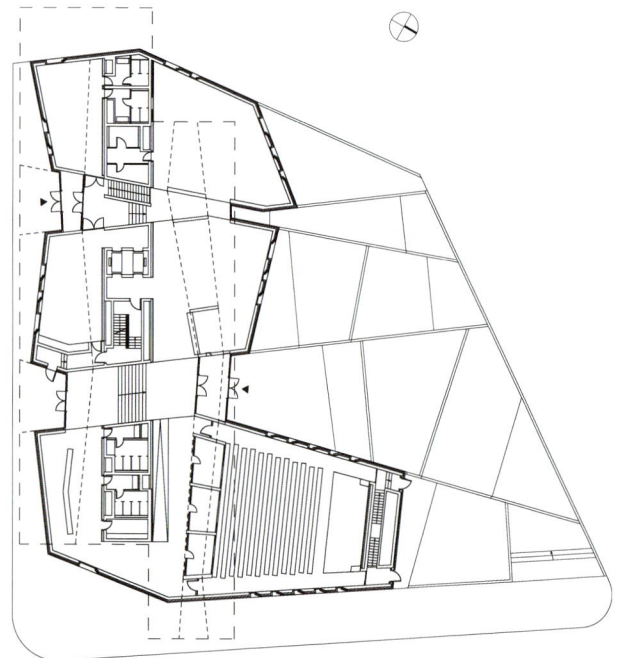

Grundriss Erdgeschoss   **Ground-floor plan**

Lobby   **Lobby**

Treppenbrücken   **Stairway bridges**

Büroebene **Office level**

Auditorium **Auditorium**

Marie-Elisabeth-Lüders-Haus mit Paul-Löbe-Haus, Deutscher Bundestag, Berlin
Marie-Elisabeth Lüders House with Paul Löbe House, Deutscher Bundestag, Berlin

Stephan Braunfels

■ Am Anfang war und am Ende ist das geschriebene Wort: Mit dem überwiegend als Parlamentsbibliothek dienenden Marie-Elisabeth-Lüders-Haus (MELH) ist das auf einen Entwurf von Axel Schultes und Charlotte Frank zurückgehende ›Band des Bundes‹ im Berliner Regierungs- und Parlamentsviertel vorläufig vollendet. Gemeinsam mit dem ebenfalls von Stephan Braunfels entworfenen Paul-Löbe-Haus (PLH), das es funktional und baulich ergänzt, bildet es den östlichen Teil jenes 102 Meter breiten und über einen Kilometer langen ›Bandes‹, der baulichen Versinnbildlichung der Wiedervereinigung Deutschlands.

Im PLH am westlichen Spreeufer, dem Pendant des von Schultes und Frank entworfenen Bundeskanzleramts, brachte Stephan Braunfels 510 Abgeordneten- und 390 Büros für Ausschusssekretariate, Besucherbetreuung und Öffentlichkeitsarbeit, 21 Sitzungssäle, acht Seminarräume und zwei Restaurants unter. Ursprünglich hätten dort zusätzlich die Bundestagsbibliothek, ein öffentlicher Anhörungssaal und weitere 600 Büros unter anderem für den wissenschaftlichen Dienst Platz finden sollen. Nachdem im Herbst 1994 Braunfels als Sieger aus einem internationalen Wettbewerb hervorgegangen war, ergab eine Überarbeitung seines Entwurfs, dass das angestrebte Raumprogramm nur schwer auf dem vorgesehenen Baugelände unterzubringen war. Der Architekt schlug deshalb einen zweiten ›Spreesprung‹ und eine Verteilung der Funktionen auf zwei formal verwandte Bauten beiderseits des Flusses vor.

Im Gegensatz zu Schultes und Frank – die für das Kanzleramt zwar ebenfalls lange, dort durch Wintergärten gegliederte Büroriegel als architektonische Manifestation des ›Bundesbandes‹ entworfen, aber eben mit durchlaufenden Fassaden – lockerte Braunfels bei beiden Bauten das Ordnungsgefüge durch eine regelmäßige Kammstruktur auf. Die dreiseitig von Büros beziehungsweise Sonderflächen (beim PLH insbesondere von den acht Zylindern, in denen sich Sitzungssäle für Bundestagsausschüsse und Anhörungen befinden) eingefassten, abgesenkten und unterschiedlich gestalteten Höfe gewährleisten vielfältige Ein- und Durchblicke – und eine optimale natürliche Belichtung der Nutzflächen. Gleichwohl wird das ›Band des Bundes‹ durch die Kopfenden der Bürotrakte, den durchlaufenden Attikabalken und die schmalen Mittelpfeiler im Bereich der Höfe, allesamt aus Sichtbeton, baulich ablesbar nachgezeichnet.

PLH und MELH unterstreichen mit vielfältigen Bezügen ihre bauliche Verbundenheit. So lassen die großen Glasfronten tief ins Innere, aber auch in das jeweilige Gegenüber blicken. Das MELH greift die Dreiteilung des PLH, die zusätzlich durch das Auskragen des Dachs in der Mittelachse unterstrichen wird, nicht nur auf, sondern betont sie durch die Herausstellung dreier formal verwandter, aber – auch funktional – eigenständiger Kopfbauten an der Spree: ein Würfel mit großen runden Öffnungen (Anhörungstrakt), die durch Grünglas in ihrer Transparenz erheblich eingeschränkte zentrale Halle mit frei eingestellter Rotunde (Bibliothek) und schließlich eine dem südlichen Bürotrakt vorgelagerte und durch schmale Sichtbetonpfeiler

In the beginning was, and in the end is, the written word: the Marie-Elisabeth Lüders House (MELH), which primarily serves as the parliamentary library, marks the interim completion of the so-called "federal belt" in the Berlin government district, based on a design by Axel Schultes and Charlotte Frank. Together with the Paul Löbe House (PLH), also designed by Stephan Braunfels, which it complements in terms of both function and architecture, it forms the eastern part of the 102 metre broad and more than one kilometre long "federal belt" that symbolises the reunification of Germany.

The PLH on the west bank of the Spree forms the counterpart to the Bundeskanzleramt (federal chancellery) by Schultes and Frank. In it, Stephan Braunfels has housed 510 offices for members of parliament, 390 offices for committee secretaries, visitor liaison and public relations, 21 meeting rooms, eight seminar rooms and two restaurants. Originally, this building was also meant to house the parliamentary library, a public hearing chamber and another 600 offices for research and other staff. However, after Braunfels had won the international design competition for the building in 1994, the project was revised to an extent that made it extremely difficult to accommodate all the envisaged facilities on the earmarked site. The architect proposed a second "Spree crossing" with the facilities divided between two formally related buildings on either side of the river.

In contrast to Schultes and Frank, who had designed long office tracts interspersed with winter gardens and uninterrupted facades as an architectural manifestation of the "federal belt", Braunfels relaxed the structural order of both buildings by means of a serried, comb-like structure. The various sunken courtyards flanked on three sides by offices and special spaces (notably, in the case of the PLH, the eight cylinders housing the parliamentary committee and hearing chambers) provide ever-changing views and vistas, as well as being a superb source of natural light. At the same time, the "federal belt" is echoed visibly in the narrow ends of the office tract, the continuous parapet and the slender pillars in the courtyards, all of them in unfaced concrete.

The PLH and the MELH underline their architectural affinity with a rich variety of references. For instance, the huge expanses of glass frontage afford views far inside the building as well as towards the building opposite. The MELH not only reiterates the tripartite structure of the PLH, further underlined by the cantilevered roof section in the central axis, but actually emphasises it by presenting three formally related but nevertheless architecturally and functionally discrete components on the banks of the Spree: a cube with large round apertures (hearing tract), a central hall featuring green tinted glass to limit its transparency with a freestanding rotunda (library) and finally, fronting the southern office tract, a terrace with a sweeping stairway framed by slender pillars of unfaced concrete and parapets. From this terrace there are stunning views of some of Berlin's most fascinating urban spaces: the new squares and piazzas along the bank of the Spree flanked by the two new buildings,

Architekten Architects Stephan Braunfels Architekten, München/Berlin, www.braunfels-architekten.de; Team: Ramsi Kusus, Karin Melcher & Günter Kaesbach, Philipp Jamme, Philippe Vernin & Christoph Bräutigam, Stefan Heigl, Frank Hüpeden, Jasmine Jivanjee, Gerhard Karschner, Lutz Keßels, Josef Konrad, Andreas Kopp, Thomas Kortyka, Christian Müller, Eckhard Palm, Berthold Pesch, Nerantzi Pussert, Hans Sabel, Maureen Schäffner, Matthias Schwarz, Karin Weigang, Jörg Wich, Isa Wiesenthal, Michael Zeuner **Bauherr** Client Im Auftrag der Bundesrepublik Deutschland für die Bundesregierung vertreten durch die Bundesbaugesellschaft Berlin mbH Commissioned by the Federal Republic of Germany for the federal government represented by Bundesbaugesellschaft Berlin mbH **Tragwerk** Structural SSP Sailer, Stepan & Partner GmbH, München **HL-Technik** Technical HL-Technik AG, München; CBP – Cronauer Beratung Planung Beratende Ingenieure GmbH, München **Freianlagen** Landscape Stephan Braunfels Architekten, München/Berlin; Adelheid Schönborn, München **Wettbewerb** Competition 1994 **Ausführung** Construction 1997–2003 **Standort** Location Paul-Löbe-Allee 2, Otto-von-Bismarck-Allee, Berlin

und -attikabalken gerahmte Terrasse mit Freitreppe. Diese Terrasse bietet vielfältige Ausblicke auf einen der facettenreichsten Stadträume Berlins: die entlang der Spreeufer neu entstandenen Plätze, die von den beiden Neubauten, dem Reichstagsgebäude und dem Jakob-Kaiser-Haus mit integriertem ehemaligen Reichstagspräsidentenpalais eingefasst werden.

Ein Steg im obersten Geschoss für Abgeordnete und Mitarbeiter und eine sanft geschwungene Brücke für Passanten verbinden die beiden Braunfelsbauten miteinander. Im Gegensatz zum PLH, bei dem der Haupteingang schon von weitem unter dem auskragenden Vordach der westlichen Stirnseite zu vermuten ist, liegt der – allerdings provisorische – Eingang des MELH etwas versteckt am Ende des ersten nördlichen Hofs. Kaum eingetreten, befindet sich der Besucher im Herz des Hauses. Die Rotunde der Bibliothek vor sich, kann er sich nun nach rechts zum vorgelagerten Anhörungstrakt oder nach links zu einer gewaltigen Treppe wenden. Diese führt ihn auf die obere Ebene der zentralen Halle, in der er sich, ohne es zu wissen, bereits zuvor befunden hat. Was er allenfalls ahnt: Unter dem höheren Hallenniveau befindet sich ein viergeschossiges 8000 Quadratmeter großes Magazin. Was er dagegen sieht: Eine lichtdurchflutete Halle, deren lasierter hellgrauer Sichtbeton eine kühle, angenehme Atmosphäre erzeugt und deren östliche Stirnseite einen Ausblick auf das Baufeld eines möglichen Erweiterungsbaus gewährt. Mit ihren frei eingestellten, weitgehend in Glas aufgelösten Sonderbaukörpern für den wissenschaftlichen Dienst und mit ihren acht geschlossenen Aufzugstürmen, die gleichfalls abstrakt an Häuser erinnern, wirkt die Halle wie eine gebaute Manifestation eines städtischen (Außen-)Raums, in dem die öffentliche Versammlung und mithin der Mensch im Mittelpunkt steht. Hier können Mitarbeiter und Besucher ihren Gedanken, Worten und Blicken freien Lauf lassen.

Der aufregendste und zugleich irritierendste Raum dieses kompakten und facettenreichen Gebäudes, ist von hier, wenngleich im Zentrum der Sichtachse, nur zu erahnen: der Lesesaal der Bundestagsbibliothek in der Rotunde. Von einer doppelten Sichtbetonschale umhüllt (im Zwischenraum befinden sich Treppen, kleine ›Klosternischen‹ für das konzentrierte Arbeiten und Nebenräume), erstrecken sich über insgesamt fünf Ebenen und Galerien zahlreiche Leseplätze – und über allem ›schwebt‹ eine um 45 Grad gedrehte Rasterdecke aus Glas und Sichtbeton, die dem ohnehin schon komplexen Raum zusätzlich Dynamik verleiht. Nur die Bücherregale vor den geschlossenen Wandflächen gewähren dem Auge ein wenig Ruhe. Erst nach einiger Zeit durchschaut der Betrachter das Vexierspiel: Nicht die Rasterdecke, sondern der gesamte Lesesaal ist um 45 Grad aus der Hauptachse gedreht, um einen optimalen Ausblick auf den Spreeplatz, das Reichstagsgebäude und nicht zuletzt das Paul-Löbe-Haus zu gewährleisten, dessen bauliche Ergänzung mit dem Marie-Elisabeth-Lüders-Haus in kongenialer Weise gelungen ist.

Oliver G. Hamm

the Reichstag and the Jakob Kaiser House integrating the former palace of the Reichstag president.

The two Braunfels buildings are linked by a footbridge on the uppermost floor for the use of members of parliament and staff, and a gently curved bridge for passers-by. In contrast to the PLH, whose entrance is discernible from afar under the cantilevered roof section on the western narrow side, the (provisional) entrance of the MELH is tucked away at the end of the first northern courtyard. On entering, visitors immediately find themselves at the very heart of the building, facing the rotunda of the library, where they can turn right towards the hearing tract or left towards a massive stairway leading to the upper levels of the central hall where, in fact, they have already been, probably without even realising it. Under the higher hall level is a four-storey, 8000 square metre storage depot. While visitors to the building may suspect as much, what they actually see is a hall flooded with light, its pale grey unfaced concrete lending a pleasantly cool atmosphere, while the eastern narrow end affords views towards the site of a possible extension. With their freestanding glass building components for the research staff and their eight closed elevator towers like abstract houses, the hall looks for all the world like a built manifestation of an (outdoor) urban space in which the focus is on public assembly and the human individual. Here, staff and visitors alike can give free rein to their thoughts, words and eyes.

The most exciting, and perhaps most confusing, space in this compact and many-facetted building can only be surmised from here, even though it is right in the middle of the axis of view: the reading room of the parliamentary library in the rotunda. Clad by a double shell of unfaced concrete (between the walls are the stairs, little "monastic cells" for contemplative work, and ancillary rooms) the rotunda has five levels, with galleries and reading areas, and above it all "hovers" a gridded ceiling of glass and unfaced concrete swivelled at a 45-degree angle, lending the already complex space an even more dynamic aspect. Only the bookshelves in front of the closed wall areas give the eye some respite. It takes some time for the visitor to grasp the illusion: it is not the gridded ceiling, but the entire reading room itself, that is swivelled out of the main axis by 45 degrees, providing a stunning view towards the Spreeplatz, the Reichstag and the Paul Löbe House which so brilliantly complements the Marie-Elisabeth Lüders House.

Oliver G. Hamm

Marie-Elisabeth-Lüders-Haus mit Paul-Löbe-Haus, Deutscher Bundestag, Berlin
Marie-Elisabeth Lüders House with Paul Löbe House, Deutscher Bundestag, Berlin

79

Spreeplatz   **Spreeplatz**

1 Paul-Löbe-Haus   **Paul Löbe House**
2 Marie-Elisabeth-Lüders-Haus
  Marie-Elisabeth Lüders House
3 Reichstag   **Reichstag**
4 Bundeskanzleramt   **Bundeskanzleramt**

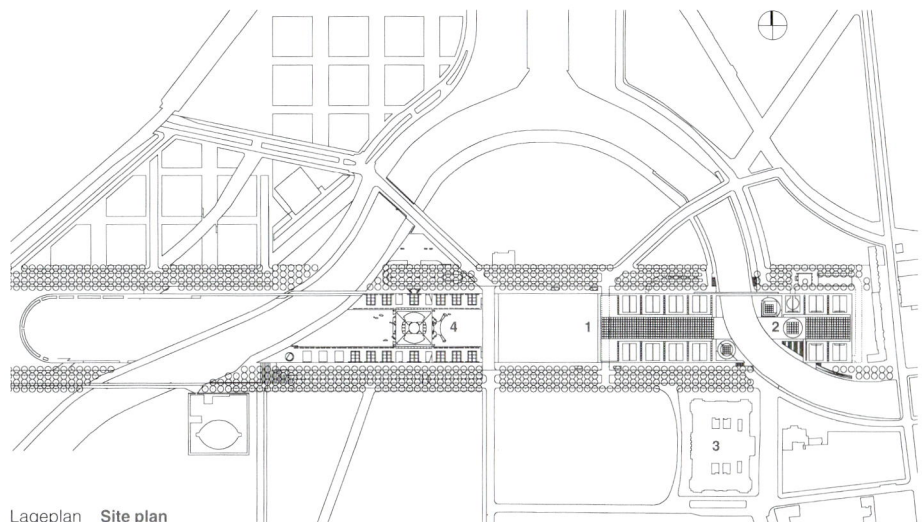

Lageplan   **Site plan**

Paul-Löbe-Haus, Ansicht von Südosten   **Paul Löbe House, view from the south-east**

Marie-Elisabeth-Lüders-Haus mit Paul-Löbe-Haus, Deutscher Bundestag, Berlin
Marie-Elisabeth Lüders House with Paul Löbe House, Deutscher Bundestag, Berlin

81

Paul-Löbe-Haus, zentrale Halle
Paul Löbe House, central hall

Paul-Löbe-Haus, Europasaal   **Paul Löbe House, Europasaal**

Marie-Elisabeth-Lüders-Haus, Ansicht von Südwesten   **Marie-Elisabeth Lüders House, view from the south-west**

Marie-Elisabeth-Lüders-Haus, Freitreppe
Marie-Elisabeth Lüders House, stairway

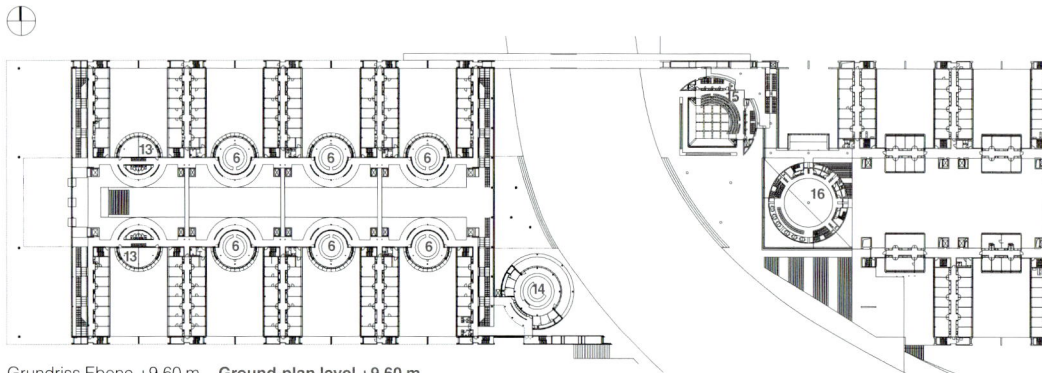

Grundriss Ebene +9,60 m   **Ground-plan level +9,60 m**

1   Spreeplatz   **Spreeplatz**
2   Eingang   **Entrance**
3   Halle   **Hall**
4   Tunnel zum Reichstag
   Tunnel to Reichstag
5   Seminarräume   **Seminar rooms**
6   Sitzungssäle   **Conference halls**
7   Restaurant   **Restaurant**
8   Mauermahnmal   **Berlin Wall memorial**
9   Veranstaltungsfoyer   **Functions foyer**
10 Sporthalle   **Sports hall**
11 Ausstellungsfläche   **Exhibition space**
12 Magazin   **Depot**
13 Besprechungsräume   **Meeting rooms**
14 Europasaal   **Europasaal**
15 Besuchertribüne Anhörungssaal
   Visitors' gallery in plenary chamber
16 Bibliothek   **Library**

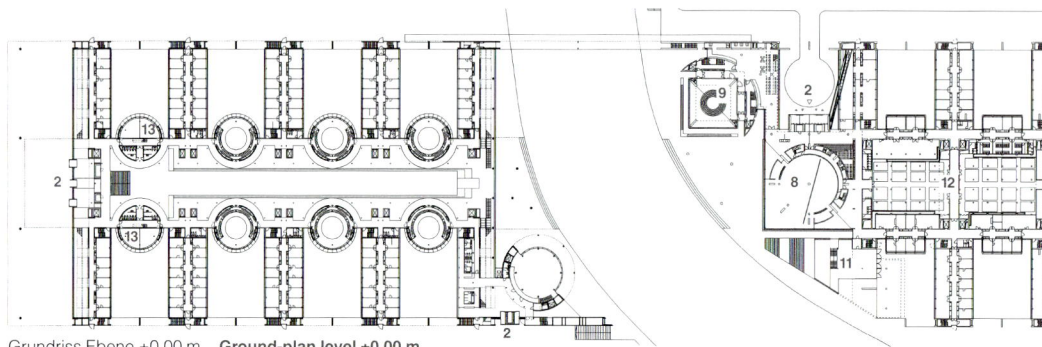

Grundriss Ebene ±0,00 m   **Ground-plan level ±0,00 m**

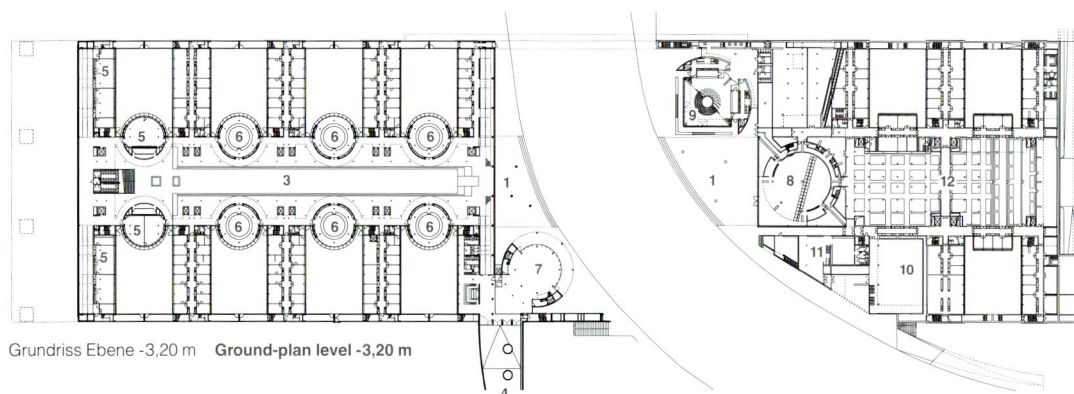

Grundriss Ebene -3,20 m   **Ground-plan level -3,20 m**

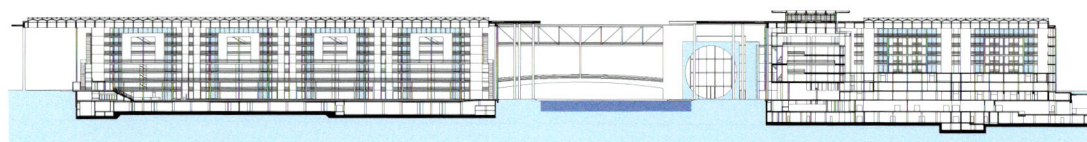

Schnitt   **Section**

Marie-Elisabeth-Lüders-Haus, Bibliothek
Marie-Elisabeth Lüders House, library

Marie-Elisabeth-Lüders-Haus, Anhörungssaal
Marie-Elisabeth Lüders House, plenary chamber

Marie-Elisabeth-Lüders-Haus, zentrale Halle   **Marie-Elisabeth Lüders House, central hall**

Marie-Elisabeth-Lüders-Haus, Aufgang zur Halle
Marie-Elisabeth Lüders House, stairs to hall

Wohnhaus im Hinterhof, Düsseldorf
One-family-house in rear courtyard, Düsseldorf

buddenberg.architekten

■ Ich dachte, ich sei vorbereitet. Ein blaues Haus in der Düsseldorfer Tannenstraße. Und nun stand ich hier, im Stadtteil Derendorf, und fand es nicht, das leuchtend blaue, frei stehende Einfamilienhaus. Hier soll das sein? Rechts der Straße eine Kaserne in Backstein, wohl in der zweiten Hälfte des 19. Jahrhunderts erbaut, links ein Blockrand aus gründerzeitlichen Wohnhäusern, die schon bessere Zeiten gesehen hatten. In den Erdgeschossen Läden, Kneipen und – ein Architekturbüro. Im Schaufenster, mit Panoramablick auf die Schreibtische der Kreativen, ein Plakat, darauf das gesuchte Objekt der Begierde. Also doch richtig. Ein kurzer Plausch mit dem Architekten und Bewohner des ungewöhnlichen Wohnhauses, dann geht es gemeinsam zum Grundstück. Das Auto kann stehen bleiben, denn der einzig mögliche Weg ist nicht weit: nur eben raus aus dem Laden, zweimal links herum und durch den Hausflur des sparsam ornamentierten Mietshauses von 1898 in den Hinterhof.

Hier, im Innern eines allseits geschlossenen Straßenblocks, auf dem knapp bemessenen Grundstück zwischen Brandwänden und Hofmauern, haben Oliver Buddenberg und Inge Tauchmann ihr Haus gebaut, für sich und die beiden Kinder. Sie sind dabei sehr pragmatisch vorgegangen: trotz ihres knappen Budgets wollten sie in der Stadt wohnen und arbeiten, zentral und doch ruhig. Kein leichtes Unterfangen bei den Grundstückspreisen in der nordrhein-westfälischen Landeshauptstadt. So entstand der Plan, sich auf die eigenen Fähigkeiten zu besinnen und etwas zu kaufen, dessen Potenzial nur für Fachleute erkennbar war. Man suchte – und fand im wenig eleganten Norden das leicht heruntergekommene Mietshaus mit dem kleinen grünen Hinterhof, günstig zu erwerben und teilweise leer stehend. Die Architekten griffen zu, sanier(t)en das Mehrfamilienhaus behutsam, zogen mit dem eigenen Büro ins Erdgeschoss und bauten sich ihr Domizil im langen, schmalen Hof. Da sich nachweisen ließ, dass hier, direkt auf der Grundstücksgrenze, früher ein Schuppen gleicher Kubatur stand, gab es weder Probleme mit der Baugenehmigung noch mit den Nachbarn. Die einzige Schwierigkeit, eine im Weg stehende, zum Fällen eigentlich zu große Zeder wurde in der Silvesternacht 2001/02 Opfer eines Blitzschlags. Es konnte also losgehen. Buddenberg und Tauchmann bauten den klaren Kubus aus Porenbeton – »außen leicht, innen schwer« – in nur fünf Monaten und zogen im Herbst 2002 ein.

Betritt man nun das Haus im Hinterhof, wird auf den ersten Blick klar, dass es sich um eine äußerst individuelle Lösung handelt: kein Windfang, kein Flur, keine Zimmertüren! Die gut hundert Quadratmeter Wohnfläche verteilen sich im Grunde auf je einen großen Raum pro Geschoss. Ein haushoher Luftraum im Zentrum verbindet zudem die beiden Ebenen optisch und akustisch. Hier öffnet sich das Haus bis unter das (begrünte Flach-) Dach zum Garten, hier ist die Schnitt- und Schaltstelle des ›Ein-Raums‹. Frei steht der betonierte Küchenblock im Raum und zoniert das Erdgeschoss, ebenso frei steht der halbhohe Schrankblock im Obergeschoss und trennt das elterliche ›Schlafzimmer‹ vom Spiel- und Schlafbereich der Kinder. Aus der Not

I thought I was prepared. A blue house on Tannenstrasse in Düsseldorf. And here I am, standing in the Derendorf district of the city. But I can't find the bright blue detached family house. Isn't this where it's supposed to be? To the right I see brick-built barracks, probably dating from the late nineteenth century. To the left a row of slightly dilapidated Victorian tenements that have seen better times, with ground floor shops, pubs and – yes, an architectural practice. In the window, through which I can plainly see the desks of the creative staff who work there, is a poster showing the very thing I'm looking for. So I must be right after all. After chatting briefly to the architect, who also happens to live in this unusual house, we set out together to see the site. No need for the car – we just walk out of the door, turn left twice and go through the hall of the sparsely decorated 1898 tenement into the rear courtyard.

Here, tucked away inside a closed block, on the tiny site between firewalls and masonry walls, Oliver Buddenberg and Inge Tauchmann have built a home for themselves and their two children. They have taken a highly pragmatic approach. In spite of a shoestring budget, they were determined to live in the city, in a central but quiet location. No easy task, given the property prices in Düsseldorf, regional capital of North Rhine Westphalia. So they decided to pool their talents and buy something whose potential would be recognisable only to a few specialists. The hunt was on – and in the unfashionable north of the city, they found a slightly dilapidated tenement with a little green backyard at an affordable price. Some of the flats were empty. They restored it sensitively, put their office on the ground floor and built themselves a home in the long, narrow backyard. Having found evidence that a structure of similar size had

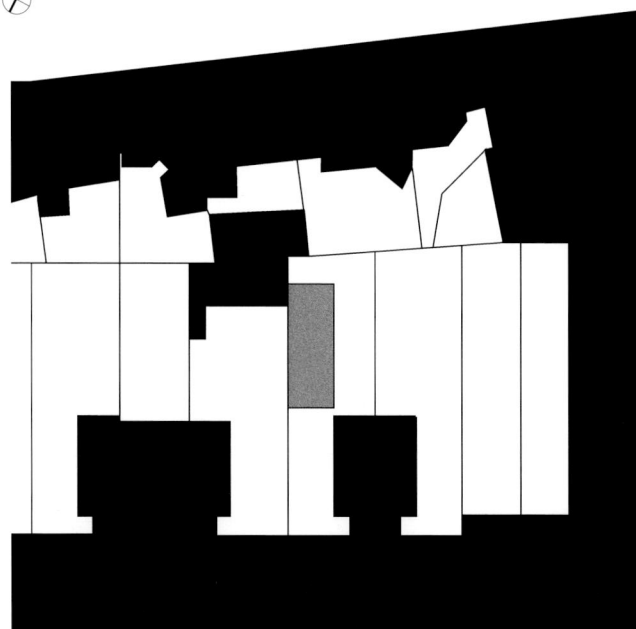

Lageplan **Site plan**

Architekten Architects buddenberg.architekten, Düsseldorf, www.buddenberg-architekten.de; Oliver Buddenberg, Inge Tauchmann **Bauherr** Client Oliver Buddenberg, Inge Tauchmann, Düsseldorf **Tragwerk** Structural Dipl.-Ing. Wolfgang Klees, Hilden **Ausführung** Construction 2002 **Standort** Location Tannenstraße 9, Düsseldorf

der fensterlosen Wand zum Nachbargrundstück machten die Architekten eine Tugend: über die ganze Länge des Hauses zieht sich hier eine mit Schiebetüren abtrennbare ›begehbare Wand‹, die im Erdgeschoss Gästetoilette, Garderobe, Abstellraum, Treppe, Küchenschrank, Medientechnik sowie im Obergeschoss Kinderbetten und -schränke, Waschküche und schließlich das Bad enthält. Bei geöffneter Schiebetür ist von der Wanne beinahe das gesamte Obergeschoss überschaubar, verschlossen plätschert man hingegen ganz für sich, mit Blick in den Garten. Die Servicezonen erweitern bei Bedarf den ›Ein-Raum‹, nicht nur funktional, sondern auch räumlich. Viele Möglichkeiten, immer wieder anders, tun sich auf. Klar und unprätentiös wie das Haus selbst sind auch die Materialien und selbst entwickelten Details, seien es die schweren Multiplex-Schiebeläden vor den Fenstern oder die leichten Schiebetüren der ›begehbaren Wand‹. Selbst der nach einem Schweizer Verfahren behandelte Beton mit seiner samtig-schwarzen Oberfläche und die fein geschreinerten Einbaumöbel aus Lärche bleiben wohltuend selbstverständlich, sind gestaltet, nicht designt.

Trotz der beengten Hinterhofsituation bietet das kleine Haus eine erstaunliche Großzügigkeit, innen und außen. Den fast vollständigen Verzicht auf individuelle Rückzugsmöglichkeiten betrachten die Bewohner gelassen, ja sogar als Chance auf ein besseres Miteinander. Und wenn die Kinder einmal größer sind und die Teeniemusik des Jahres 2015 gar zu schrecklich: es gibt ja immer noch die beiden Mini-Apartments im Erdgeschoss des Altbaus!

Christof Bodenbach

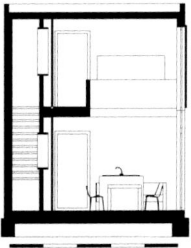

Schnitt   **Section**

once stood on the site, there were no problems with planning permission or with the neighbours. The only major difficulty was a cedar tree that was too big to fell. On New Year's Eve 2001 it was struck by lightning – and there was nothing to stop them. Buddenberg and Tauchmann built the aerated concrete cube ("light outside, heavy inside") in just five months, and moved in in the autumn of 2002.

On entering this house, it is immediately clear that they have gone for a highly distinctive solution – no porch, no corridor, no interior doors! The one hundred square metres of living space are basically made up of one huge room on each floor. A full-height clear space in the centre links the two levels visually and acoustically, opening the house right up to the flat greened roof and creating an interface between the open-plan levels. The freestanding concrete kitchen island structures the ground floor into zones, while the half-height storage island on the upper floor divides the parents' "bedroom" from the children's play and sleeping area. The architects have made a virtue of necessity by turning the windowless wall that runs the entire length of the house and backs onto the neighbours' property into a "walk-in wall space" with a sliding door housing the guest toilet, wardrobe, storage space, utility room, stair, pantry and media on the ground floor, while on the upper floor it holds the children's beds and wardrobes, the laundry room and bathroom. Whoever is soaking in the tub can see almost the entire upper floor if the sliding door is left open, or enjoy an intimate bath with idyllic garden views if it is closed. These service zones not only optimise the open-room living space in terms of function, but also expand it visually. The possibilities are endless. The materials used are as unpretentious as the house itself, and the owners have come up with some interesting details, from the heavy multiplex window shutters to the light sliding doors of the "walk-in wall space". Even the concrete, which has undergone a special Swiss treatment to lend it a velvety black surface, and the finely crafted built-in larchwood furnishings are pleasantly understated.

In spite of the limitations of the site, this tiny house seems remarkably spacious both inside and out. The architects are quite relaxed about the relative lack of privacy, which they see as an opportunity for better family interaction. And anyway, once the children are old enough to need more space to listen to whatever ear-splitting horrors the 2015 pop charts may hold, they can always move into the two mini apartments on the ground floor of the original tenement.

Christof Bodenbach

Ansicht von Süden **View from the south**

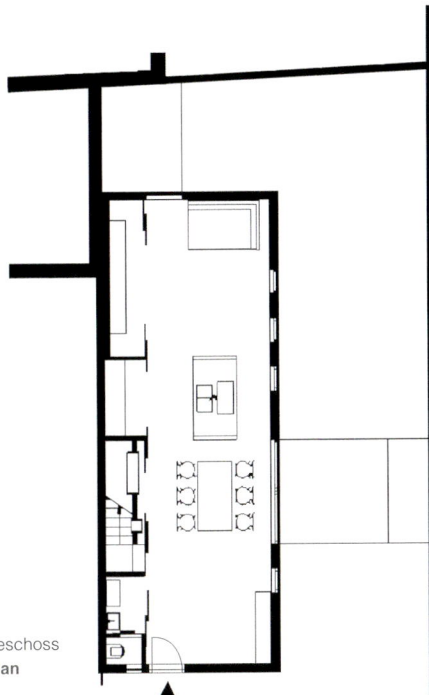

Grundriss Erdgeschoss
Ground-floor plan

Grundriss Obergeschoss
Upper-floor plan

Innenraum Erdgeschoss   **Interior, first floor**

Wohnbereich
Living area

Innenraum Obergeschoss   **Interior, upper floor**

Badezimmer
Bathroom

Bender, Wohn- und/oder Geschäftshaus, Berlin
Bender, apartment/office building, Berlin

Deadline

■ Die Hessische Straße liegt mitten in Berlin und doch kennt sie niemand. Die in einem langen Bogen gekurvte Straße wird als stark befahrene Abkürzung zwischen Invaliden- und Friedrichstraße benutzt, die der Autofahrer üblicherweise schnell durchquert und deren Umgebung auch die Fußgänger kaum wahrnehmen – ein Ort des Übergangs. Immerhin hat der Neubau mit der Nummer 5 einen prominenten Nachbarn fast in Sichtweite: die schwergewichtige Neorenaissance des Naturkundemuseum von August Tiede.

Das Haus war noch nicht ganz fertig, aber längst bewohnt, als die Besichtigung stattfand. An jenem Juninachmittag waren von der Straße wie zufällig in jedem Geschoss Menschen zu sehen, als hätte man sie kunstvoll in der vertikal gegliederten Fassade arrangiert. Nicht nur, dass dieses Haus mit seinem keck nach außen kragenden Überhang und seinen scharf abgeschnittenen Rundungen eine formale Inszenierung deutlich macht. Auch die Bewohner schienen bei diesem theatralischen Arrangement mitzuspielen. Erst später wurde deutlich, dass die auffällige Belebung der Räume auf eine nachträgliche Nutzungsänderung zurückzuführen war. Neben Wohnungen und Büros beherbergt das Gebäude auch ein so genanntes Lofthotel: Apartments, deren Vermietung per Internet die Architekten selbst in die Hand genommen haben.

Das deutsch-kanadische Architektenpaar Britta Jürgens und Matthew Griffin hat vor fünf Jahren den lang nach hinten gezogenen Bauplatz mit einem schmalen Querflügel gekauft – mit dem Ziel, eigene Vorstellungen vom Wohnen und Arbeiten in der Stadt umzusetzen. Der Umbau vollzog sich in zwei Phasen – zuerst die Sanierung des Querflügels, dann der jetzt fertig gestellte Neubau zur Straße. Jeder Gebäudeteil hat seinen eigenen Namen. Der Umbau des Querflügels heißt *slender* was nicht überrascht, wenn man nach oben blickt und vor einer Brandmauer die schmalen, terrassenförmig zurückspringenden Fassadenstreifen sieht, hinter denen gewohnt wird. Der Neubau zur Straße hört auf den Namen *bender*. Das Wort kann Nonsens! meinen, hat aber auch eine homoerotische Bedeutung, vor allem heißt es Saufgelage. Was hat dieser Name mit dem Haus zu tun? Vielleicht bloß dies: Wie der sperrige Name, der über einen fremden Ort gestülpt wurde, so zeigt das Haus eine Fülle von Entwurfsideen, über deren Realisierungsfähigkeit sich die Architekten zu Anfang vielleicht nicht immer sicher waren.

Schon von Ferne machen die fülligen Fassadenkurven, die edelstahlglänzenden Umrandungen und die grafisch gegliederten Fensterflächen deutlich, dass hier ein bescheidener Standort mit entwerferischen Mitteln üppig instrumentiert wurde. Die Architekten haben keine Angst vor solcher Fülle. Die Umfassung der beiden hintereinander gestaffelten Fassadenabschnitte zum Beispiel besteht aus silberglänzendem Edelstahl, die senkrechten Fassadenrippen sind goldeloxiert. Im grellen Nachmittagslicht, das der nach Südwesten in die Straße gerückte Bau auf sich zieht, verschwimmen die warmen und kalten Farben der Stahlverkleidung zu einem fast einheitlichen Ton. Im Innern der Lofts trifft man auf ein ähnliches

Hessische Strasse is right in the centre of Berlin, yet nobody knows it. The street curves in a long arc and is frequently used as a quick shortcut between Invalidenstrasse and Friedrichstrasse. Drivers and pedestrians alike take little notice of their surroundings in this place of transition. However, the new building at No. 5 does have a prominent neighbour almost within sight: the ponderous neo-renaissance Natural History Museum by August Tiede.

The building was not quite finished, but already in use when we viewed it. On that afternoon in June, looking at the building from the street, you could see people on every floor, as though they had been artistically arranged throughout the vertically structured facade. Not only does this building clearly suggest a theatrical sense of staging with its bold cantilevered protrusion and its sharply cropped curves, but even the people who live there seem to be part of the play. Only later did it become evident that the striking vitality of the rooms was actually due to a later change of use. Apart from apartments and offices, the building also includes a "loft hotel" – apartments rented out by the architects themselves on the internet.

German-Canadian architect team Britta Jürgens and Matthew Griffin purchased the deep, narrow building site with a narrow transverse wing five years ago with the aim of realising their own ideas of living and working in the city. The conversion took place in two phases – first the renovation of the transverse wing, then the recently completed new building fronting the street. Each part of the building has its own name. The renovated transverse wing is called *slender* – aptly enough, when you look up at it from below and see the narrow, stepped facade strips like terracing in front of a firewall, with the apartments behind it. The new building towards the street is called *bender*. Like the odd name imposed upon an unfamiliar place, the building itself is teeming with design ideas which the architects themselves may not even have been initially certain would be feasible.

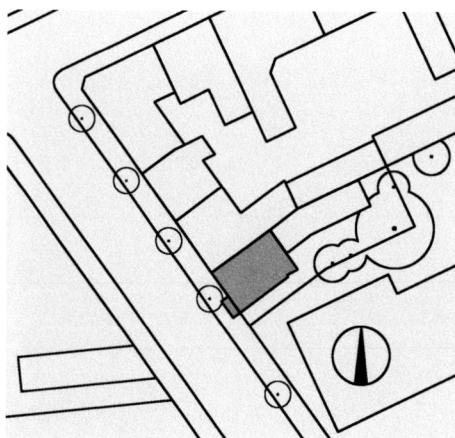

Lageplan **Site plan**

Architekten Architects Deadline, Berlin, www.deadline.de; Matthew Griffin, Britta Jürgens; Team: Matthew Griffin, Britta Jürgens, Stefan Bullerkotte, Kristine Verdier, Hans Christian Wilhelm **Bauherr** Client Jürgens, Jürgens, Griffin GbR, Berlin **Tragwerk** Structural Eisenloffel. Sattler + Partner, Berlin **Ausführung** Construction 2003/04 **Standort** Location Hessische Straße 5, Berlin-Mitte

Nebeneinander, das die Wahrnehmungsfähigkeit des Betrachters zu testen scheint. Viele der verputzten Wände sind kalt weiß, aber daneben gibt es auch einige in Chamois, durchsetzt mit Partikeln aus Stroh und Sand. Manches am Innenausbau sieht aus wie ein Prototyp, an dessen Ausführung man sich kein zweites Mal wagen will: etwa im zweigeschossigen Atelier-Büro, die Stahltreppe aus einer gekurvten Wange, die so viel wiegt wie ein Kleinwagen. Die Leinengardinen hingegen, die in den Lofts dem Schwung der Fassadenkurve folgen, haben einen anderen, provisorischen Charme.

Dieses Haus zeigt den Spezialfall einer Planung, bei der sich die Architekten – auch aufgrund der ökonomischen Zwänge – fast alles zugemutet haben. In selbst gewählter Ämterhäufung fungierten sie als Entwerfer, Marktbeobachter, Developer, Facility Manager und schließlich als Wohnungsvermarkter und Hotelier.

Das fertige Haus ist das Ergebnis einer mutig geführten Auseinandersetzung zwischen der Wunschproduktion der Architekten und der Grenze, bis zu der die behördlich organisierte Gesellschaft diese dann akzeptiert. Das Finanzierungsmodell beispielsweise kollabierte fast während des Bauprozesses an den Obergrenzen zur Vermietung, die als Folge einer rückwirkend gültigen Milieuschutzsatzung einzuhalten waren – die Lösung in letzter Minute war das erwähnte Lofthotel. Die Frage, ob der aufwendige Rohbau nach neuer oder alter Betonnorm berechnet werden muss, führte fast zum Baustopp und die ungewöhnliche Form des Baukörpers – die Architekten sprechen von 3-D in der Lücke – erforderte zahllose Ausnahmegenehmigungen und so weiter.

Für Matthew Griffin ist der »Umgang mit dem Mittelmaß« die entscheidende Erfahrung des turbulenten Bauverlaufs. Damit ist vermutlich auch der ernüchterte Blick auf jenen Begriff des Gewöhnlichen gemeint, dessen architektonische Faszination die englische Schule im Gefolge der Smithsons so überzeugend vermittelt hat. Welche Gewöhnlichkeit und Normalität könnte heute Herausforderung sein? Die eingespielten Baustandards jedenfalls, Surrogat jener Normalität, auf deren ungestörtes Ablaufen sich alle Beteiligten heute verlassen, sind es nicht. Das Schöne an dem Bau in der Hessischen Straße ist, dass er trotz seiner opulenten Außenform in seinen Details ein weitgehend ›normales‹ Haus geblieben ist. Bis auf den Unterschied, dass auch diese Details erzählen, welche Anstrengung es die Architekten gekostet hat, die üblichen Standards jenes Stück weit zu verrücken, das zu ihrer Bewusstmachung notwendig ist.

Kaye Geipel

Even at a distance, the curves of the facade, the shining stainless steel contours and the graphically structured window areas clearly indicate that creative design concepts have been lavishly implemented on this otherwise modest site. The architects have no qualms about such lavishness. The stepped facade sections, for instance, are framed in shining silvery stainless steel, and the vertical facade ribs are gold anodised. In the bright afternoon light that falls on the building as it juts into the street in a south-westerly direction, the warm and cold colours of the steel cladding meld into an almost uniform tone. Inside the lofts, there is a similar juxtaposition that seems to test the observer's powers of perception. Many of the plastered walls are in cold white, but some of them are chamois, mixed with particles of straw and sand. Some aspects of the interior design are reminiscent of a prototype one would be reluctant to tackle a second time: for instance the steel stair on a curved stringer, weighing as much as a small car, in the two-storey studio office. The linen curtains, on the other hand, that follow the sweeping curve of the facade in the lofts, have a rather different, more provisional charm.

This building illustrates the special case of a plan in which the architects, partly due to economic constraints, have dared to do almost anything. They have chosen to wear many hats: designers, market researchers, developers, facility managers and, finally, estate agents and hoteliers.

The finished building is the result of a courageous confrontation between the architects' own visions and the limits to which bureaucratically organised society was willing to accept these visions. Funding, for example, almost fell through during the building process because of problems relating to rental legislation as a result of a retroactively applied property usage clause. The last-minute solution they came up with was the loft hotel. The question as to whether the complex shell of the building should be calculated according to the new or old standards for concrete almost brought the entire project to a complete standstill, while the unusual form of the building – the architects describe it as 3D in the gap – called for countless exemption permits, and so on.

For Matthew Griffin, dealing with the average has been the most crucial experience of this turbulent building project. This probably also means taking a sober look at the concept of "ordinariness", whose architectural fascination has been so persuasively conveyed in English architecture by the followers of Peter and Alison Smithson. What kind of ordinariness and normality could possibly be a challenge today? Certainly not the tried and tested building standards that are surrogates for the sort of normality everyone tends to rely upon these days. The beauty of the building on Hessische Strasse is that, in spite of its opulent exterior, it has remained a more or less "normal" house in its details. This is the case despite the fact that these details, too, tell of the architects' enormous effort to push conventional standards that little bit further – just far enough for us to become aware of them.

Kaye Geipel

Ansicht von Südosten **View from the south-east**

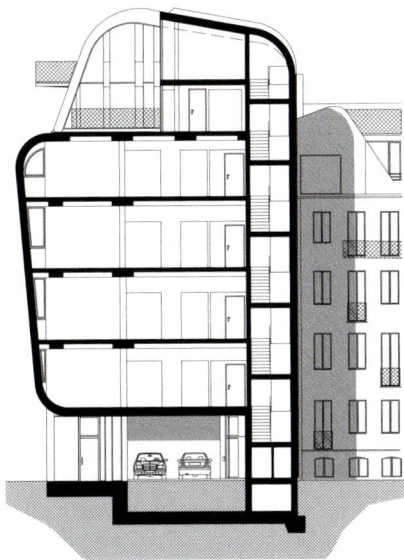

Längsschnitt **Longitudinal section**

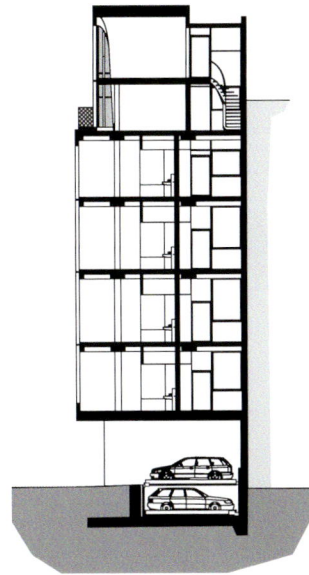

Querschnitt **Cross section**

Ansicht von Westen   **View from the west**

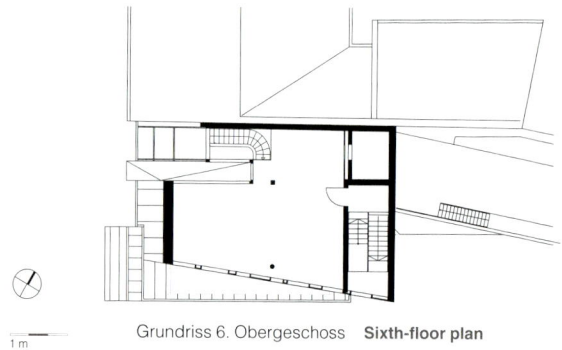

1 m

Grundriss 6. Obergeschoss   **Sixth-floor plan**

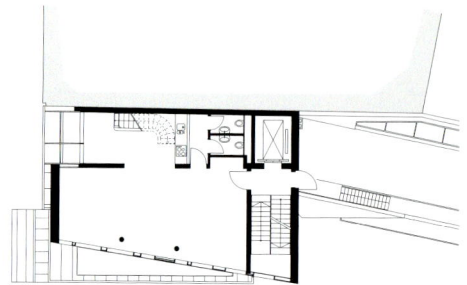

Grundriss 5. Obergeschoss   **Fifth-floor plan**

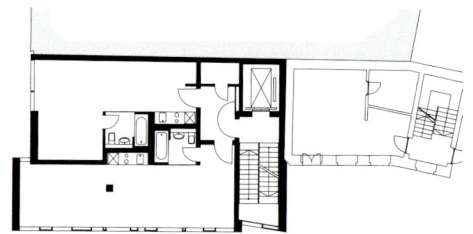

Grundriss 1.–4. Obergeschoss   **First- to fourth-floor plan**

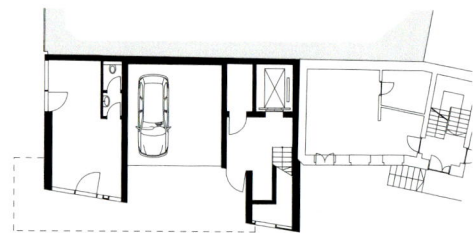

Grundriss Erdgeschoss   **Ground-floor plan**

Ansicht von Südwesten
View from the south-west

Miniloft **Miniloft**

Ausblick Miniloft **View from Miniloft**

Umbau und Aufstockung der ehemaligen Jade-Fabrik, Frankfurt am Main
Conversion and extension of former Jade factory, Frankfurt/Main

Jo. Franzke

■ Der Osten boomt – aber nur der Osten Frankfurts am Main. Die Hanauer Landstraße, Ausfallstraße aus der Frankfurter Innenstadt nach Osten, gehörte bis vor wenigen Jahren zu den unattraktiven Gegenden der Mainmetropole. Hier siedelten sich im 19. Jahrhundert Gewerbe und Industrie an, deren Gebäude in den letzten Jahrzehnten immer mehr herunterkamen. Mit der Auflösung der Weseler Werft, mit neuen Wohnquartieren und insbesondere mit der Entscheidung der Europäischen Zentralbank, auf dem Gelände der Großmarkthalle ihren neuen Hauptsitz zu errichten, hat sich in den letzten Jahren der an die Innenstadt angrenzende Teil der Hanauer Landstraße bereits verändert. In die Gewerbebauten sind Grafikbüros und Werbeagenturen eingezogen, während sich in den Erdgeschossen Designerläden und Outletstores breit machen. Dieser langsame Strukturwandel erfasst auch die weiteren Bereiche bis nach Fechenheim.

Ab 1870 ließen sich am Rande des Fischerdorfs in der Mainschleife verschiedene Industriezweige nieder. Zu den ersten Firmen gehörte das Cassella-Farbwerk. Von dem Industriekomplex, der sich in den Gründerjahren schnell entwickelte, sind heute noch große Teile erhalten. Hierzu zählt auch das 120 Meter lange, 25 Meter tiefe viergeschossige Gebäude, wohl aus dem Jahr 1923, das mit seiner südlichen Schmalseite unmittelbar an die Ausfallstraße grenzt. Bis in die neunziger Jahre wurden dort Kosmetika der Firma Jade/Mouson hergestellt, weswegen das Gebäude bis heute Jade-Fabrik genannt wird.

2000 kaufte die Frankfurter Goldman Holding die leer stehende Fabrik, um sie in ein Bürogebäude umzuwandeln. Nachdem mehrere Frankfurter Architekten um Gestaltungsvorschläge gebeten worden waren, erging noch im selben Jahr der Auftrag an das Büro von Jo. Franzke. Dem Architekten war es wichtig, trotz der neuen Nutzung den ursprünglichen Fabrikcharakter des Bauwerks zu erhalten, um so auch einen optischen Bezug zu dem auf der gegenüberliegenden Straßenseite sich erstreckenden Firmenkomplex zu bewahren.

Die Entstehungsgeschichte des in massivem Ziegelmauerwerk ausgeführten Gebäudes ist weitgehend unbekannt. Vermutlich wurde um 1923 zunächst ein elfachsiger Fabrikbau errichtet, dessen Ecken sowie mittlere Achsen mit schmalen, bossierten Risaliten betont wurden. Zu einem späteren Zeitpunkt muss das Gebäude dann noch einmal um 13 Achsen verlängert worden sein. An der Nahtstelle ist auch im Innern ein Stützenwechsel zu beobachten. Im Zweiten Weltkrieg von einer Bombe getroffen, wurde das ehemalige Walmdach durch ein sehr flaches Dach mit Sheds ersetzt. So besaß das Gebäude bereits seit den fünfziger Jahren gegenüber seinem ursprünglichen Erscheinungsbild ein strenges kubisches Äußeres. Dieses Charakteristikum betont die neuerliche Aufstockung um zwei weitere Geschosse noch in besonderer Weise. Zwar gewinnt der Bau in der disparaten Umgebung – eingeschlossen zwischen Eisenbahntrasse und Schnellstraße – an Fernwirkung, doch seine Proportionen bleiben unbefriedigend.

The east is booming – but only the east of Frankfurt/Main. Only a few years ago, Hanauer Landstrasse, the main artery leading eastwards out of the city centre, was one of the city's most unattractive areas. Industrial and commercial enterprises had moved here in the nineteenth century, and in recent decades their buildings had become increasingly dilapidated. With the closure of the Weseler Werft river wharf and the creation of new apartment complexes and, more importantly, with the decision to use the grounds of the Grossmarkthalle, the former fruit and vegetable market, for the new headquarters of the European Central Bank, this part of Hanauer Landstrasse bordering on the city centre has already been transformed. Graphic artists and advertising agencies have moved in to the loft spaces of the former industrial buildings. Designer boutiques and outlet stores are burgeoning on the ground floors. This gradual structural change has now rippled out as far as Fechenheim.

From 1870 onwards, various branches of industry began to settle on the edge of this former fishing village nestled in a bend of the River Main. One of the first to arrive was Cassella-Farbwerk. A considerable proportion of the company's industrial complex, which rapidly expanded around the turn of the twentieth century, is still in existence. It includes the 120 metre long, 25 metre wide four-storey building, probably erected in 1923, whose south end borders directly on the major through road. Until the 1990s, it was a factory producing cosmetics for the Jade/Mouson company, and is still known today as the Jade Factory.

In the year 2000, the Frankfurt-based Goldman Holding acquired the empty factory with the aim of turning it into offices. After approaching several Frankfurt architects to submit designs, the conversion was awarded to Jo. Franzke. Franzke was determined to retain the factory-style character of the building in spite of its new function, in order to maintain a visual balance with the company complex on the opposite side of the street.

Little is known of the history of this solid brick-built factory. It was probably constructed around 1923 as a factory on eleven axes, with the corners and central axes emphasised by slender, rough-hewn projections. At some later point in time, the building

Lageplan **Site plan**

Architekten Architects Jo. Franzke Architekten, Frankfurt am Main, www.jofranzke.de; Jo. Franzke, Magnus Kaminiarz; Team: Martin Böhler & Hans-Peter Hackh, Harald Etzemüller, Thomas Dröll **Innenausbau Kantine** Canteen interior Mack + Partner Architekturbüro, Frankfurt am Main **Bauherr** Client Benjamin Goldmann Nachlass, Frankfurt am Main **Tragwerk** Structural TPK Tragwerksplanung Kostic, Frankfurt am Main **Freianlagen** Landscape Gabriele Schultheiß Landschaftsarchitektur, Berlin **Licht** Lighting ag Licht Gesellschaft beratender Ingenieure für Lichtplanung, Bonn **Ausführung** Construction 2001–2003 **Standort** Location Hanauer Landstraße 523, Frankfurt am Main

Zunächst entfernte man alle späteren An- und Einbauten. Die über den Dachansatz hinausragenden Treppentürme auf der Ostseite wurden gekappt. Übrig blieb ein längsrechteckiger Quader, auf den die beiden neuen Geschosse aufgesetzt wurden. Das neue Flachdach wurde ein wenig nach innen versenkt, so dass es am Außenbau nicht in Erscheinung tritt. Die Aufstockung – eine Stahlbeton-Fertigkonstruktion – ist im Wechsel mit dunkelgrauen Lamellen und einem Edelstahlgewebe verkleidet. Der Rhythmus nimmt Bezug auf die darunter liegenden Fensterachsen des historischen Baus. Trotz dieser Bezüge entwickelt die Aufstockung aufgrund ihrer gänzlich anderen Materialität und Farbigkeit eine ausgeprägte Flächigkeit sowie gleichzeitig einen eigenen horizontalen Rhythmus.

Im Innern wurde das Gebäude bis auf die Stützen entkernt. An der Schnittstelle des Stützenwechsels zwischen Altbau und späterer Verlängerung platzierte der Architekt ein zentrales Treppenhaus. So ist der Baukörper quasi in zwei Hälften geteilt, die auch auf jedem Stockwerk separat vermietet werden können. Jede Gebäudehälfte erhielt einen kleinen Lichthof. Den zweigeschossigen Eingangsbereich, der von außen über eine großzügige Rampe erreicht werden kann, beherrschen zwei leuchtend rote Einbauten. In einem sind die Fahrstühle untergebracht. An den Stirnseiten des Bauwerks befindet sich jeweils ein Ladenlokal, weshalb dort die ursprüngliche Kleinteilung der Fenster durch große Glasscheiben ersetzt wurde.

Die Aufstockung der Jade-Fabrik hat dem alten Gebäude ein völlig neues Gesicht gegeben – ein Gesicht mit einem Tages- und einem Nachtantlitz. Tagsüber wirken die Gitternetze und Lamellen wie eine hermetische Hülle, hinter der die beiden neuen Geschosse nur zu erahnen sind. Nachts aber wird die Hülle transparent, und die beiden Stockwerke schweben gleichsam über einem dunklen Sockel.

Ursula Kleefisch-Jobst

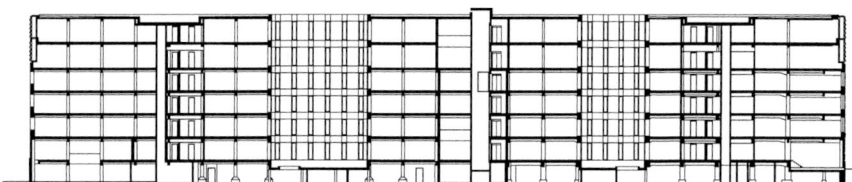

must have been extended by a further thirteen axes. On the interior, a change in the load-bearing system is evident at the join. Struck by bombs during the war, the former hipped roof was replaced by a flat roof with sheds. As a result, by the 1950s, the building had a stringently cuboid exterior in contrast to its original appearance. This particular characteristic also further underlines the recent addition of two storeys. Although the building on this rather oddly defined site between a railway line and an expressway has now gained greater presence as a landmark visible from afar, its proportions are not entirely satisfying.

First, all later extensions and additions were removed. The stairwell towers jutting above the eaves on the eastern side were capped. What was left was a long, rectangular block on which the two new storeys were constructed. The new flat roof was slightly sunken so that it could not be seen from the outside. The additional two storeys, built using a reinforced concrete prefabricated structure, are clad alternately in dark grey slatting and stainless steel weave. The rhythm relates to the window axes of the historic building below. In spite of these references, the added storeys have a certain planarity and a horizontal rhythm of their own because of the use of entirely different material and colour.

On the inside, the building has been completely gutted, but for the supports. The architect has positioned a central stairwell at the interface where the load-bearing system changes between the original structure and its later elongation. This divides the building into two halves, as it were, which can be rented out as separate units on each floor. Each half of the building has been given its own little atrium. The two-storey entrance area, accessed from the outside by a large ramp, is dominated by two bright red installations. One of these houses the lifts. At each narrow end of the building, there is a retail outlet, which is why the original mullioned windows there have been replaced by large panes of glass.

Adding two new storeys to the Jade Factory has given the old building a completely new look – a look that has a "night-time face" and a "day-time face". During the day, the metal grids and slats give it a hermetically self-contained shell, behind which the two new storeys can only be guessed at. But at night the shell becomes transparent, and the two new storeys seem to hover on a dark plinth.

Ursula Kleefisch-Jobst

Schnitt **Section**

Ansicht von Süden **View from the south**

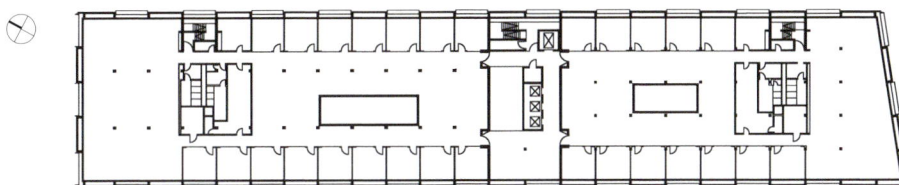

Grundriss 5. Obergeschoss **Fifth-floor plan**

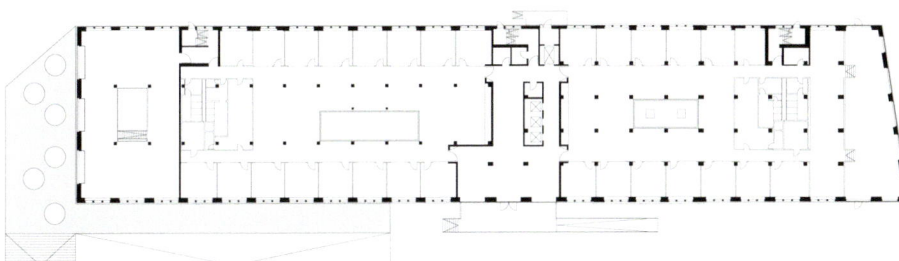

Grundriss Erdgeschoss **Ground-floor plan**

5

Innenraum   **Interior**

Foyer   **Foyer**

Lichthof   **Atrium**

Wohnhaus Weiler, Falkenhagen/Brandenburg
Weiler House, Falkenhagen/Brandenburg

Peter Grundmann

■ Sogar einen Laden gibt es im uckermärkischen Falkenhagen, zwar eigentlich ein umgenutztes Wohnzimmer und wohl mehr als Nachbarschaftshilfe und Nachrichtenbörse gedacht, wo man auch am Sonntagnachmittag noch ein paar Flaschen Bier und den neusten Klatsch eingepackt bekommt. Doch sonst wird nicht viel geboten: eine Hauptstraße ohne Durchgangsverkehr, die Backsteinkirche, ein paar Kossätenhäuser, einige nicht mehr bewirtschaftete Vierseithöfe. Die wenigen Menschen mit Arbeit pendeln tagsüber ins nahe Prenzlau, das pulsierende Zentrum zwischen Schwedt und Neubrandenburg.

Mitten im Dorf, gleich neben der Kirche liegt einer der alten Höfe, abgemauert zur Straße hin. Man tritt durch das Tor: ein Hof mit Katzenkopfpflaster, linker Hand das marode Wohnhaus, offenbar nicht mehr in Gebrauch, rechter Hand der frühere Kuhstall, in dem es vernehmlich rumort. Ponys stehen dort, ein Esel, ein Reitpferd und eine Hand voll Ziegen, offenkundig kein wirklich landwirtschaftlicher Betrieb. Die Rückseite des Gevierts bildet eine schrundige Backsteinwand, Relikt der voluminösen Scheune, die früher den Hof nach Osten abschloss.

Szenenwechsel: Die sanft hügeligen Felder der Uckermark, Mais, Wintergerste, am Ortsrand ein eingezäunter Bauerngarten, Baustellenreste, eine sandige Wiese, die auf Pflege wartet, eine einsame Robinie. Und dann das Artefakt aus einer anderen Welt: transparent, leicht, schwebend, ein gläserner Bungalow, präzise gezeichnet, ungeniert raumgreifend.

Die beiden so unterschiedlichen Szenarien gehen zusammen, denn der Bungalow gehört zum Hof, steht versteckt hinter der Backsteinwand an Stelle der Scheune, in seiner gläsernen Erscheinung durch die Öffnungen der Wand vom Hof aus mehr erahn- als wahrnehmbar.

Ein Musikerehepaar mit drei Kindern hatte den reichlich heruntergekommenen Hof erworben. Das Wohnhaus zu klein und unkomfortabel, die Scheune ruinös, bot sich die Chance für einen Neubau. Peter Grundmann, Architekt aus Neubrandenburg, ließ die Reste der Scheune bis auf die West- und Südwand abtragen und suchte an deren Stelle eine Position für den Neubau. 99 von 100 Architekten hätten die Backsteinwände in den Neubau einbezogen. Grundmann rückte ihn ab und gewann einen Zwischenraum, 3,00 Meter an der Längsseite, 1,40 Meter an der Schmalseite, eine Übergangszone, breiter als ein Gang, schmaler als ein nutzbarer Hof. Und er gewann Distanz zwischen Wohnhaus und Hof, der künftig halböffentlich für Veranstaltungen genutzt werden soll.

Das Haus selbst reduziert sich auf drei Elemente: die Bodenplatte, einerseits in das leicht nach Norden abschüssige Gelände eingetieft, andererseits aufgeständert, schwebend; dann die im Plattenwerk vorfabrizierten Innenwände aus Stahlbeton und schließlich die Dachplatte, eine leichte, zweischalige Holzrahmenkonstruktion. Statt der Außenwände umläuft ein Glasvorhang den Grundriss, hier eingeknickt, um eine Eingangssituation zu markieren, da ausgefaltet,

Falkenhagen in Uckermark even has a shop. Strictly speaking, it is more of a converted living room, a meeting place for neighbours to exchange news and help each other, where you might well get a few bottles of beer and the latest gossip thrown in on a Sunday afternoon. Otherwise, there isn't much to see: a sleepy main street, a brick-built church, a few traditional cottages and some disused courtyard farms. The few people here who do have jobs commute to busy nearby Prenzlau, which lies between Schwedt and Neubrandenburg.

In the middle of the village, just beside the church, is an old courtyard farm, walled off to the street. The gateway leads into a cobbled courtyard with the dilapidated and clearly disused dwelling house on the left, and a former cowshed on the right. There is quite a noise – ponies, a donkey, a horse and few goats – but this does not seem to be a working farm. The rear section of the square is formed by a rough brick wall, a relic of the huge barn that once formed the eastern boundary of the courtyard.

Change of scene: the gently rolling fields of Uckermark, maize, winter barley, a fenced-off farm garden, the remains of a building site, an untended sandy meadow, a lone robinia. And then this artefact from another world: transparent, light, hovering, a glass bungalow with precise lines that fills the space confidently.

These two very different scenes go together, for the bungalow belongs to the farm. It stands tucked away behind the brick wall in place of the barn; more sensed than visible from the courtyard through the wall apertures.

A couple of musicians with three children bought the farm, which required considerable renovation. As the house was too small and uncomfortable for them, and the barn in ruins, the obvious choice was to opt for a new build. Neubrandenburg-based architect Peter Grundmann had the remains of the barn demolished but for the west and south walls, and set about positioning the new building. Out of 100 architects, 99 would have integrated the brick walls in the new building. Grundmann set it at a distance, creating an interim space of 3 metres on the long side and 1.40 metres on the narrow side: a transitional zone broader than a corridor but narrower than a courtyard. In this way, he also created a space that separates the house from the courtyard, which is to be used for semi-public performances in future.

The house itself is reduced to three elements: the floor panel, sunk into the slightly northward-sloping site on the one hand, underpinned and floating on the other hand; secondly the prefabricated interior partitions of reinforced concrete, and finally the roofing slab, which is a light, double-leaf wooden framed structure. Instead of the external walls, there is a glass curtain wall around the floor plan, with a crease marking the entrance area, a protrusion folding out to lend the bedroom the character of a pavilion, and an indentation creating an internal courtyard that separates the living area and parents' area both acoustically and functionally from the children's tract.

Architekten Architects Peter Grundmann, Neubrandenburg **Bauherr Client** Ursula Weiler, Carsten Schlottke, Falkenhagen/Brandenburg
Tragwerk Structural Ingenieurbüro Senckpiel, Altentreptow **Ausführung Construction** 2002/03 **Standort Location** Quillowstraße 47, Falkenhagen/Brandenburg

um dem Schlafraum einen pavillonartigen Charakter zu verleihen, dort eingezogen, um einen Innenhof zu formen, der den Wohn-Eltern-Trakt akustisch und funktional vom Kinderhaus trennt.

Der ›fließende Raum‹ des Wohnbereichs weitet sich durch den unbegrenzten Ausblick in die Landschaft. Wind und Wetter sind als Wohngenossen eingeladen, doch anders als bei Werner Sobeks gläsernem Wohnwürfel in Stuttgart gibt es Vorhänge, die bei Bedarf Zurückgezogenheit ermöglichen.

Man könnte das Haus als unverschlüsselte Reminiszenz an Ludwig Mies van der Rohes Farnsworth House lesen, wäre da nicht die Sache mit dem Knick im Dach. Was aussieht wie die kopflose Flucht vor dem Übervater Mies ist pures Kalkül, denn durch das Absenken der Kinderzimmerdecke und das Anheben des Dachs über dem Esszimmer wird die Ungunst der Himmelsrichtung ausgeglichen und viel Südlicht in den Wohnbereich geleitet. Und wo Mies sein Dach noch auf Stützen stellte, kommt Grundmann scheinbar ohne aus, denn die schmalen Fensterpfosten tragen gleichzeitig das Dach und die Scheiben sind rahmenlos angeklebt.

Goldene Wasserhähne sind in dem Haus nicht zu finden, im Gegenteil. Baukosten von weniger als 200 000 Euro für 250 Quadratmeter lassen erahnen, dass der Ausbaustandard minimiert wurde. Die Innenwände bleiben betonsichtig, der Fußboden beige gestrichener Estrich, rohe MDF-Platten dienen als Türen und Schrankwände. Die Badewanne ist eine Vertiefung im Boden, abgedeckt durch einen Holzrost, der gleichzeitig als Duschwanne dient. Geheizt wird über eine Fußbodenheizung mittels eines Holzkessels im benachbarten Schuppen.

Die ›Ehrlichkeit‹ des unverhehlten Materials passt freilich zur rigorosen Konzeption des Hauses, das es in der Konsequenz seiner Haltung vielleicht mit Mies aufnehmen kann, allerdings beim Raffinement des Finishs passen muss. Auf eine betuchte Bauherrin wie Edith Farnsworth wird der Architekt wohl noch etwas warten müssen.

Falk Jaeger

The "fluid space" of the living area is visually extended by the unlimited views across open country. Wind and weather are welcome guests here, but unlike Werner Sobek's glazed cube in Stuttgart, this home has curtains that can provide some privacy if needed.

The house might be read as an uncoded reminder of Ludwig Mies van der Rohe's Farnsworth House, were it not for the fold in the roof. What may look like a spontaneous attempt to flee from the shadow of Mies van der Rohe is in fact carefully calculated, for by lowering the ceiling of the children's room and raising the roof over the dining room, the otherwise potentially unfavourable alignment of the house is countered so that lots of southern light is channelled into the living area. And whereas Mies van der Rohe placed his roof on supports, Grundmann appears to manage without them, for the slender window mullions also support the roof and the panes seem to be attached without frames.

There are no gold-plated taps to be found in this house. On the country, built on a budget of less than 200,000 Euros for 250 square metres, the interior fittings are pared down to the minimum. The walls are unfaced concrete, the floors are screed painted beige, the doors and cupboard walls are made of MDF. The bathtub is a recess in the floor covered by wooden slats, which serve as a shower basin. Underfloor heating is provided by a wood-fired burner in the adjacent shed.

The "honesty" of these undisguisedly simple materials fits perfectly with the rigorous design of the house. The sheer consistency of this approach is indeed comparable with the work of Mies, though it may lack his sophisticated finish. It looks as though the architect will just have to wait a little longer for a such a wealthy client as Edith Farnsworth to come along.

Falk Jaeger

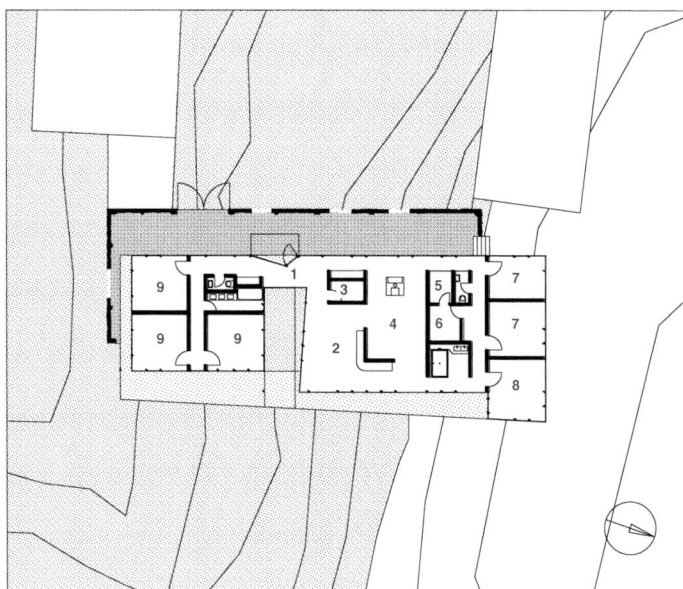

1 Eingangsbereich **Entrance area**
2 Essbereich **Dining area**
3 Speisekammer **Larder**
4 Wohnbereich **Living area**
5 Kleiderkammer **Walk-in wardrobe**
6 Hauswirtschaftsraum **Utility room**
7 Musikzimmer **Music room**
8 Schlafzimmer **Bedroom**
9 Kinderzimmer **Children's room**

0   20 m

Grundriss **Ground plan**

Ansicht von Osten **View from the east**

Westlicher Leerraum **Western space**

Ansicht von Südosten   **View from the south-east**

Tür zum Schlafzimmer   **Door to bedroom**

Blick vom Bad in den Essbereich
View from bath to dining area

Legal/Illegal, Wohn- und Geschäftshaus, Köln
Legal/Illegal, apartment and office building, Cologne

Manuel Herz

■ Das Haus von Manuel Herz in Köln-Bayenthal ist ein Haus der extremen Gegensätze, und es gibt sich keine Mühe, dies zu verbergen. Es liegt in einem nicht minder extremen Umfeld: einem ehemaligen Industrieviertel, das sich heute als ein Patchwork aus gründerzeitlichen Produktionsgebäuden, Bürohochhäusern aus den siebziger Jahren und neueren Wohnanlagen präsentiert. Sich ständig wandelnde Materialien, Typologien und Maßstäbe formen eine wenig fotogene, dafür aber lebendige urbane Landschaft, die in ihrer Entstehung stark von den Interessen der Stahlindustrie geprägt war. Die Produktionsanlagen nahmen den größten Teil des Viertels ein, die Erweiterungsgebiete einen fast noch einmal so großen, die Arbeiterwohnviertel schließlich den kleinsten. Mit dem Rückzug der Industrie in der Strukturkrise und dem gleichzeitigen Exodus der Städter in die Peripherie beschloss die Stadt 1970 einen Bebauungsplan, demzufolge die Industriebrachen mit Einfamilienhäusern gefüllt und die Stadtflüchtlinge zur Rückkehr bewegt werden sollten. Um Platz für Vorgärten zu schaffen, sollten die Straßen verbreitert und die Bauflucht zurückgesetzt werden. Die Dichte wurde auf die einfamilienhauskompatible Geschossflächenzahl von 1,1 heruntergesetzt, was eine wirtschaftliche Bebauung der Grundstücke bis heute so gut wie ausschließt. Aufgrund der vielerorts noch vorhandenen »erhaltenswerten Altbauten« ist der Bebauungsplan bis heute nie zur Anwendung gekommen. Gültig ist er nichtsdestotrotz, und so muss sich hier jeder Neubau zunächst mit diesem Phantomschmerz der Planung auseinander setzen.

Diese Szenerie des Absurden hat den Architekten Manuel Herz dazu bewogen, die widerstreitenden Kräfte, die auf das Grundstück wirken, architektonisch abzubilden. Daraus ist ein Gebäude aus zwei siamesischen Körpern entstanden: Der eine repräsentiert die nach dem Baugesetz maximal zulässige Kubatur, der andere das wirtschaftliche Interesse des Bauherrn.

▨ The house of Manuel Herz in the Bayenthal district of Cologne is a house of extreme contrasts, and it doesn't try to hide the fact. Indeed, the location itself is no less extreme: a former industrial estate that is now a patchwork of turn of the century production complexes, seventies office high-rises and modern apartment buildings. Constantly changing materials, typologies and scales create a vibrant, though hardly pretty, urban landscape shaped primarily by the interests of the steel industry. The production complexes once took up most of this district, their extensions almost as much again, with the worker housing accounting for the smallest share. Industrial recession, together with urban exodus to the suburbs, prompted the city to draw up a development plan in 1970 which involved filling up the industrial gap sites with one-family houses in a bid to entice people back to the city. In order to make room for front gardens, the streets were to be widened and the building alignment set further back. Density was reduced to allow a floor area factor of just 1.1, which has virtually precluded any industrial development of the sites right up to the present day. Given the number of existing old buildings of "architectural interest", the development plan has never been carried out. However, the guidelines still apply, and so any new building here still has to cut through a mass of planning department red tape.

This absurd situation prompted architect Manuel Herz to mirror the conflicts and contradictions of the site in architecture. The result is a building made up of Siamese-twin-like components: one represents the maximum cubic volume permitted under current planning legislation, while the other represents the economic interests of the client.

This dialectical division of the building into a "legal" body and an "illegal" body is also echoed in the architectural design: on the one hand, a transparent box glazed from floor to ceiling, and on the

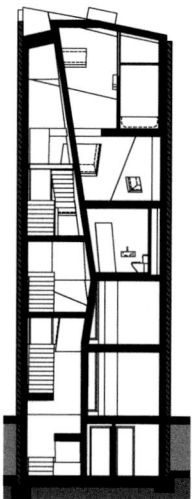

Querschnitt **Cross section**   Längsschnitt **Longitudinal section**

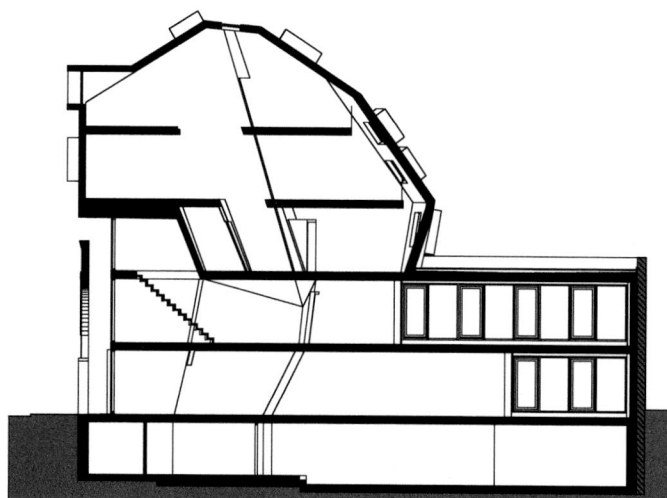

Architekten Architects Manuel Herz Architekt, Köln, www.manuelherz.com; Team: Emmanuelle Raoul, Sven Röttger   **Bauherr** Client TURRIS Immobilien GmbH & Co. KG, Köln   **Bauleitung** Construction Management Martin Schäfer, Köln   **Tragwerk** Structural Arup GmbH, Düsseldorf   **HL-Technik** Technical Ingenieurbüro Rapita, Mönchengladbach   **Ausführung** Construction 2002/03   **Standort** Location Goltsteinstraße 106, Köln-Bayenthal

Diese dialektische Teilung des Gebäudes in einen ›legalen‹ und einen ›illegalen‹ Körper findet in der architektonischen Gestaltung ihre Entsprechung: hier die transparente Kiste mit raumhoher Verglasung, da die opak geschlossene Raumskulptur, deren schreiend roter Polyurethanüberzug den gläsernen Widerpart ziemlich farblos aussehen lässt. Auch im Innern stellen sich die beiden Volumina antipodisch dar: Der ›legale‹ Baukörper ist formal ein eher zurückhaltender Raum und öffnet sich dank der raumhoch verglasten Fassaden stark nach außen. Vor allem in dem schmalen Raumband, in dem gekocht und gegessen wird, hat man das Gefühl, schon draußen zu sein; übergangslos entgrenzt sich das Interieur in den Außenraum von Terrasse und anschließendem Hof. Der ›illegale‹ Baukörper ist dagegen sehr plastisch gestaltet und orientiert sich eher nach innen. Durch geschickte Eingriffe hat Herz die dreigeschossige Wohneinheit als ein kontinuierliches Raumgebilde artikuliert. Zur Hofseite sind die Geschossdecken ein Stück weit von den geneigten Wandflächen zurückgesetzt, so dass der Raum von einer Etage zur anderen ›weiter fließen‹ kann. Dieser Effekt wird verstärkt durch den vertikalen Luftraum, der zentral alle Geschosse durchschneidet. Mit Hilfe dieser Maßnahme gelangt nicht nur viel Tageslicht in die innen liegenden Bereiche, der Leerraum erzeugt auch vielfältige Blickbeziehungen zwischen den einzelnen Wohnräumen.

In seiner Konsequenz bringt dieses duale System den Raum jedoch auch um die Früchte einer möglichen Differenz. Aufgrund der Festlegung, den ›legalen‹ Körper in Glas zu bauen, ist der ebenso ungewöhnlich wie reizvoll in die Vertikale entwickelte Schlafraum ziemlich wehrlos den vieläugigen Blicken des gegenüberstehenden Bürohochhauses ausgeliefert. Umgekehrt vermisst man etwas von dieser Transparenz im ›illegalen‹ Körper, dessen interne Großzügigkeit abrupt an den Wänden aufhört, weil die engen Lochfenster nur wenig räumliche Kommunikation mit dem Außen zulassen. Diese konzeptionelle Starrheit ist nicht unbedingt zum Vorteil des Projekts, lässt sie doch die Frage unerforscht, was an der Stelle passiert, wo die beiden Gegensätze aufeinander stoßen. Man wartet vergebens auf jenes Dazwischen, das Eigenschaften von beidem enthält, jenen Unschärfebereich der Realität, in dem Verbotenes unmerklich legalisiert und Erlaubtes mit Tabu belegt wird: Die Grammatik der Grauzone also, die im örtlichen Brauchtum der alltäglichen Rechtsbeugung (in Köln auch Klüngel genannt) zum virtuos beherrschten Savoir-faire des gesellschaftspolitischen Handelns gehört. Nicht zuletzt deswegen wirkt der Colorcode des ›illegalen‹ Bauteils – das Rot der Verkehrsampel – arg plakativ. Offenbar geht es Herz ganz wesentlich um die Darstellung der Überschreitung von Regeln, wodurch die Frage des konkreten räumlichen Mehrwerts, der durch diese Überschreitung erzeugt wird, in den Hintergrund gerät.

Ilka & Andreas Ruby

other hand an opaque closed spatial sculpture whose lurid red polyurethane cover makes its glass counterpart look almost insipid. The interior, too, contrasts these two volumes: the "legal" component is formally more subtle, with its full-length glazing opening it outwards. In particular, the narrow strip earmarked for cooking and dining gives a sense of being outdoors, with the interior flowing seamlessly towards the exterior, the terrace and the courtyard. The "illegal" building, on the other hand, is very sculptural, and more inward-looking. Herz has cleverly articulated the three-story living unit as a continuous spatial entity. On the side facing the courtyard, the ceilings are set back slightly from the tilted walls so that the space can "flow" from one storey to the next. This effect is further emphasised by the vertical clear space that cuts centrally through all the floors. Not only does this allow lots of daylight to pour into the inner areas, but the empty space also generates many varied views between the individual rooms.

But the rigorous consistency with which this approach has been applied also tends to suffocate the potential for more distinctive spatial differentiation within this dual system. The decision to build the "legal" component in glass has made the unusual and appealing vertically oriented bedroom quite vulnerable to the many-eyed gaze of the office high-rise opposite. On the other hand, there is a lack of transparency in the "illegal" building, whose internal space, generous as it is, stops abruptly at the walls because the narrow window apertures allow little spatial communication with the exterior. Such conceptual inflexibility does not necessarily work to the advantage of the project as a whole, for it does not address the question of what happens at the point where these two opposites meet. We search in vain for an "in-between" zone containing the characteristics of both buildings – an unclearly defined area of reality in which the forbidden is imperceptibly legalised and the permitted becomes taboo. In other words, we miss the "grammar of the grey area" that is so ingrained in the local tendency to bend the rules with a skilfully mastered savoir-faire of socio-political mores that there is even a word for it in Cologne: "Klüngel". For this reason alone, the colour coding of the "illegal" component in traffic-light red seems a little too obvious. Herz is clearly interested primarily in portraying the breaking of rules, while the question of the actual added spatial value generated by this transgression takes a back seat.

Ilka & Andreas Ruby

Ansicht von Westen **View from the west**

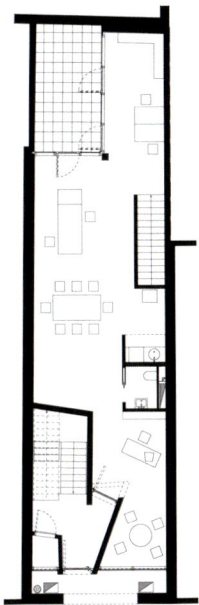

Grundriss Erdgeschoss
Ground-floor plan

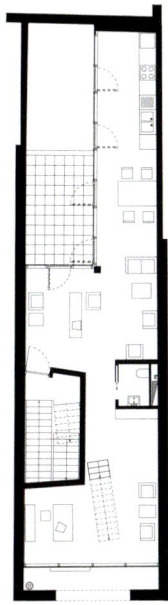

Grundriss 1. Obergeschoss
First-floor plan

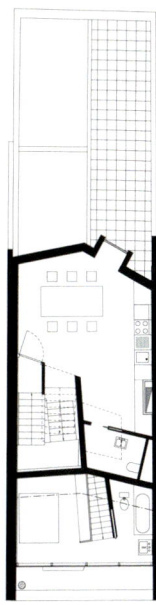

Grundriss 2. Obergeschoss
Second-floor plan

Grundriss 3. Obergeschoss
Third-floor plan

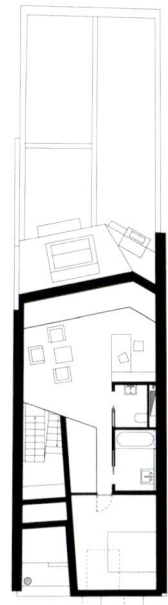

Grundriss 4. Obergeschoss
Fourth-floor plan

Rückwärtiger Luftraum 2.– 4. Obergeschoss   **Rear space, second to fourth floor**

Straßenseitiger Wohnbereich 1. Obergeschoss
Street-facing living area, first floor

Rückwärtige Wohnbereiche 1. Obergeschoss
Rear living area, first floor

Zentraler Luftraum 2.– 4. Obergeschoss
Central space, second to fourth floor

Soundchambers, architektonisch-musikalischer Pavillon, Porto, Portugal
Soundchambers, architectural and musical pavilion, Porto, Portugal

Nikolaus Hirsch/Michel Müller

■ Oberhalb des Douro auf der Hochfläche zwischen dem Zentrum von Porto und dem Küstenvorort Foz do Douro gelegen, bildet der Park Serralves eine grüne Enklave im wachsenden Siedlungsgebiet der nordportugiesischen Metropole. In den dreißiger Jahren des vergangenen Jahrhunderts war er im Auftrag eines vermögenden Textilfabrikanten von dem französischen Landschaftsarchitekten Jacques Gréber angelegt worden; am Rand des Areals errichtete der Architekt Charles Siclis eine Villa im Stil des Art déco. Park und Villa sind seit 1989 öffentlich zugänglich – als Domizil der Fundação Serralves, dem ersten Museum des Landes, das ausschließlich der zeitgenössischen Kunst gewidmet ist. Dabei beschäftigt sich die Institution nicht allein mit bildender Kunst, sondern gleichermaßen mit Musik und Tanz. Da die Räume in der bestehenden Villa für all diese Aktivitäten nicht ausreichend Platz boten, beauftragte die Stiftung Álvaro Siza mit dem Bau eines neuen Museums, das Ausstellungssäle, aber auch Aufführungsräume umfassen sollte und in der zweiten Hälfte der neunziger Jahre realisiert werden konnte.

Das Interesse der Museumsleitung an interdisziplinären Kunstprojekten hatte den für Musik zuständigen Kurator 2002 zum Besuch der Ausstellung *Frequenzen [Hz]. Audiovisuelle Räume* in die Frankfurter Schirn geführt. Dort waren die einzelnen Sound-Installationen in eine kontinuierliche Struktur aus weißen Wänden integriert, die als Mäander einzelne Kojen entstehen ließen – eine Gemeinschaftsarbeit der Architekten Nikolaus Hirsch und Michel Müller, des Grafikdesigners Markus Weisbeck sowie des Komponisten und Musikers Ekkehard Ehlers. Das Team hatte ein Konzept entwickelt, das für das Klangerlebnis einen funktionalen und neutralen Hintergrund bot und mit den Prinzipien der Repetition und Modulation auf einer den Installationen adäquaten Strategie basierte.

Als Hirsch daraufhin von der Fundação Serralves zu einer neuen Arbeit im Grenzbereich zwischen Architektur und Musik eingeladen wurde, entschied er sich aus gutem Grund, seine Intervention nicht im Museum selbst – es zählt nicht zu den stärksten Werken von Siza –, sondern im Park zu realisieren. Das ausgedehnte Areal mutet zu weiten Teilen eher informell und romantisch im Sinne der englischen Gartentradition an, während andere Bereiche, insbesondere in der Nähe der Villa, im Stil des französischen Parks formal gestaltet sind und innerhalb der Gesamtanlage wie artifizielle Einschlüsse wirken.

Das Team um Hirsch, verstärkt durch den Trompeter Franz Hautzinger und den Gitarristen Josef Suchy, wählte den nahe der Villa gelegenen Rosengarten für die Realisierung der Soundchambers: eine axialsymmetrische Anlage, die aus verschiedenen durch Hecken umgrenzten Pflanzfeldern besteht. Die zentrale Wegachse führt gleichsam in eine Apsis über dem Grundriss eines halben Achtecks.

Das Team begann mit einer Kartierung des Gartens: Im Sinne eines Mapping wurden sämtliche der von Hecken umschlossenen Flächen erfasst und anschließend in eine dreidimensionale Grafik übertragen. Dabei manipulierte man gewisse Parameter, um zu

Set above the Douro on the high plain between the centre of Porto and the coastal suburb of Foz do Douro, the Serralves Park forms a green enclave within the growing urban sprawl of the northern Portuguese city. The park was created in the 1930s by a wealthy textile manufacturer, who commissioned the French landscape architect Jacques Gréber to design it. At the edge of the park, the architect Charles Siclis built an Art Déco villa. Both the park and the villa have been open to the public since 1989 as the seat of the Fundação Serralves – the first museum in the country dedicated entirely to contemporary art. The institution showcases not only the visual arts, but also music and dance. As the existing villa simply did not have enough room for all these activities, the foundation commissioned Álvaro Siza to build a new museum capable of housing exhibition spaces and auditoriums. It was completed in the late 1990s.

In 2002, the museum directorate's interest in inter-disciplinary art projects prompted the curator in charge of music to visit to the exhibition *Frequenzen [Hz]. Audiovisuelle Räume* at the Schirn Kunsthalle in Frankfurt/Main. There, individual sound installations were integrated into a continuous structure of white walls whose

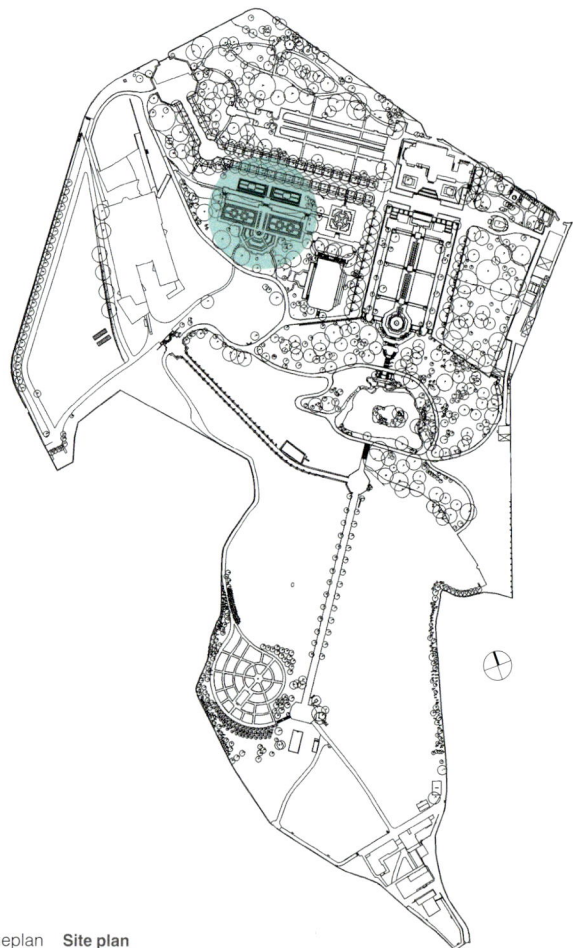

Lageplan **Site plan**

Architekten Architects Nikolaus Hirsch/Michel Müller, Frankfurt am Main; Team: John Lau, Tobias Katz, Daniel Dolder **Bauherr Client** Museu Serralves, Porto, Portugal **Musik Music** Ekkehard Ehlers, Franz Hautzinger, Josef Suchy **Grafik Graphics Design** Markus Weisbeck **Ausführung Construction** 2002/03 **Standort Location** Museu Serralves, Rua D. João de Castro 210, Porto, Portugal

Elementen von handhabbarer Größe zu gelangen. Die dergestalt ›extrudierten‹ Elemente ließen sich aus Blöcken von grünem Blumensteckschaum ausschneiden und in Form einer aus fünf Lagen bestehenden, begehbaren Gangstruktur in der Mittelachse des Rosengartens aufschichten. Locker gefügt, so dass sich Durchblicke nach außen ergaben, wurden die Blöcke beidseits des Durchgangs aufgestapelt und auf der obersten Ebene miteinander verbunden. Das fünfteilige Musikstück, durch kleine Lautsprecher in den Gang übertragen, basiert ebenfalls auf dem Modell der sequenziellen und sich überlagernden Anordnung vorgegebener Elemente, ohne sich jedoch auf eine schematische Übertragung einer diagrammatischen Anordnung in ein anderes Medium zu beschränken.

Mit ihrer temporären synästhetischen Installation war den Beteiligten eine eindrucksvolle Arbeit gelungen, die mit ihrer Transformation von Elementen des Gartenplans in eine andere Ordnung und von der Horizontalen in die Vertikale die strenge Geometrie des Rosengartens zugleich stärkte und störte: Innen und außen verzahnten sich in dem von Tönen erfüllten Durchgang. Man mochte an eine zeitgenössische Variante der Follies denken, jener kleinen Bauten des englischen Landschaftsgartens, welche die Besucher um spezifische ästhetische, mitunter irritierende Erfahrungen bereichern sollten. Das Grün der Natur kehrte wieder, verwandelt im artifiziellen Grün des Blumensteckschaums, der sich üblicherweise nahezu unsichtbar unter dem Blattwerk verbirgt, hier aber als ›natürliche‹ Kunst der künstlichen Natur gegenübergestellt wurde. So wie aber die in ständiger Wandlung befindliche Natur gegenüber dem präzisen Gartenlayout eine gewisse Autonomie zu bewahren vermag, so verhinderte auch das weiche aufgeschäumte Baumaterial der Soundchambers, dass die von den Architekten entworfenen Formen in kalte Sterilität transformiert wurden. Die Lebendigkeit entsteht durch ein Moment der Unschärfe, welches auch der Musik eigen ist.

Hubertus Adam

meandering form created individual booths – a joint project designed by architects Nikolaus Hirsch and Michel Müller, graphic designer Markus Weisbeck and the composer and musician Ekkehard Ehlers. The team had developed a concept that offered a functional and neutral background for the sound experience, based on a strategy suited to the installation using the principles of repetition and modulation.

When the Fundação Serralves subsequently invited Hirsch to create a new work on the borderline between architecture and music, he chose, for good reason, not to realise the project in the museum itself (it is not one of Siza's best) but in the park. This expansive area has the informal and romantic air of the traditional English garden, whereas other areas, especially those close to the villa, adopt the formal style of a French garden, and seem like artificial inserts within the park as a whole.

Hirsch's team, with trumpeter Franz Hautzinger and guitarist Josef Suchy, chose the rose garden near the villa as the site for the Soundchambers. It has an axially symmetrical layout consisting of various beds bounded by hedgerows. The central pathway leads to what is reminiscent of an apse over the plan of a half-octagon.

The team began by mapping the garden. All the areas surrounded by hedges were charted and transposed into a three-dimensional graphic scheme. At the same time, some of the parameters were manipulated in order to create elements of a manageable size. The elements that had been "extruded" in this way could be cut out from blocks of green foam (of the kind used for flower arranging) and stacked in a five-layered corridor structure along the central axis of the rose garden. Loosely positioned to permit outward views, the blocks were stacked on either side of the corridor and linked at the top. The five-part musical composition broadcast in the corridor through small loudspeakers is also based on the principle of a sequential and layered arrangement of given elements, but is not limited to the schematic transposition of a diagrammatic order into another medium.

With this temporary synaesthetic installation, the team succeeded in creating an impressive work that transferred elements of the garden layout into a different order and transformed them from the horizontal to the vertical, simultaneously strengthening and undermining the stringent geometry of the rose garden: interior and exterior dovetailed in the sound-filled corridor. What springs to mind here is a contemporary variation on the idea of the folly – those little buildings in English landscaped gardens that were meant to provide the visitor with a specific aesthetic experience, at times a confusing one. The green of nature was repeated, transformed into the artificial green of the foam that is normally hidden beneath an array of foliage, but which forms a contrast here between "natural" art and artificial nature. But just as nature, in constant flux, is able to maintain a certain autonomy from the precision of the garden layout, so too did the soft foam of the Soundchambers prevent the forms designed by the architects from turning into cold sterility. Vitality is created by a moment of unclarity that is also inherent in music.

Hubertus Adam

Soundchambers, architektonisch-musikalischer Pavillon, Porto, Portugal
Soundchambers, architectural and musical pavilion, Porto, Portugal

123

Innenraumwirkung   **Interior view**

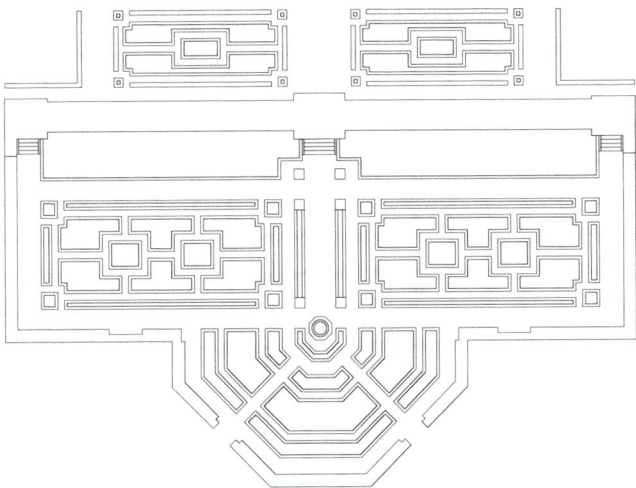

Kartierung der Hecken   **Mapping of hedgerows**

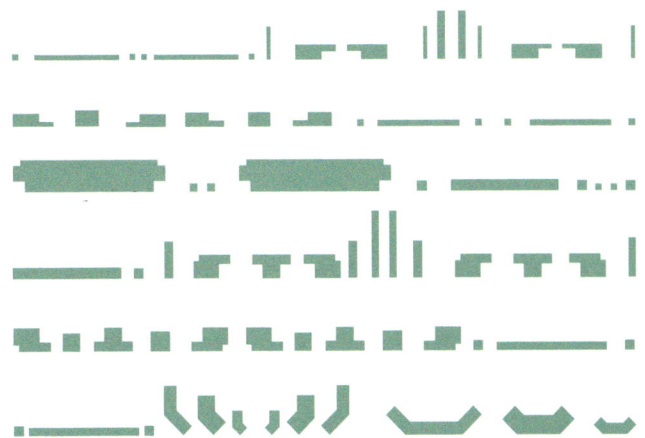

Ansicht von Nordwesten   **View from the north-west**

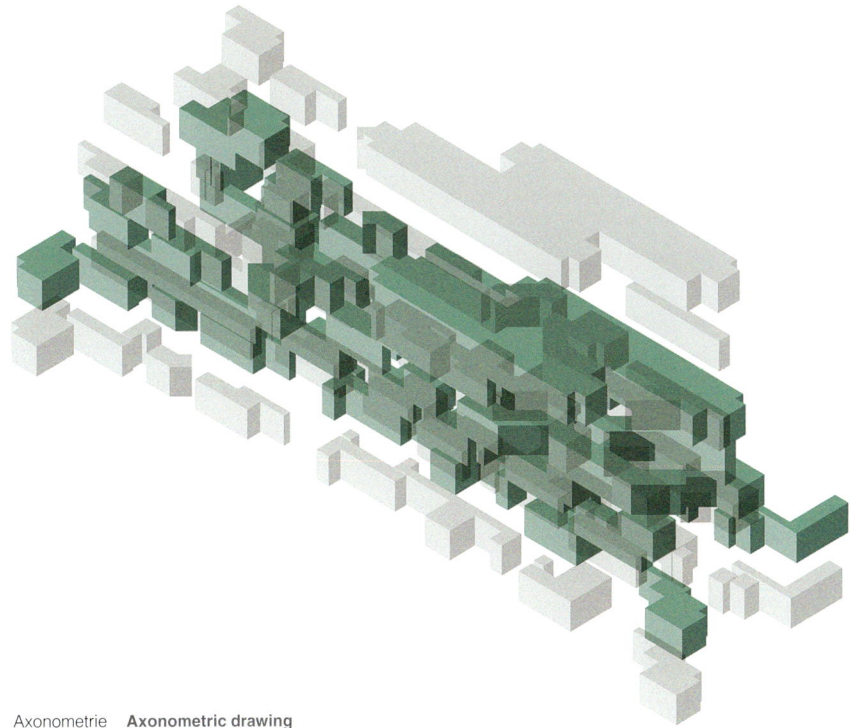

Axonometrie **Axonometric drawing**

Konventhaus Kloster St. Ansgar, Travenbrück-Nütschau
Convent of St. Ansgar, Travenbrück-Nütschau

Gisberth M. Hülsmann mit with Elmar Sommer

■ Das hätten wir uns an der Hochschule nicht getraut: Eine Tragstruktur aus gewölbten Betonfertigteilen wird in der Mitte, im Zenit, durch eine Raumtrennwand geteilt! Der Balken, auf dem die Fertigteile aufliegen, ruht auf einer Stütze im Flur, vor der Tür; sie teilt, schön symmetrisch, die Flurwand – und wie wir noch vom griechischen Tempel wissen: Eine ungerade Zahl von Säulen an der Front verstellt den Eingang.

Dieser ist verstellt. Der Architekt, Gisberth M. Hülsmann, zeigt – und begründet das aus der Baugeschichte – den einzelnen Raum als Teil eines Ganzen, nicht als in sich geschlossene Einheit. Jeder im Essraum erkennt, dass dieser Raum eigentlich jenseits der Wand noch weitergeht, dass er Teil von etwas Größerem ist. Der große Speisesaal der Mönche, das Refektorium, nimmt dagegen mit seiner größeren Raumtiefe die Flucht der Stützen auf, die den Flur vor dem Gästespeiseraum teilt. Das Refektorium ist für das Leben des Klosters weit wichtiger und inszeniert das mit seinem Eingang: Durch zwei Säulen beidseits der Tür wird er zum Portal. Diese stehen auf einer Betonstufe in einem Bett aus groben Kieseln, das von den Mönchen selbst gelegt wurde. Die Säulen erhalten so eine Basis, die sich vom Betonfußboden abhebt. Auf der Betonstufe, in den Flur hineinragend, liegt eine naturbelassene Holzplatte. Sie schwebt über dem Boden und wird durch ein schmales, senkrecht stehendes Stahlprofil gehalten. Die große Portalöffnung wird durch eine massive, aus Holz waagerecht gefügte Fläche geschlossen, die, vom Innenraum erkennbar, seitlich über die gemauerte Raumwand greift.

Beton, manchmal weiß gestrichen, Eichenholz und Esche aus dem klostereigenen Wald – das sind die dominierenden Materialien des Klosteranbaus in Nütschau. Nur die Leuchtkörper und Geländer, sämtlich Sonderanfertigungen, sind aus Metall. Auch alle Möbel wurden eigens für das Kloster entworfen und werden von einem der Mönche, einem gelernten Tischler, gefertigt.

Das ist das Prinzip: Mit eigenen Mitteln, so einfach wie möglich. Nun entsprechen ja bewusste Askese und Reduktion der formalen Mittel einer heute aktuellen ›Neuen Einfachheit‹. Auf den ersten Blick sieht der Anbau an das aus dem 16. Jahrhundert stammende, dreigieblige Herrenhaus so aus, als erfülle er deren stilistische Vorgaben. Die programmatische ›Neue Einfachheit‹ in der Architektur aber folgt einem anderen Prinzip: so einfach wie möglich, koste es, was es wolle. Das hätte sich das Kloster nicht leisten können, und dennoch geht es nicht um eine ›Architektur der Armut‹. Denn wer arm ist, will in der Regel nicht eine Architektur, die das Einfache betont. Hier ist die ›Armut‹ finanzielle Notwendigkeit, religiöse Überzeugung und formale Disziplin.

1951 wurde das Kloster nach der Ordensregel des hl. Benedikt und seinem Gebot »ora et labora« gegründet. Die Räume für das Leben der Mönche und die Seminar- und Unterbringungsräume für Gäste entstanden in den sechziger und siebziger Jahren – in einer mit ihren bescheidenen Flachbauten sich dem Herrenhaus unterordnenden Bauweise, meist mit weiß geschlämmten Ziegelsteinmauern.

It's something we wouldn't have dared to suggest when we were students: a load-bearing structure of vaulted prefabricated concrete components divided in the middle, at the very zenith, by a partition wall! The beam carrying the prefabricated components rests on a support in the corridor, in front of the door. It divides the corridor wall nicely symmetrically. As we all know, the entrance to an Ancient Greek temple is obscured by an uneven number of columns at the front.

This entrance, too, is obscured. Architect Gisberth M. Hülsmann has looked to historic architecture, presenting the individual room as part of a whole, rather than as a self-contained unit. Everyone in the dining room is fully aware that this room continues beyond the wall and that it forms part of a larger entity. The refectory, on the other hand, is a space with greater depth, echoing the row of columns that divides the corridor from the guests' dining room. The important role played by the refectory in the life of the monastery is reflected in its entrance: the door is turned into a portal by positioning two columns on either side. The columns stand on a concrete step embedded in rough pebbles placed there by the monks themselves, creating a base that is distinct from the concrete floor. A panel of untreated wood on the concrete step juts into the corridor. Hovering over the floor, it is held by a slender vertical steel profile. The large portal aperture is closed by a massive horizontal area of wood that continues sideways across the masonry wall and is visible from inside the room.

Concrete, some of it painted white, oak and ash from the monastery's own woodlands – these are the predominant materials used in the new extension at Nütschau. Only the lighting and railings, all of which have been custom designed, are made of metal. All the furnishings have been specially designed for the monastery and are being made by one of the monks who is a trained cabinetmaker.

The underlying principle is one of maximum simplicity using the resources available. Deliberate asceticism and pared-down form are very much in keeping with today's New Simplicity. At first glance, the extension seems to conform stylistically with the triple gabled sixteenth-century main building. But architecture's programmatic New Simplicity follows a different principle: maximum simplicity, at any price. The monastery could not have afforded that, but nevertheless this is no "architecture of poverty". For those who are poor do not generally want an architecture that emphasises simplicity. In this case, "poverty" is a question of financial necessity, religious conviction and formal discipline.

The monastery was founded in 1951 according to the rules of the Order of St. Benedict and his principle of ora et labora. The monks' rooms, the seminar rooms and the guest accommodation were created in the 1960s and 1970s in flat-roofed buildings of whitewashed brick that were plainly dominated by the architecture of the main building. As the seminar facilities expanded and repairs to the main

Architekten Architects Prof. Gisberth M. Hülsmann, Wachtberg, www.gisberthhuelsmann.de, mit with Elmar Sommer, Monschau; Team: Ulrich Hahn, Bettina Schröder
Bauleitung Construction Management Elmar Sommer, Monschau **Bauherr Client** Benediktiner-Priorat St. Ansgar, Travenbrück-Nütschau **Tragwerk Structural**
Wetzel & von Seht Ingenieurbüro für Bauwesen, Hamburg **HL-Technik Technical** Büro für Energie- und Lichtplanung, Dipl.-Ing. Christoph Roggendorff, Hamburg
Ausführung Construction Erster Bauabschnitt First building phase 1998/99; Zweiter Bauabschnitt Second building phase 2003–2006 **Standort Location**
Schlossstraße 30, Travenbrück-Nütschau

Mit der Ausweitung des Seminarbetriebs, dem Sanierungsdruck beim Herrenhaus und mit funktionalen Erfordernissen wie einer Pforte als bewusstem Zugang zu einem Kloster wurde eine Neuordnung nötig, die die Architekten in einem Gutachten 1995 vorlegten. Im Diskurs mit den Mönchen wurde es bis zur heutigen, noch nicht vollständig realisierten Form weiterentwickelt. Der nächste Bauabschnitt umfasst die Sanierung des Herrenhauses, des Gemeinschaftsbereichs der Mönche mit Bibliothek, Noviziat und einer kleinen Kapelle, sowie den Bau der Pforte. Diese wird durch eine hohe, frei stehende Wandscheibe markiert werden, die die Nahtstelle zwischen Herrenhaus und dem 1999 fertig gestellten Seitenflügel für die Mönche besetzen soll. Dieser bildet mit der vorhandenen Kirche zwei Seiten eines ›Kreuzgangs‹, der mit Hecken vorläufig unter freiem Himmel angelegt wird.

Der neue Seitenflügel umfasst den für das Klosterleben wichtigsten Bereich: Auf drei Ebenen liegen 19 Zellen, Priorat und Krankenstation, dazu die Speiseräume. Hier können sich die Mönche auf sich zurückziehen – ein Bereich, der sich bewusst nicht der Arbeit und der Öffentlichkeit öffnet.

Die Nahtstelle zwischen Herrenhaus und Seitenflügel wird nach ihrer Fertigstellung der architektonisch anspruchsvollste, ein räumlich höchst komplexer Teil sein – dort, wo drei Wege zusammenkommen. Der Ort, an dem die Verbindung zur Welt draußen hergestellt wird (Pforte) und der, wo klösterliche Gemeinschaft und mönchische Zurückgezogenheit zusammentreffen. Auch der Neubau nimmt an dieser Stelle Rücksicht auf das Alte, wie seine schräge Giebelwand bezeugt, die dem Alten nicht zu dicht auf den Pelz rücken will. Das zeigt Respekt – Respekt aber heißt nicht Unterordnung, und so bildet das Ensemble eine in Form übersetzte, selbstbewusste Neu-Begründung des klösterlichen Lebens in heutiger Zeit.

Gert Kähler

building became increasingly urgent a reappraisal of the layout was needed to include such functional necessities as a gate marking the entrance to the monastery. In 1995, the architects presented a proposal. In close cooperation with the monks, this proposal was developed and amended to its current, as yet unfinished, form. The next building phase involves refurbishing the main building, the communal areas such as the library, novitiate and small chapel, and the construction of the entrance gate. The entrance gate is to be marked by a high, freestanding wall at the intersection between the main building and the side wing for the monks, completed in 1999. Together with the existing church, this forms two sides of a "cloister", currently open-air and planted with hedgerows.

The new side wing houses the most important components of monastic life: 19 cells, priory and infirmary on three levels, as well as dining rooms. The monks can withdraw here into an atmosphere deliberately sheltered from work and the outside world.

Once it is completed, the intersection between the main building and side wing will be the most architecturally sophisticated and spatially complex part of the monastery, as the fulcrum point of three separate paths. It is the point at which the connection with the outside world is visible (the entrance gate) and also the point at which monastic community meets monastic seclusion. The juxtaposition of new and old is handled sensitively here, as in the angled gable wall that does not encroach too closely on the old building. This shows respect. Respect, however, is not submissive – and, consequently, the ensemble is a self-assured statement that brings monastic life into the present day, translating it into built form.

Gert Kähler

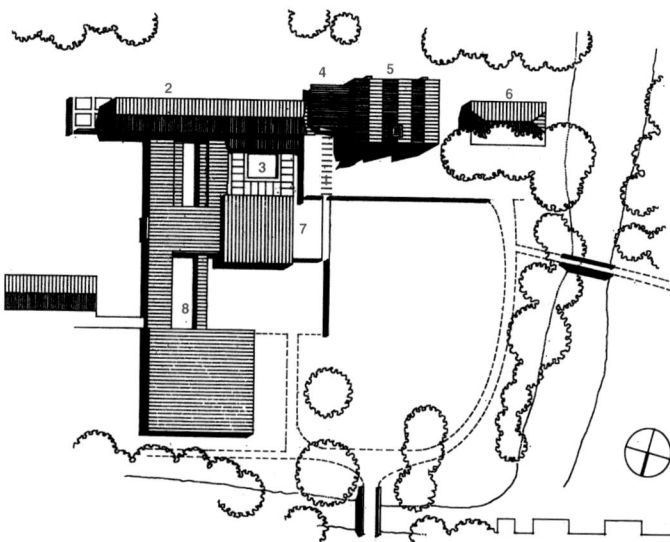

1 Pforte **Gate**
2 Konventhaus **Convent**
3 Kreuzgang **Cloister**
4 Bibliothek **Library**
5 Herrenhaus **Main house**
6 Gästewohnen **Guest accommodation**
7 Kirche **Church**
8 Hotellerie **Hostelry**

Lageplan **Site plan**

Ansicht von Südosten **View from the south-east**

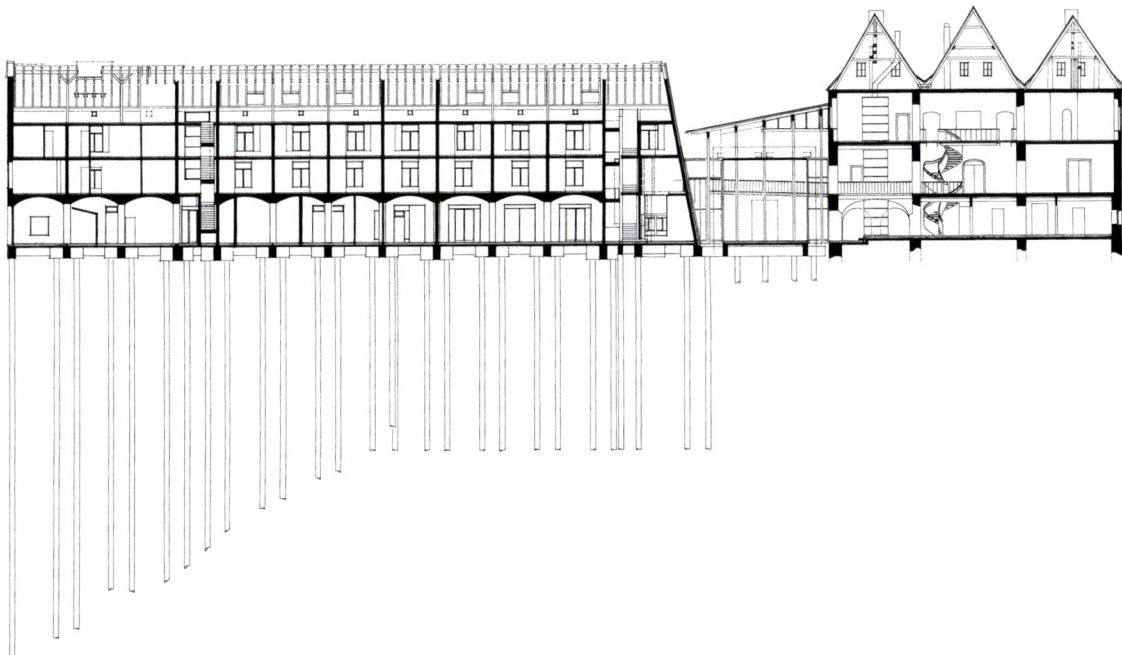

Schnitt **Section**

Nordansicht, 1. und 2. Bauabschnitt **North elevation, first and second building phase**

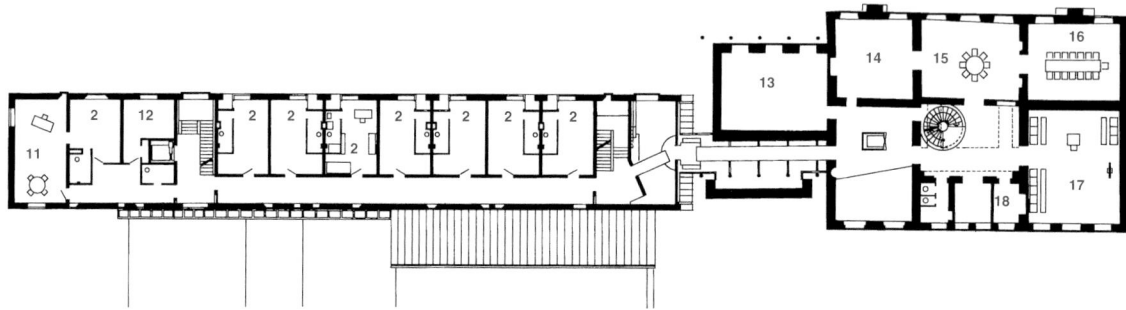

Grundriss Ebene +1 **Ground-plan level +1**

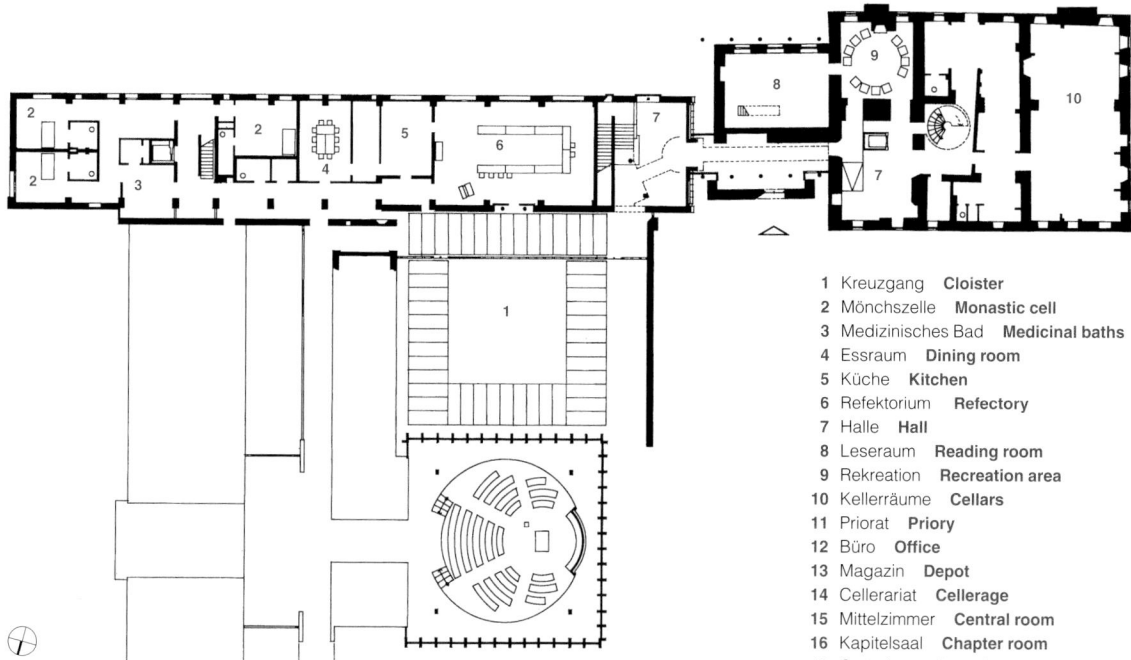

0   5   10 m

Grundriss Ebene 0 **Ground-plan level 0**

1 Kreuzgang **Cloister**
2 Mönchszelle **Monastic cell**
3 Medizinisches Bad **Medicinal baths**
4 Essraum **Dining room**
5 Küche **Kitchen**
6 Refektorium **Refectory**
7 Halle **Hall**
8 Leseraum **Reading room**
9 Rekreation **Recreation area**
10 Kellerräume **Cellars**
11 Priorat **Priory**
12 Büro **Office**
13 Magazin **Depot**
14 Cellerariat **Cellerage**
15 Mittelzimmer **Central room**
16 Kapitelsaal **Chapter room**
17 Oratorium **Oratorium**
18 Sakristei **Sacristy**

Südfassade **South facade**

Kreuzgang, 1. Bauabschnitt **Cloister, first building phase**

Fensterdetail in der Halle
Detail of hall window

Speiseraum für Gäste   **Dining room for guests**

Refektorium   **Refectory**

Detail der gemauerten Treppenbrüstung in der Halle
Detail of masonry parapet in hall

Jugend- und Pfarrheim, Thalmässing
Youth centre and parsonage, Thalmässing

meck architekten

■ Das Klischee will es so: Bayern ist barock und katholisch. Im oberfränkischen Thalmässing, 50 Kilometer südlich von Nürnberg gelegen, liegen die Dinge anders. Zwar sind die drei Kirchen, zwischen denen sich der kleine Ort aufspannt, mehr oder weniger barock, doch katholisch sind sie nicht. Seit der Reformation ist Thalmässing eine evangelische Enklave. Um zur katholischen Kirche zu gelangen, ist man auf einen kleinen Wegweiser angewiesen, der in eine Sackgasse zeigt.

Als ein paar zugezogene Katholiken 1924 ihre kleine Kirche St. Peter und Paul bauten, gaben sie sich redlich Mühe nicht aufzufallen. Ein sympathisches kleines Neoirgendwas blickt mit zwei runden Fensteraugen aus schmuckloser Fassade und zeugt vom Versuch, sich den in Franken verbreiteten – evangelischen – Markgrafenstil anzueignen, einer Mixtur aus französischem Klassizismus, einer Prise bayrischem Barock und viel fränkischer Strenge. Mehr noch als ihre stilistische Mimikry zeugt der Standort der Kirche von der katholischen Diaspora. Zur Bauzeit führte eine Bahnlinie wenige Meter am Gebäude vorbei, das noch heute von Koppeln und Gärten umgeben ist. Die Anschrift des 1948 rückwärtig angebauten Pfarrhauses lautet Kirchenweg 1. Es war das bisher einzige Haus der Straße.

2001 gewannen meck architekten den eingeladenen Wettbewerb um ein Jugend- und Pfarrheim in direkter Nachbarschaft der Kirche. Abweichend von den anderen Teilnehmern platzierten sie den neuen Baukörper nicht vor die Kirche, sondern daneben – an die Stelle, wo bis vor 30 Jahren noch Züge rollten. Der eingeschossige stark geschlossene Neubau schiebt sich parallel zum Gotteshaus in den leichten Hang. »Farbe und Ornament überlassen wir der Kirche«, sagt Andreas Meck zu den Fassaden aus Sichtbeton, die von je einer großen Öffnung durchbrochen sind. Die Längsseiten bleiben nur knapp unter der 50-Meter-Marke. Durch eine Art Loggia blickt der

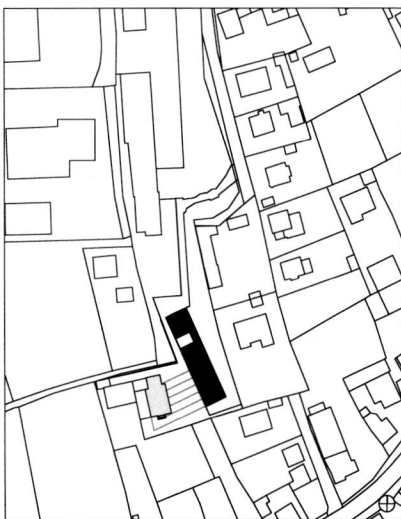

Lageplan **Site plan**

When we think of Bavaria, we think of baroque and Catholicism. But in the Upper Franconian town of Thalmässing, 50 kilometres south of Nuremberg, that cliché does not hold true. Although the three churches that are the fulcrum points of this little town are indeed more or less baroque, they are not Catholic. Thalmässing has been a Protestant enclave since the days of the Reformation. To get to the Catholic church, you have to follow a tiny sign pointing down a cul-de-sac.

When a handful of Catholic newcomers founded the church of St. Peter and Paul in 1924, they did all they could to keep a low profile. A pleasant little neo-something-or-other with two round eye-like windows gazing out of an unadorned facade bears witness to their attempt to adopt the margravian style so prevalent in the (Protestant) region of Franconia – a blend of French neo-classicism with a hint of Bavarian baroque and a generous helping of Franconian stringency. Yet it is the location of the church, rather than its stylistic mimicry, that tells of the Catholic diaspora. When it was built, there was a railway line running just a few metres from the building which, even today, is still surrounded by paddocks and gardens. The address of the chaplaincy built just behind it in 1948 is Kirchenweg 1. It was the only house in the street at the time.

In 2001 meck architekten won the competition for a youth and pastoral centre adjacent to the church. Unlike the other architects invited to submit designs, they did not position the new building in front of the church, but beside it – in the place where trains had still been rolling thirty years before. The single-level, self-contained new building projects into the gentle slope parallel to the church. "We have left the choice of colour and ornament to the church," says Andreas Meck, referring to the unfaced concrete facades that are each pierced by one large aperture. The long sides are just under the 50 metre mark. The full length of the parish hall looks towards the church through a kind of loggia, which also forms the entrance to the vestibule before the hall. Seen from inside, the hall itself and the space before it seem to merge into a single room through the glass wall, so that the side of the church becomes like the wall of the room. Seen from outside, the recessed aperture is anything but modest and welcomes the approaching visitor with a gesture of magnificent pretentiousness verging on the baroque. All the other rooms are screened from the outside world. Two rooms for youth groups face each other across a little courtyard of monastic simplicity. Two offices and a music room in the basement are lit by the glazed end wall to the north, while the kitchen and entrance vestibule are lit by a skylight.

The building was constructed under the auspices of the Diözesanbauamt, or diocesan building authorities, in Eichstätt, some 30 kilometres from Thalmässing – a body renowned for its high architectural standards. Meck had already worked with this ecclesiastical client. In 1998 he built the nearby pastoral centre at Lenting. In Thalmässing, the young parish priest Josef Bader not only looks

Architekten Architects meck architekten, München, www.meck-architekten.de; Prof. Andreas Meck; Team: Susanne Frank & Erwin Steiner, Johannes Bäuerlein, Peter Sarger **Bauleitung Construction Management** meck architekten mit with Karlheinz Beer, Weiden **Bauherr Client** Katholische Pfarrgemeinde St. Peter und Paul, Thalmässing; Betreuung under supervision of Diözesanbauamt Eichstätt **Tragwerk Structural** Ingenieurbüro Hans-Ludwig Haushofer, Markt Schwaben **Freianlagen Landscape** meck architekten; Werkplanung mit works planning with Hermann Salm Landschaftsarchitektur, München **Wettbewerb Competition** 2001 **Ausführung Construction** 2002–2004 **Standort Location** Kirchenweg 3, Thalmässing

Pfarrsaal über seine volle Länge zur Kirche. Von hier betritt man auch das dem Saal vorgelagerte Entree. Von innen gesehen verschmelzen durch die Glaswand Saal und Vorplatz zu einem Raum, wird die seitliche Kirchenfassade zur Saalwand. Von außen ist die eingezogene Öffnung alles andere als bescheiden und empfängt den sich nähernden Besucher mit prätentiöser, nahezu barocker Geste. Alle anderen Räume dürfen sich außen nicht zeigen. Zwei Jugendgruppenräume blicken sich über ein klösterliches Höfchen gegenseitig an. Zwei Büros und ein Musikraum im Keller belichtet die verglaste nördliche Kopfseite, Küche und Entree ein Oberlicht.

Den Bau betreute das Diözesanbauamt Eichstätt, knapp 30 Kilometer von Thalmässing entfernt und für baukulturellen Anspruch bekannt. Meck hat bereits Erfahrung mit dem geistlichen Bauherrn: 1998 baute er das nahe gelegene Pfarrheim in Lenting. In Thalmässing betreut der junge Pfarrer Josef Bader neben seiner 800-Seelen-Gemeinde noch ein großes Gebiet als Jugendseelsorger, was letztlich auch den Ausschlag für den Neubau des Jugend- und Pfarrheims gab. Er ist stolz auf sein neues Haus, in dem in Zukunft auch überregionale Begegnungen stattfinden sollen, wie die beliebten Filmtage. Zunächst sei es nicht einfach gewesen, den Leuten das Aussehen des neuen Gebäudes zu vermitteln, so der Schlagzeug spielende Priester. Je mehr das Innere der ›Betonkiste‹ jedoch Gestalt annahm, desto mehr wich der Zweifel der Gemeinde: sorgsam gefertigte Türen und Einbauschränke aus Eichenholz, ein Boden aus grünlich schwarzem, glänzend geschliffenem Gussasphalt, der – scheinbar monolithisch – auch Treppenstufen und die Brüstung des Kellerabgangs überzieht. Das auffälligste Material des Hauses ist jedoch die geflochtene ›Korbwand‹ des Saals. Sie bedeckt, über Foyer und Gang bis hinunter in den Keller, die gesamte Länge der östlichen Innenwand. Zwei Weidenflechter waren sechs Wochen mit ihrem Handwerk beschäftigt. Als dreidimensionale Tapete bleibt das Material zwar in seinen Eigenschaften wie Lichtdurchlässigkeit und Stabilität unausgeschöpft, taucht jedoch den Innenraum in eine warme Stimmung und sorgt für eine gute Akustik.

»Mit dem Weidengeflecht wuchs noch etwas anderes«, meint Pfarrer Bader mit der seinem Berufsstand eigenen Liebe zur Bildhaftigkeit: Die Identifikation der Gemeinde mit ihrem neuen Haus. Die wahre Feuerprobe steht dem Gebäude allerdings noch bevor. Die Frauen der Gemeinde lassen es sich nicht nehmen, das neue Pfarrheim in Form einer Generalreinigung in Besitz zu nehmen und gründlich auf Tauglichkeit zu prüfen. Erste Kritik gab es schon für die schwarz gestrichenen Wände des Kellergangs und die unterirdischen Toilettenräume in einem leuchtenden Rot. Das weckt bei Katholiken doch etwas irritierende Assoziationen.

Axel Simon

after some 800 parishioners, but also provides pastoral care for young people over a wider area. In fact, it was this aspect of his work that led to the idea of building a new youth and pastoral centre. He is proud of the new building, which will also house events of more than just local importance in future, such as the ever popular Filmtage screenings. According to the young parish priest, who is also a keen drummer, it was no easy task at first to persuade people to accept the look of the new building. But their doubts began to fade as the interior of the "concrete box" took shape, with beautifully crafted doors and built-in cupboards of oak, and a greenish-black floor of brilliantly polished cast asphalt throughout, even covering the stairs and parapet of the basement stairway and generating an almost monolithic look. The most striking material in the building is the woven "basket wall" of the hall which covers the entire length of the eastern inner wall, through the foyer and corridor right down into the basement. It took two basket-weavers six weeks to complete. Although some of the properties of this three-dimensional wall covering – such as its stability and the way it filters the light – may not be exploited to the full, it does lend the interior an atmosphere of warmth, as well as ensuring good acoustics.

"The wickerwork brought something else as well," explains Father Bader with that awareness of symbolism so typical of his vocation: it helped the people of the parish to identify with their new building. But the building has yet to go through its real "baptism by fire". The women of the parish have insisted on testing its functionality by taking over the building for a thorough spring cleaning. They have already voiced their criticism of the black walls in the basement corridor and the bright red walls of the basement toilets. That particular colour combination does have some perturbing connotations for Catholics.

Axel Simon

Ansicht von Süden **View from the south**

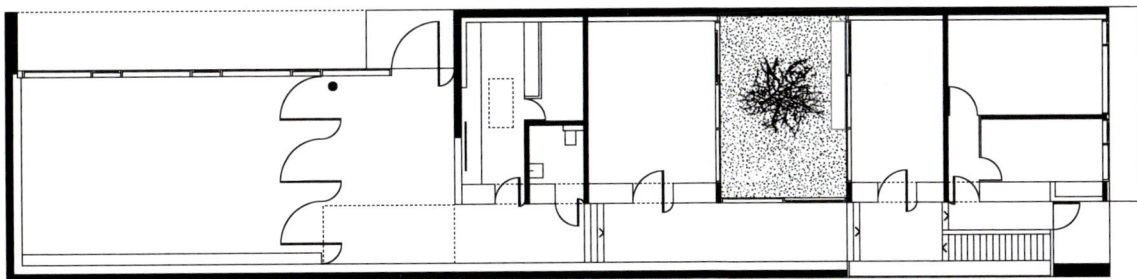

Grundriss Erdgeschoss **Ground-floor plan**

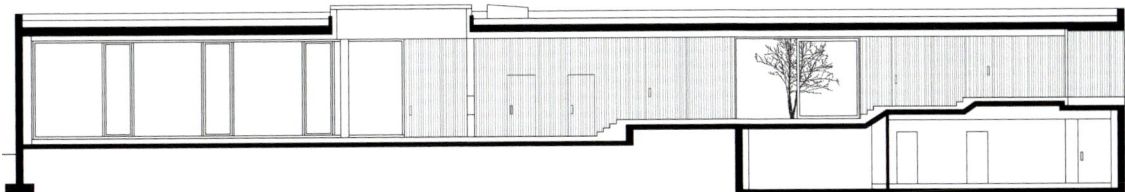

Schnitt **Section**

Ansicht von Nordwesten   **View from the north-west**

Innenhof   **Courtyard**

Pfarrsaal **Parish hall**

Blick vom Gang ins Foyer **View from corridor to foyer**

Niederländische Botschaft, Berlin
Netherlands Embassy, Berlin

OMA – Office for Metropolitan Architecture

■ Vielleicht liegt es an den endlosen Marschwiesen, in denen sich über Kilometer kein Erdhügel erhebt; vielleicht daran, dass die Niederlande die höchste Besiedlungsdichte Europas haben und der Einfamilienhausbrei über die letzten unbebauten Wiesen und Felder schwappt; vielleicht liegt es an der horizontalen Ausrichtung des Wohnens in Holland, dass hier wie nirgendwo in Europa an einer Vertikalisierung der Stadt und des Wohnens gearbeitet wird. Eine der ersten experimentellen ›Vertical Cities‹ war der holländische Pavillon auf der Weltausstellung 2000 in Hannover: Ein futuristisches Sandwich aus gestapelten Landschaften, erbaut von den jungen Architekten des Rotterdamer Büros MVRDV – Schülern des Architekten, der in Berlin das spektakulärste Botschaftsgebäude errichtet hat.

Rem Koolhaas' niederländische Botschaft leuchtet in der stillsten Gegend der alten Mitte metallisch rot, gleißend weiß, golfrasengrün in die Nacht hinein wie ein metallischer Zauberapparat – und steht dort wie ein Experimentallabor eines neuen räumlichen Denkens.

Es ist nicht das erste Mal, dass Koolhaas in Berlin baut – 1989 entstand am Checkpoint Charlie ein dunkler Wohnbau mit kühn schwingendem Betondach, das aussieht, als wolle es den Beton der Grenzbefestigung mit in die Luft reißen. Im folgenden Jahr wurde Koolhaas in die Jury für die Neugestaltung des Potsdamer Platzes berufen und verließ wenig später frustriert die Stadt, nicht ohne sich über das »kleinbürgerliche, altmodische, reaktionäre, banale, provinzielle und vor allem dilettantische Bild« (*Berliner Zeitung*, 02.03.2004) Berlins zu beschweren.

Vielleicht war sein Denken zu wild für eine Stadt, die Ruhe und Orientierung im Vergangenen suchte. Der 1944 geborene Architekt, Theoretiker und Pritzker-Preisträger, der in Schriften wie *S,M,L,XL* immer wieder die moderne Stadt erforschte, arbeitet in Regionen, die zahlreiche Berliner Stadtbauer nicht einmal mit Schutzbrille betrachten würden. Koolhaas analysierte die städtische Selbstorganisation in den anarchisch wuchernden Metropolen Asiens und Afrikas und plante für die zukünftigen Megalopolen mit seinem Office for Metropolitan Architecture spektakuläre Wolkenkratzerstädte. Die Stadt wird dabei aus der Horizontalen in die Vertikale gekippt, Fahrstühle und Rampen übernehmen die Rolle der Straße.

Eine Miniaturausgabe dieser großen vertikalen Stadtvisionen ist die neue Niederländische Botschaft – obwohl sie, wenn man das, was in ihr passiert, noch mit Stockwerken beschreiben könnte, nur etwa zehn Etagen hat.

Tritt man näher an den frei stehenden Zauberwürfel, scheint er sich zu winden und zu pulsieren, als habe jemand versucht, ihn auseinander zu drehen: Verglaste Rampen drücken durch die Metallfassade, so als arbeite in der silbernen Kiste ein Organ, das es auseinander zu sprengen droht.

Die wahre Sensation ist das Innere: ein silbern glänzender, ganz mit Aluminium verkleideter Korridor windet sich, einmal als Treppe, einmal als Rampe, wie ein wild gewordener Wurm durch das Gebäude, öffnet sich zu kleinen Sitzungssälen, drückt aus der Fassade

It may have something to do with the endless floodplains, stretching for miles without the slightest hillock. It may have something to do with the fact that this is Europe's most densely populated country, its huddle of one-family homes sprawled over every available meadow and field. Everything seems geared towards the horizontal in the Netherlands. This may explain why here, more than anywhere else in Europe, they are striving so hard to introduce verticality into home-building and the urban landscape. One of the first experimental Vertical Cities was the Dutch pavilion at the Expo 2000 in Hanover: a futuristic sandwich of layered landscapes built by the young architects of the Rotterdam-based firm MVRDV – students of the architect responsible for giving Berlin its most spectacular foreign embassy.

Rem Koolhaas' Dutch Embassy shines out in the quietest area of Berlin-Mitte: a metallic red, searing white, golf-course green, magical entity shining in the night. It looks for all the world like some experimental laboratory of a new spatial awareness.

This is not the first time that Koolhaas has built in Berlin. In 1989 he created a dark apartment building with a sweeping concrete roof near Checkpoint Charlie, as though seeking to draw the very concrete of the border defences in its wake. The following year, Koolhaas was appointed to the jury in charge of redeveloping Potsdamer Platz. He left the city shortly afterwards, complaining of Berlin's "petty-bourgeois, old-fashioned, reactionary, banal, provincial and above all dilettante notion" (*Berliner Zeitung*, 2 March 2004).

Perhaps his ideas were too maverick for a city that seeks a sense of calm and direction by looking to the past. Born in 1944, Koolhaas is an architect, theoretician and Pritzker laureate who has repeatedly analysed the modern city in writings such as *S,M,L,XL* and who has worked in regions that many a Berlin urban planner would not so much as cast a glance at without donning protective goggles. Koolhaas has analysed autonomous urban organisation in the anarchic metropolitan sprawls of Asia and Africa and, with his Office for Metropolitan Architecture, has planned spectacular high-rise cities for the megalopolises of the future. He does so by tilting the city from the horizontal into the vertical, letting elevators and ramps take on the role of the street.

The Dutch Embassy is a miniature version of these vast, vertical, urban visions – even though (if we could still describe what happens on the inside in terms of storeys) the building has only ten or so floors.

As we approach the freestanding magic cube, it seems to twist and pulsate, as though someone had tried to unscrew it: glazed ramps press through the metal facade as though there were some organ at work within the silver box, threatening to explode it.

The real sensation, however, is the interior: a shining silver corridor clad entirely in aluminium meanders through the building – sometimes in the form of stairs, at other times in the form of a ramp

Architekten Architects Office for Metropolitan Architecture, Rotterdam, Niederlande Netherlands, www.oma.nl; Rem Koolhaas; Team: Ellen van Loon, Erik Schotte & Michelle Howard, Gro Bonesmo & Beth Margulis, Anu Leinonen, Daan Oievaar, Robert Choeff, Christian Muller, Adrianne Fisher, Oliver Schütte, Fernando Romero Havaux, Matthias Hollwich, Katrin Thornhauer, Barbara Wolff, Bruce Fisher, Anne Filson, Udo Garritzman, Jenny Jones, Mette Bos, Adam Kuhrdahl, Stan Aarts, Julien Desmedt, Annick Hess, Rombout Loman, Antti Lassila, Thomas Kolbasenko, Moritz von Voss, Paolo Costa, Carolus Traenkner, Susanne Manthey, Christiane Sauer, Tammo Prinz, Nils Lindhorst, Felix Thoma, Shadi Rahbaran; Recherchen Research Bill Price, Marc Guinand **Bauherr** Client Niederländisches Außenministerium Netherlands Ministry of Foreign Affairs – Dienst Gebouwen Buitenland, Den Haag The Hague, Niederlande Netherlands **Tragwerk** Structural Royal Haskoning, Rotterdam, Niederlande Netherlands; Arup GmbH, Berlin **HL-Technik** Technical Huygen Elwako Raadgevende Ingenieurs bv, Rotterdam, Niederlande Netherlands; Arup GmbH, Berlin **Projektsteuerung** Project Management Royal Haskoning, Rotterdam, Niederlande Netherlands **Ausführung** Construction 2000–2003 **Standort** Location Klosterstraße 50, Berlin

heraus und bohrt sich schräg durch das Gebäude bis auf das Dach empor. Sitzungssäle und Büros zweigen von diesem wilden Mäander ab. Das öffentliche Leben der Miniaturstadt findet im Dachgeschoss statt, wo sich unter anderem die Kantine für die Mitarbeiter befindet. Im Sommer fährt das Dach auf, man isst unter freiem Himmel. Im kleinen Maßstab werden hier die »culture of congestion« und die Utopie der vertikalen Stadt ausprobiert, die seit *Delirious New York* – der surrealistisch wilden Architektursoziologie, die Koolhaas 1978 als Stadtpoeten und Theoretiker berühmt machte – ein zentraler Aspekt seiner Arbeit ist.

Koolhaas' Botschaft ist ein Denkgebäude für eine andere Architektur. Der binäre Code des Etagenbaus, der vom Fahrstuhl geprägt wurde, wird geknackt, der Bau folgt einem weicheren, wuchernden Rhythmus ineinander verschachtelter Ebenen. Es sind vielleicht nicht tausend Plateaus, die Koolhaas hier als Alternative zum Geschossbau anbietet – dennoch ist dieses Gebäude nicht weniger als die Ablösung des klassischen Bürohauses durch eine gebaute Arbeitslandschaft; was man hier auf mehr als zweihundert Metern durchwandert, ist eher ein abstrahiertes Bergdorf als ein normales Büro.

Koolhaas hat das Motiv der Rampe, des Gleitens durch die Ebenen, schon in früheren Projekten thematisiert, und stets war nicht Mies van der Rohe, auf den sich Koolhaas offen bezieht, sondern Le Corbusier derjenige, dessen Theorie weitergedacht wurde. Es war Le Corbusier, der Etagen mit Rampen verband, der ein Museum der Weltwahrheiten, das Mundaneum, entwarf, an dessen Außenfassade man auf einer Rampe emporstieg und während dieser ›Promenade Architecturale‹ See und Berge, die Naturgesetze von Erosion, Sturm und Witterung entdecken sollte. In Berlin hebt der Trajekt die Stadt auf eine andere Ebene und lässt den Besucher das Zentrum mit all seinen historischen Brüchen entdecken. Wie auf einem historisch-ästhetischen Lehrpfad werden Berlins schwierige Schönheit und Geschichte bewusst gemacht: Man steigt auf der geteerten Rampe zur Stadtloggia auf, deren glitzernder Metallmantel hart und technisch ist und einen wunderbaren Blick auf die Spreeinsel ermöglicht; dann, während man auf grünem Glas emporwandert, blickt man auf den staubigen Neoklassizismus des Verwaltungsbaus aus den dreißiger Jahren. Nach einer Wendung in dem polierten Metallschlauch öffnet sich plötzlich eine monumentale Sichtachse auf die Kugel des Fernsehturms – so, als bohre sein Licht einen Laserstrahl durch die stählerne Architektur des Hauses. Oben schließlich, aus der Skylobby, blickt man auf die wirre, straßenköterhafte Mischung von historischer Architektur und modernen Hochhäusern – und in dieser Mischung der Stile und der Epochen, in dieser stillen bis unwirtlichen Gegend der Stadt offenbart sich jener selbstbewusst großstädtische Charakter, der anderswo in Berlin verzweifelt inszeniert und doch nicht gefunden wird.

Niklas Maak

– like a worm gone wild, opening up to reveal little meeting rooms, pushing out of the facade and boring at an angle through the building right up to the roof. Meeting rooms and offices branch off from this unruly meandering. The public life of this miniature city happens at rooftop level, where the staff canteen is located. In summer, the roof is opened up for al fresco dining. It is a small-scale experiment in the "culture of congestion" and the utopia of the vertical city that has been a key aspect of Koolhaas' work ever since his 1978 *Delirious New York*, the surrealistically wild sociology of architecture that made him famous as an urban poet and theoretician.

Koolhaas' Embassy is a thought construct for a different kind of architecture. He has broken the binary code of floor-by-floor building determined by the elevator: the building follows a softer, more sprawling rhythm of interlinked levels. While Koolhaas may not exactly be offering a thousand plateaus as an alternative to layered storeys, this building marks nothing less than the turning point from the classic office block to built working landscape. The landscape we walk through for more than two hundred metres here is more abstract mountain village than conventional office.

Koolhaas has already adopted the motif of the ramp, of floating through different levels, in previous projects – and invariably, it was not Mies van der Rohe, to whom Koolhaas openly refers, but Le Corbusier, whose theories have been taken one step further here. It was Le Corbusier who used ramps to link floors, and it was Le Corbusier who designed a Museum of World Truths, the Mundaneum, featuring an external ramp on which the sea and the mountains, the natural laws of erosion, storm and weather, could be discovered in the course of a "promenade architecturale". In Berlin, the trajectory lifts the city to another level, allowing visitors to discover the centre with all its historic breaks. Berlin's problematic beauty and history become evident, as though on a historic-aesthetic tour. We step onto the tarred ramp leading up to the urban loggia, whose glittering metal cladding is hard and technoid, and affords a magnificent view of the Spreeinsel; then, as we wander upwards on green glass, we look upon the dusty neo-classicism of the 1930s administration building. A turn in the polished metal tube suddenly opens out onto a monumental view of the television tower's sphere – as though its light bored through the steel architecture of the building like a laser beam. Finally, at the top, from the Skylobby, we look out over the mad, motley mix of historic architecture and modern high-rises – and in this hotchpotch of styles and eras, in this quiet, almost uninhabitable district of the city, we perceive that confident big-city quality that other parts of Berlin so desperately seek, in vain, to achieve.

Niklas Maak

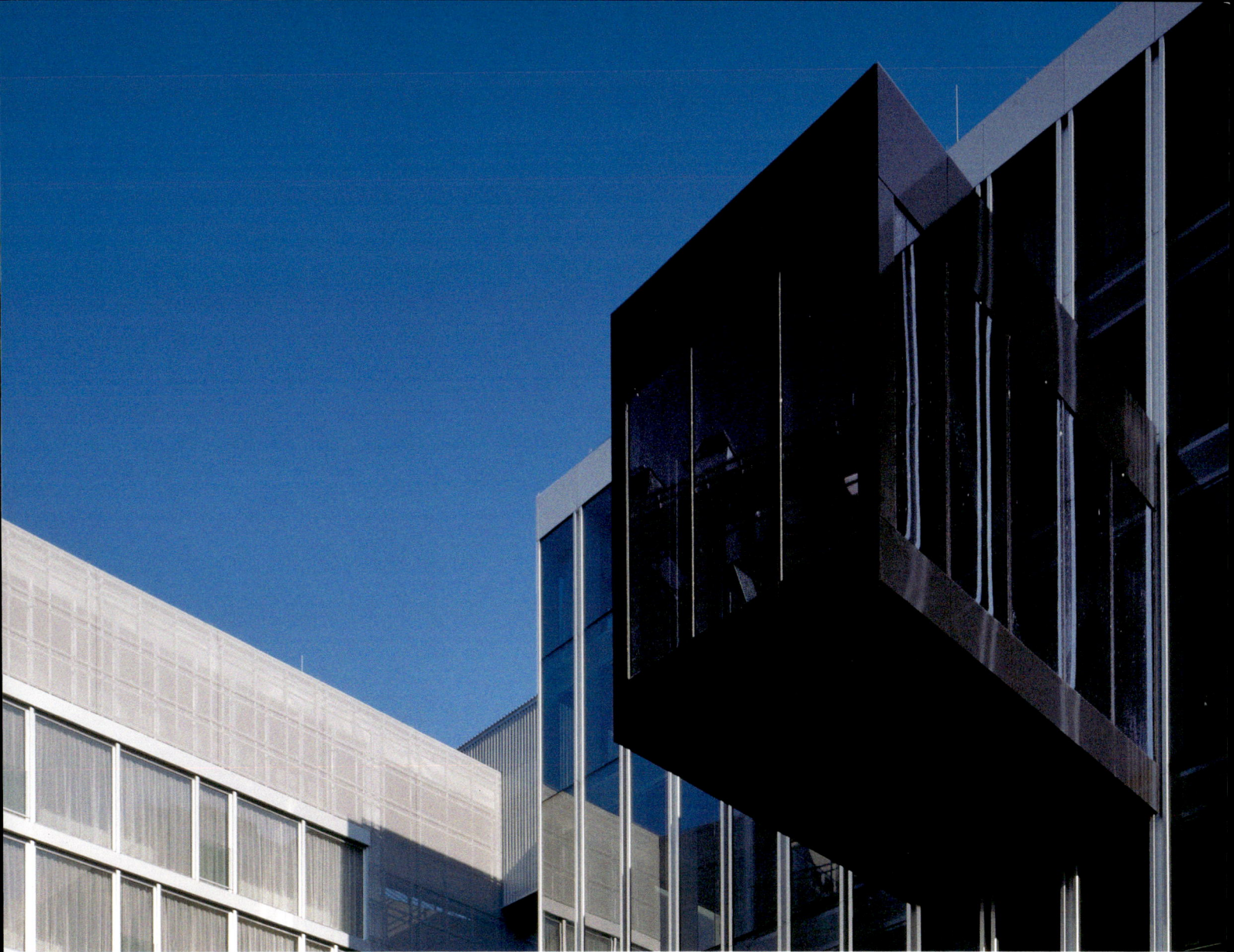

Skybox **Skybox**

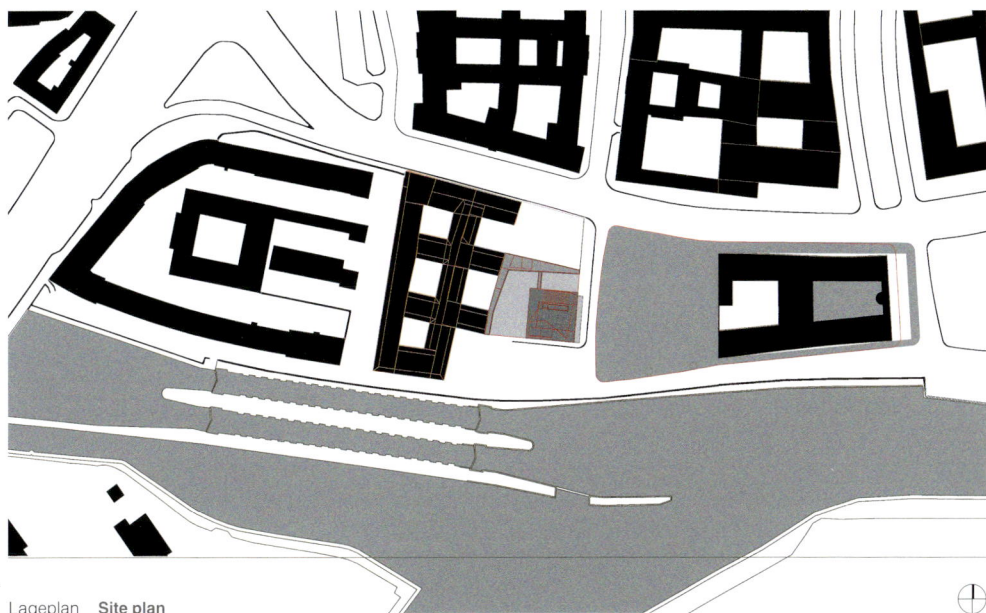

Lageplan **Site plan**

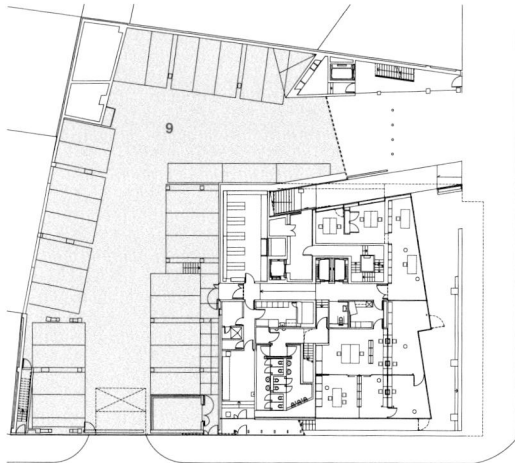

Grundriss Konsularabteilung
Floorplan of consular department

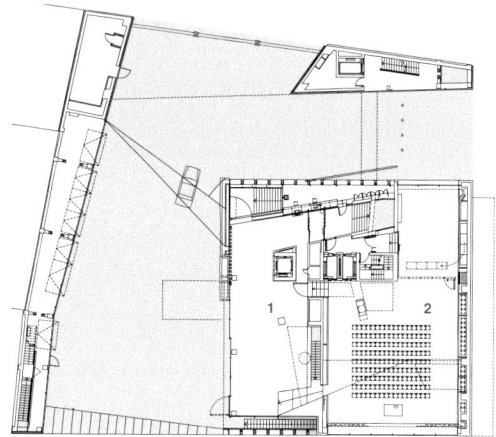

Grundriss Eingangsebene
Floorplan of entrance level

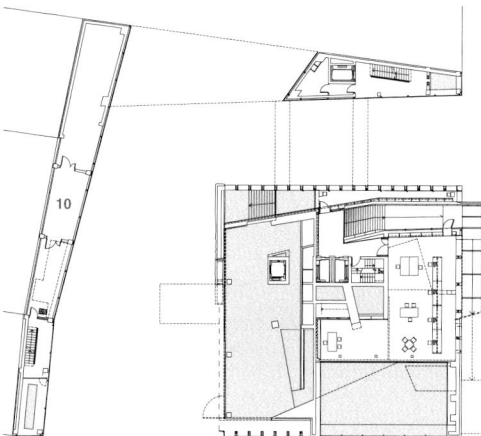

Grundriss Kulturabteilung
Floorplan of cultural department

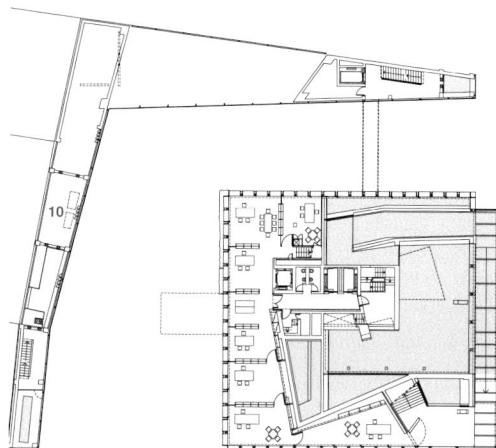

Grundriss Militärabteilung, Presseabteilung
Floorplan of military department, press office

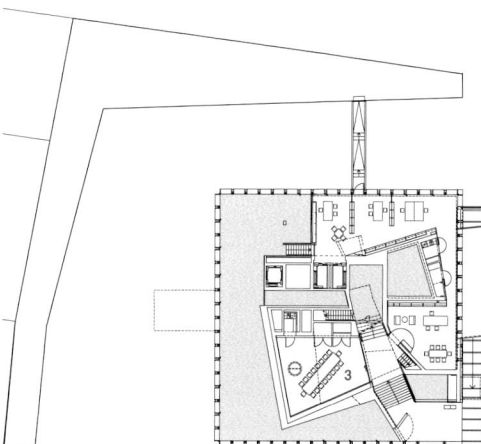

Grundriss Verkehrsabteilung
Floorplan of traffic department

1 Foyer **Foyer**
2 Multifunktionssaal
  Multi-functional room
3 Besprechungsraum
  Meeting room
4 Fitnessbereich
  Fitness area
5 Kantine
  Canteen
6 Wohnung 1
  Apartment 1
7 Wohnung 2
  Apartment 2
8 Wohnung 3
  Apartment 3
9 Parkgarage
  Car park
10 Technik
  Technical services

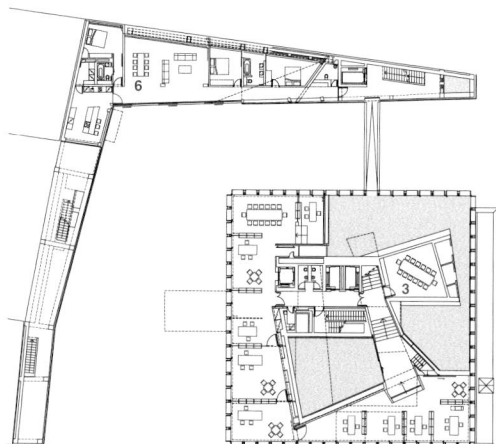

Grundriss Landwirtschaftsabteilung
Floorplan of agricultural department

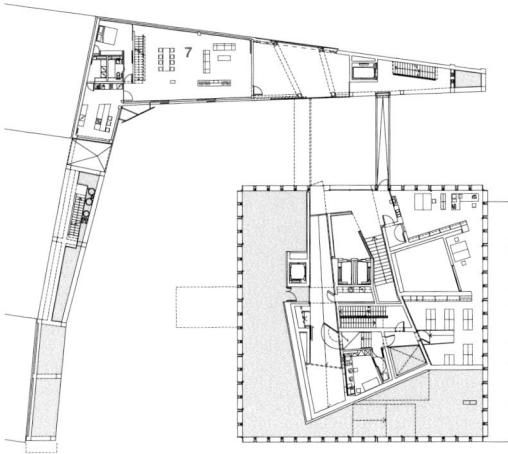

Grundriss Poststelle
Floorplan of postal department

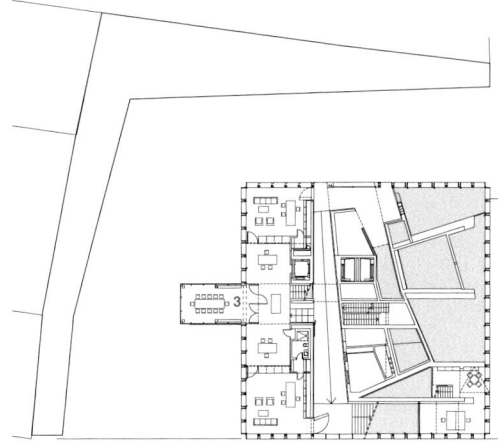

Grundriss Büro des Botschafters
Floorplan of ambassador's office

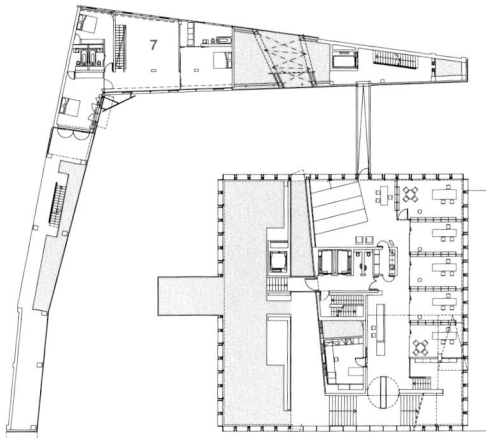

Grundriss Politische Abteilung
Floorplan of political department

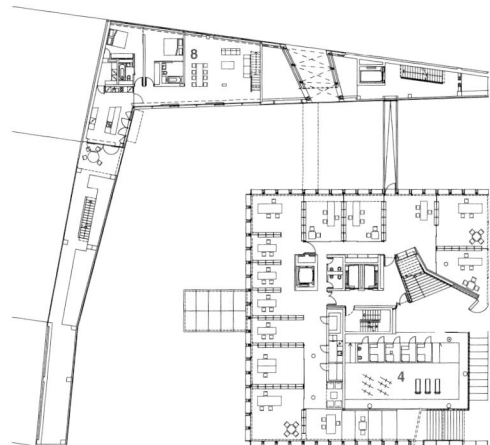

Grundriss Technische Abteilung, Wirtschaftsabteilung
Floorplan of technical department, trade and economics department

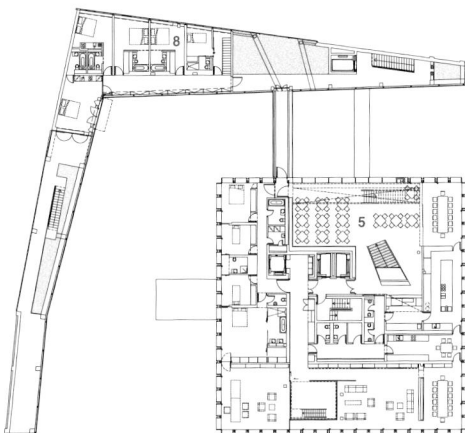

Grundriss Wohnung des stellvertretenden Botschafters
Floorplan of deputy ambassador's accommodation

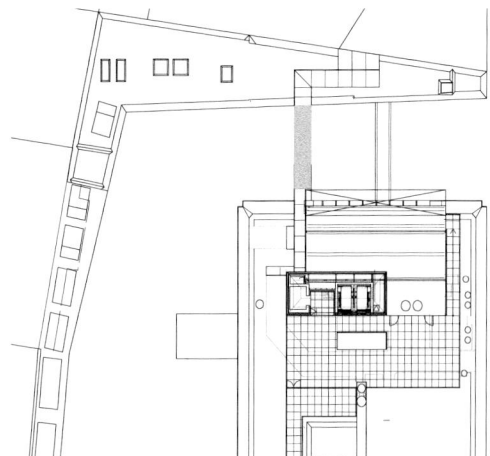

Grundriss Dachterrasse
Floorplan of rooftop patio

Auffahrt zum Haupteingang
Approach to main entrance

Blick durch die bewohnbare Wand auf den Fernsehturm
View through residential wall towards television tower

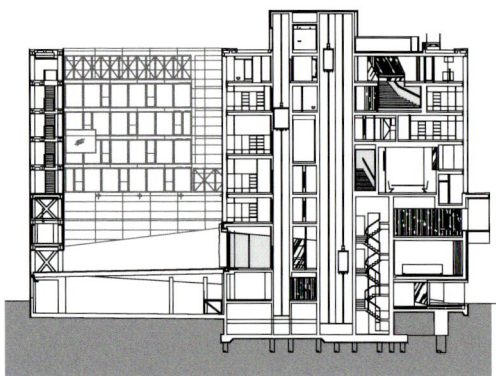

West-Ost-Schnitt   **West-East section**

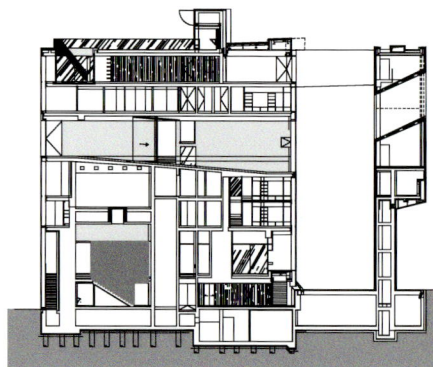

Nord-Süd-Schnitt   **North-South section**

Gläsernes Trajekt an der Ostfassade
Glass trajectory on east facade

Seiten 148/149   **Pages 148/149**
Trajekt   **Trajectory**

Skybox   **Skybox**

Besprechungsraum   **Meeting room**

Wohnung des stellvertretenden Botschafters
Deputy ambassador's apartment

Multifunktionssaal   **Multi-functional room**

Umbau und Aufstockung Waterloohain 9, Hamburg
Conversion and extension, Waterloohain 9, Hamburg

Carsten Roth

■ 1976 zerschoss der Architekt und Künstler Gordon Matta-Clark, um seiner Abneigung gegen geschlossene Raumcontainer Ausdruck zu verleihen und um für ›frische Luft‹ zu sorgen, alle Fenster des New Yorker Institute of Architecture and Urban Studies mit seinem Gewehr. Seine damaligen Kollegen schlossen ihn daraufhin aus der Architektenzunft aus. Peter Eisenman zeigte Matta-Clark sogar an.[1]

Zu derart provozierenden Aktionen neigt Carsten Roth nicht, aber rigoros ist sein Vorgehen dennoch. Aus dem Gebäude am Waterloohain 9 brach er fast alle Außenwände heraus und schnitt es durch, um es besser erschließen und mit mehr Licht versorgen zu können.

Dem Ansinnen seines Bauherrn, der PR-Agentur fischerAppelt, in diesem etwas heruntergekommenen Viertel in Hamburg-Eimsbüttel Zeichen des Wandels zu setzen, kam dieses Vorgehen, vor allem aber die Architektur, die Roth für die zwei vorgesehenen Umbauten fand, gelegen. Das Gebäude am Waterloohain 5, bereits 2001 fertig gestellt, nutzt die Agentur weitgehend selbst, das zweite, jüngere am Waterloohain 9, vermietet sie und das an kreative und umsatzstarke Betriebe wie Werbeagenturen. Ihre Dachgeschosse, beide mit bordeauxrot bis golden changierendem Metall verkleidet, weisen die Bauten als Mitglieder derselben Produktfamilie aus, dennoch sind sie, wie bei Geschwistern nicht unüblich, gut zu unterscheiden.

Am Waterloohain 9 hat sich im Vergleich zum Gegenüber viel verändert, es erinnert nur eine Außenwand und die Kubatur an die Kegelbahnen, für die dieses Bauwerk einmal errichtet wurde. Daher rührt auch noch die Geschossteilung: im nordwestlichen Teil waren drei und im südöstlichen bei gleicher Gebäudehöhe vier Ebenen untergebracht. Hier waren die Clubräume. An dieser Teilung hielt Roth fest, um differenzierbare Büroflächen anbieten zu können. Dank der Aufbrüche, Einschnitte und seiner neuen, farbenfrohen Aufstockung sind die Gedanken an die spröde Vergnügungsstätte der sechziger Jahre schnell vergessen. Dazu trägt vor allem die vollflächige Industrieverglasung der Fassade bei. Sie verdeckt die unterschiedlichen Geschosshöhen und lässt von außen nur erahnen, wo sich noch massive Wandteile befinden und wo natürliches Licht die ganze Tiefe der Geschosse erreicht. Im Dachgeschoss und in der darunter liegenden Etage helfen dabei zwei über beide Ebenen angelegte Innenhöfe. Sie spenden nicht nur Licht, sie strukturieren auch den Raum auf den Etagen.

In einigen Fällen konnte Roth auch die Gestaltung der Büros übernehmen und die Fäden seiner Architektur innen sichtbar weiter spinnen. Im Dachgeschoss betrifft das vor allem die Farbgestaltung. Im Stockwerk darunter schaffen Stein, Holz, Erdfarben und Grau als bestimmender Unterton eine Atmosphäre, die eng auf das Leitthema der Werbeagentur abgestimmt ist: Wald und Wolf. Glas, nackter Beton und immer wieder das überraschend einfallende Licht geben aber auch dieser Büroeinheit eine wohltemperierte Helligkeit und eine gut dosierte Transparenz. Ein Tonstudio am nordwestlichen Kopf des Baus profitiert besonders von der kompletten Verglasung der Fassade. Die hier nicht sehr tiefen Verwaltungsräume sind mit dem

In 1976, architect and artist Gordon Matta-Clark shot out the windows of the New York Institute of Architecture and Urban Studies with an air rifle to express his dislike of closed spaces and to let in a little "fresh air". His colleagues expelled him from their ranks. Peter Eisenman even filed a lawsuit against him.[1]

Carsten Roth may not tend towards quite such provocative acts, but his approach is no less rigorous. Breaking almost all the outer walls out of the building at Waterloohain 9, he cut through it to develop it more fully and bring in more light.

It was a move entirely in the spirit of his client, PR agency fischerAppelt. They wanted to create a sign of change in this slightly seedy district of Hamburg-Eimsbüttel, and Roth's architectural design for the two buildings that were to be converted did exactly that. The building at Waterloohain 5, completed in 2001, is used mainly by the agency. The second, more recent, building at Waterloohain 9 is rented out to creative, high-turnover clients such as advertising agencies. The attic floors, both clad in metal alternating in colour between bordeaux red and gold, marks the buildings as members of the same product family. And yet, like many siblings, it is easy to tell them apart.

At Waterloohain 9 a lot has happened in comparison to its opposite number; all that recalls the bowling alleys it once housed is a single external wall and the cuboid shape. This also dictates the division of floors: in the north-west tract, there were three levels and

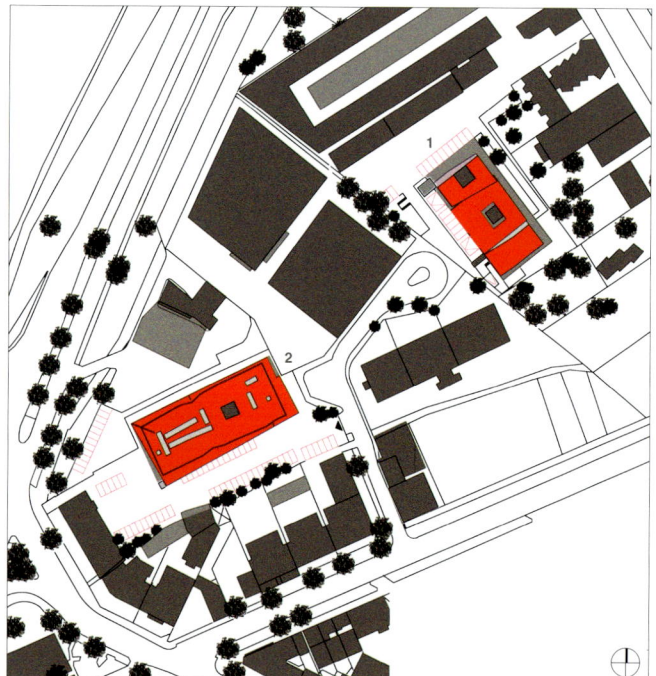

Lageplan **Site plan**

1 Waterloohain 9   **Waterloohain 9**
2 Waterloohain 5   **Waterloohain 5**

Architekten Architects Carsten Roth Architekt, Hamburg, www.carstenroth.com; Team: Christine Andreac, Peter Karl Becher, Julian Hillenkamp, Inga Krauschner, David Lagemann, Roland Thümler, Jochen Ziegler **Bauherr Client** Bernhard Fischer-Appelt c/o fischerAppelt Kommunikation GmbH, Hamburg **Tragwerk Structural** Windels Timm Morgen Partnerschaft, Hamburg **HL-Technik Technical** Klett-Ingenieur-GmbH, Fellbach **Licht Lighting** Lichtkontor, Hamburg **Ausführung Construction** 2000–2003 **Standort Location** Waterloohain 9, Hamburg

diffusen Licht, das durch die isolierten Glasprofile dringt, geradezu durchflutet. Auch die inneren Trennwände spielen mit Transparenz, geben hier und da strategische Ein- oder Ausblicke, lassen in jedem Fall aber das Licht dorthin gleiten, wo es gebraucht wird. In den Studios herrschen dunkle Holztöne vor, die in den hellen Büroräumen lediglich Akzente setzen.

Einen gravierenden Einschnitt bildet das Treppenhaus, das Roth genau am Wechsel der drei- zur viergeschossigen Gliederung angebracht hat. Der Raum musste dafür schmal gehalten werden, und so verläuft die Treppe in einem Lauf durch die ganze Tiefe des Hauses. Der gläserne Fahrstuhl schließt diesen Spalt ab, den Roth bis in das Dachgeschoss gezogen hat und dort auch in der Außenfassade sichtbar werden lässt. Durch das Dach und durch den Fahrstuhlschacht fällt also Licht in diesen Hausspalt, das die sehr sparsam profilierten Stahlstufen mit rhythmischen Schattenwürfen und Reflexionen umspielt. Exakt kalkulierte Farbverläufe von Gelb bis Grün vollenden die Harmonie dieses Treppenraums. Der Einschnitt hat sich gelohnt.

Gordon Matta-Clark setzte bei seinen Interventionen die Unbrauchbarkeit der Häuser, die er bearbeiten wollte oder bearbeitet hat, voraus. Carsten Roths Eingriffe bewirken das Gegenteil. Das Mehr an Licht und gezielten Durchblicken ist hier nicht allein künstlerische Proklamation, sondern ein Mehrwert der Nutzbarkeit. Schade, dass sich die beiden Herren nicht kennen gelernt haben.

Olaf Bartels

1 Vgl. Ludwig Seyfarth, *Abweichungen vom Standard inbegriffen. Über Häuser in der Kunst von den sechziger Jahren bis heute*, in: Felix Zdenek (Hrsg.), *HausSchau. Das Haus in der Kunst*, Ausst. Kat. Deichtorhallen Hamburg, Ostfildern-Ruit 2000, S. 19.

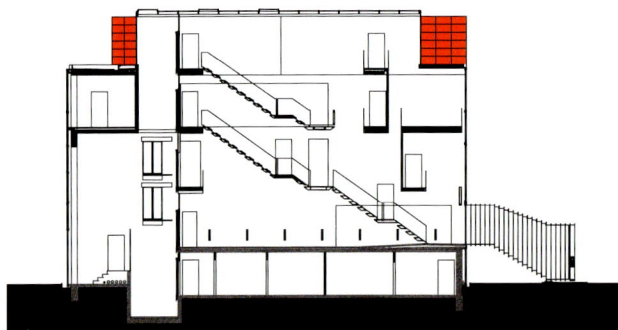

Schnitt **Section**

in the south-east tract, which is the same height, there were four. This was where the club rooms were situated. Roth kept this layout in order to provide discrete office areas. The openings, incisions and brightly coloured added levels banish all thoughts of the spartan leisure centre of the 1960s. The industrial glazing of the entire facade does the rest. It conceals the different floor heights so that from the outside one can only surmise where there are still solid walls and where natural light might be pouring in to the furthest depths of the interior. On the top floor and on the floor below it, two atrium courtyards over two storeys add to the effect. They not only provide light, but also structure the space on these floors.

In some cases, Roth has also been able to take charge of the interior design of the offices so that the threads of his architecture are spun visibly into the overall tapestry of the building. On the top floor, this applies in particular to the handling of colour. On the level below it, stone, wood, earthy colours and grey create an atmosphere closely tailored to the advertising agency's predominant theme of "wood and wolf". Glass, unfaced concrete and, time and again, unexpected sources of natural light also lend this office unit a pleasing brightness and a generous portion of transparency. A sound studio at the north-west end of the building profits particularly from the fully glazed facade. The administration offices here are not very deep, and so they are positively flooded by the diffuse light that pours in through the isolated glass profiles. The interior partition walls, too, play on the idea of transparency, with occasional strategically placed inward or outward views, allowing any amount of light to enter where it is needed. In the studios themselves, dark wood predominates, though this is used only as an accent in the bright office spaces.

The stairwell, which Carsten Roth has installed precisely at the point of transition from the three-storey to the four-storey section, is a radical incision. The space for this had to be kept narrow, and so the stair runs through the entire depth of the building. The glass lift closes off the gap that Roth has cut right up to the top floor, where it can also be seen in the exterior facade. Light falls into this gap through the roof and the lift shaft, dappling the subtly profiled steel steps with rhythmic shadows and reflections. Colouring carefully orchestrated from yellow to green completes the harmonious look of this stairway space. It was a cut worth making.

Gordon Matta-Clark's interventions were based on the notion that the buildings he wanted to change or did change were unusable. Carsten Roth's approach does the opposite. By increasing light and creating views through the building, he is not just making an artistic proclamation, but adding significantly to the user value. What a pity these two men have never met.

Olaf Bartels

1 See Ludwig Seyfarth, "Abweichungen vom Standard inbegriffen. Über Häuser in der Kunst von den sechziger Jahren bis heute", in Felix Zdenek (ed.), *HausSchau. Das Haus in der Kunst,* exhib. cat. Deichtorhallen Hamburg, Ostfildern-Ruit 2000, p. 19.

Ansicht von Südwesten **View from the south-west**

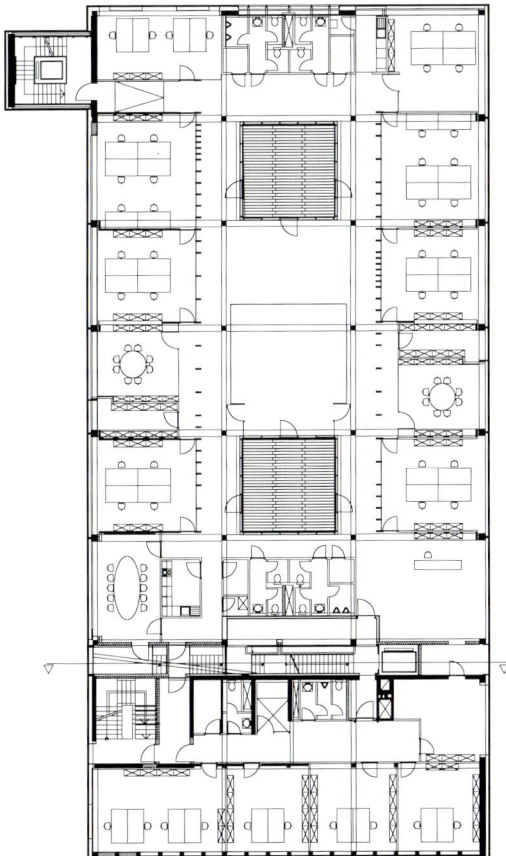

Grundriss 2. Obergeschoss **Second-floor plan**

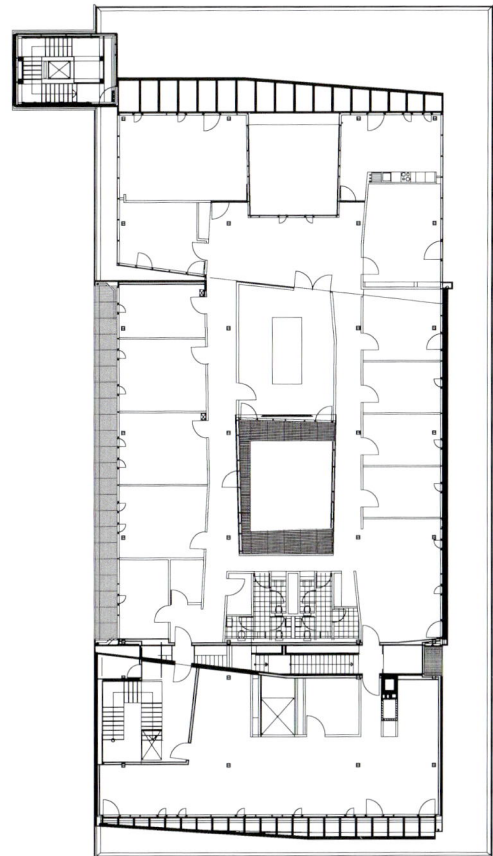

Grundriss Dachgeschoss **Top-floor plan**

Aufstockung, Südwestfassade
Extension, south-west facade

Ansicht von Nordwesten
View from the north-west

Eingangsbereich 1. Obergeschoss
Entrance area, first floor

Blick aus der Nordwestfassade 1. Obergeschoss
View from north-west facade, first floor

Innenraum 2. Obergeschoss
Interior, second floor

Treppe   **Staircase**

Rathaus, Hennigsdorf
Town hall, Hennigsdorf

sauerbruch hutton

■ Wer hier nur etwas einreichen oder abholen will und beim Warten nur das Warten fühlt, wird außer einer Schalterhalle nichts finden. Wer aber wacher Sinne ist, wer seinem Auge die Freiheit lässt, in den fünf Sitzbänken mit ihren Holzleisten auch fünf Boote, in den acht Schreibtischen mit ihren Sichtblenden auch acht Lauben und in der Zwischenfläche mit Parkett und Teppich auch ein stehendes Gewässer zu entdecken, der hat diese Architektur vielleicht besser verstanden als der versierte Kritiker mit seinen Worten vom organischen, zugleich passageren und transparenten Bürgerforum.

Jedenfalls hat sich der träumerisch Wartende die Möglichkeit geschaffen, noch diese oder jene andere Einzelheit in sein Bild zu fügen: die breite weiße Rampe und Treppe hinter ihm als Stufung und Wegung eines sandigen Abhangs; die Wände, farblich von Hellgelb nach Hellgrün schwankend, als Wälder und Wiesen in weiter Ferne; die sechs Ellipsen für das Oberlicht als Wolken; das Hellblau der Decke als Himmel; die kleinen Strahler als Sterne. Im Hintergrund erscheint sichtbar durch die gespannten Glasscheiben das beinah idyllische Panorama der alten neoromanischen Martin-Luther-Kirche, des alten neogotischen Rathauses und der alten Hauptstraße des wirklichen Hennigsdorf.

In das neue Rathaus zu gehen und es wie eine Landschaft zu sehen, bedarf einer reflektierten Naivität, die freilich durch die Architekten genährt wird. Denn Matthias Sauerbruch und Louisa Hutton haben den szenischen Charakter des Landschaftsgartens, dieses exquisiten Konglomerats von Natur und Kultur aus dem England des 18. Jahrhunderts, gern als ihr Vorbild beim Umgang mit einem Stadtraum benannt, der durch die Schnitte und Brüche der Moderne um seine Balance gebracht wurde.

Auch das Rathaus von Hennigsdorf, einer Kommune mit kaum 27 000 Einwohnern, steht an so einem Ort. Den Bahngleisen im Westen, der Hauptstraße im Osten und den Wohnzeilen im Norden fehlt die Kraft, das plane Terrain zu fassen. In dieser losen Lage wäre es jedem Neubau ein Leichtes, mit Turm, Tor oder sonstigen Signalen von Bürgerstolz sich selber wichtig und dem Postplatz – ein Quadrat mit Kaufhaus und Denkmal auf der andern Seite des Bahnhofs und Bahndamms – die Rolle streitig zu machen. Doch das Rathaus hat keine Lust, mit Funktion und Fiktion zu spielen. Was steht, liegt flach: Die Architektur ist horizontal, nicht einmal so hoch wie die noch in den Tagen der DDR gebauten Wohnhäuser der Nachbarschaft. Präsenz erreicht der Körper durch die fließende Gestaltung des Umfelds, durch die weichen Formen mit den konvexen – nein: bauschenden – Fassaden, durch die Gliederung in ein steinernes Erdgeschoss und zwei gläserne Obergeschosse. Eines auf dem andern lagernd, gleichen sie Scheiben, die untere fast so dick wie die oberen zusammen.

Hinter dem breiten Windfang mit rauschender Schiebetür zieht es Augen und Füße nach links. Die Halle des Bürgerforums ist weit und licht; sie kommt ohne Stützen aus. Rechter Hand steigen die geschweiften weißen Wangen von Rampe und Treppe empor. Oben

If you just want to deliver something or pick something up, and if all you feel when you are waiting is, well, a feeling of waiting – then you will find nothing here but a main hall. Those with a keener eye and a more fertile imagination, however, will see in the five benches with their wooden staves five boats, in the eight desks with their screens eight bowers and in the transitional area with its parquet and carpet a stretch of calm water. These are the people who may well have grasped this architecture more fully than the seasoned critic with all his talk of an organic, transitional and transparent public forum.

Those who wait and let their thoughts run free at least have the possibility of integrating the occasional additional detail into their view of things: the broad white ramp and stairway as a pathway leading down to a sandy slope; the walls, in pale yellow to pale green, as faraway woods and meadows; the six elliptical skylights as clouds, the pale blue of the ceiling as sky; the little downlighters as stars. In the background, visible through the spanned panes of glass, is the almost idyllic panorama of the neo-Romanesque Martin Luther Church, the old neo-Gothic city hall and the old main street of the real Hennigsdorf.

It takes a conscious naivety to enter the new city hall and see it in terms of a landscape, though admittedly it is a view that the architecture itself encourages. For Matthias Sauerbruch and Louisa Hutton have expressly mentioned the scenic character of the landscaped garden, that exquisite blend of nature and culture that was developed in eighteenth-century England, as something they had in mind when tackling an urban space whose balance had been undermined by the interventions and breaks of modernism.

The city hall of Hennigsdorf, a community of just 27,000, stands in just such a location. The railway tracks to the west, the main street to the east and the rows of housing to the north do not have the necessary force to bracket this flat terrain. In such a vaguely defined location, the easy solution would have been to create a new building with a tower, a gateway or some other signal of civic pride that would lend it an air of importance and draw attention away from the Postplatz – the square on the other side of the railway station and railway cutting, with its department store and memorial. But the city hall makes no attempt to play with function and fiction. It does not so much stand out as stand firm: the architecture is horizontal, and is not even as high as the neighbouring apartment buildings of the GDR era. Instead, the city hall gains its presence through the fluidity with which its surroundings are designed, through the soft forms with the convex – even billowing – facades, through the division into a stone ground floor and two glass upper floors. They are layered one on top of another like slices, the lower one almost as thick as the upper two together.

Passing through the broad windbreaker to the whish of the sliding door, we are immediately drawn towards the left. The main hall is broad and bright, and has no pillars. On the right, the sweeping

Architekten Architects sauerbruch hutton architekten, Berlin, www.sauerbruchhutton.de; Matthias Sauerbruch, Louisa Hutton, Jens Ludloff; Team: Gunnar Tausch, Wolfgang Thiessen & Wilhelm Jouaux & Julia Neubauer, Florian Völker, Jürgen Bartenschlag, Andreas Weber, David Wegener **Bauherr Client** Stadt Hennigsdorf vertreten durch die represented by Hennigsdorfer Gesellschaft für Stadtentwicklung mbH **HL-Technik Technical** Zibell Willner & Partner Ingenieurgesellschaft für Technische Gebäudeausrüstung mbH, Berlin **Tragwerk Structural** Ingenieurbüro für Bauwesen Dipl.-Ing. Herbert Fink GmbH, Berlin **Freianlagen Landscape** ST raum a. Landschaftsarchitektur, Berlin **Ausführung Construction** 2002/03 **Standort Location** Rathausplatz 1, Hennigsdorf

reiht sich Büro an Büro. Linker Hand ballen sich drei rundliche räumliche Gebilde, die kleineren zur Versorgung des Gebäudes, das größere mit dem Ratssaal. Heftig stülpt sich dieses Oval nach draußen; fünf schmale Türen öffnen sich zu einem kleinen Park. Dank der roten Wände und der blauen Decke, die auf der Hälfte des Raums einen kühnen Aufschwung wagt, spürt man die Ambition des Interieurs. Lieber als den kommunalen Politikern zu dienen, möchte der Raum ein intimes Theater oder ein Ort klassischer Konzerte sein.

Zur weiteren Bewegung trägt im gesamten Erdgeschoss das Deckenbild des Künstlers Folke Hanfeld bei. Mattweiß auf Mattblau zeigt sich eine Struktur, wie wenn zwei Steine in ein stilles Wasser plumpsen und Wellen werfen. Die Ringe wachsen und wachsen, oft nehmen die Kreise die Krümmung der Wände auf, um sie auf langen Bahnen weiterzuführen. Nicht allein im Erdgeschoss, sondern auch in den oberen Etagen knüpfen sich Netze mit Rauten, die durch Stauchung und Dehnung den Raum so prägen wie das barocke Gemälde die Kuppel der Kirche. Doch halt. In Wahrheit wirken das erste und zweite Obergeschoss eher nüchtern. Links und rechts eines Ringflurs folgt Büro an Büro. Komfort bieten diese gleichwohl. Es gibt eine rundum doppelte Fassade. Mit Blenden und Klappen und Schiebefenstern lässt sich vieles nach Wunsch steuern: Luft, Licht, Lärm.

Ähnlich den Teilen einer menschlichen Zelle wie Teilen der märkischen Landschaft: Die biologisch und topologisch inspirierte Architektur von Matthias Sauerbruch und Louisa Hutton weiß den bildlichen und räumlichen Wurzelgrund des Gebäudes stets zu abstrahieren, zu transformieren, zu sublimieren. Nur so lässt sich etwas erahnen vom Stadthafen und vom Havelland in und um Hennigsdorf, einer Kleinstadt bei Berlin.

Rudolf Stegers

white sides of the ramp and stairway rise towards the row of offices above. On the left, there are three round volumes – the smaller ones housing the service tract, the larger one the council chamber. The oval bulges outwards; five narrow doors open onto a little park. Thanks to the red walls and the blue ceiling that sweeps boldly upwards at the halfway mark, there is a distinct sense of the ambitious approach that has been applied to this interior. Rather than merely serving the needs of the local politicians, it has the air of an intimate theatre or classical concert hall.

The sense of motion is further emphasised by the ceiling painting by artist Folke Hanfeld that extends throughout the ground floor. In matte white on matte blue, it portrays the structure created by throwing two stones into a calm pool: the rings ripple out, often taking in the curvature of the walls and continuing them in long swathes. Not only on the ground floor, but also on the upper floors, nets and rhomboids compress and expand in a spatial effect reminiscent of baroque painting in a church cupola. But wait a moment. In reality, the first and second upper floors seem more restrained. Along the left and right hand sides of a ring corridor are rows of offices. They provide comfort. There is a double facade all round. Shades and vents and sliding windows allow many aspects to be controlled: air, light, noise.

Like parts of a human cell, or parts of the local landscape, the biologically and topologically inspired architecture of Matthias Sauerbruch and Louisa Hutton invariably succeeds in abstracting, transforming and sublimating the visual and spatial roots of the building. Only in this way is it possible to perceive something of the port and the Havelland in and around Hennigsdorf, a small town near Berlin.

Rudolf Stegers

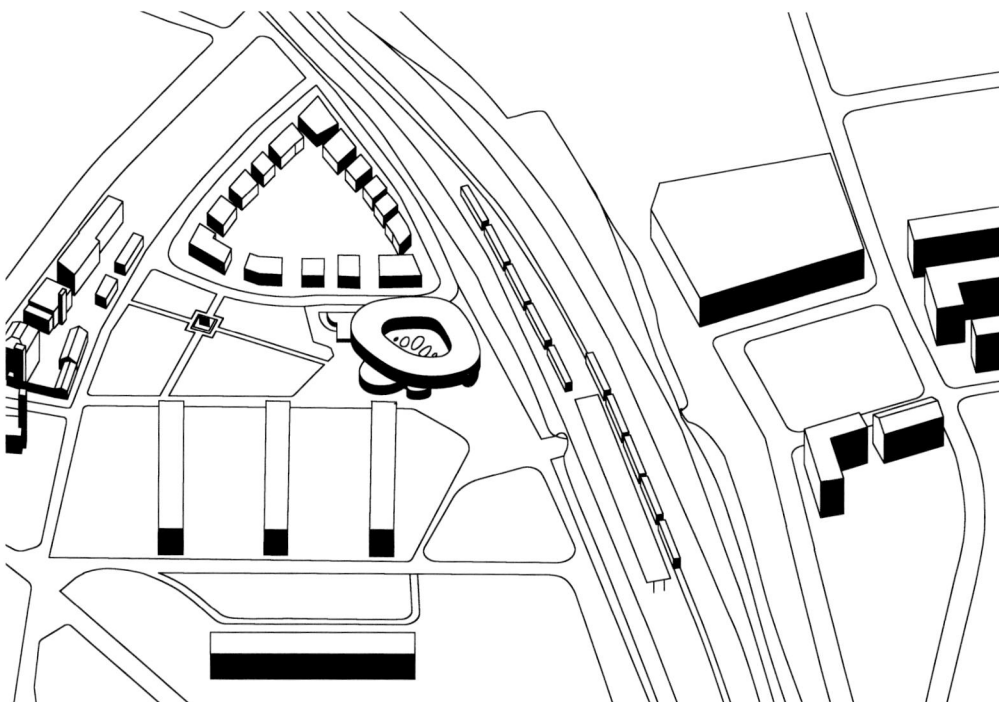

Axonometrie Lageplan   **Axonometric site plan**

Ansicht von Osten **View from the east**

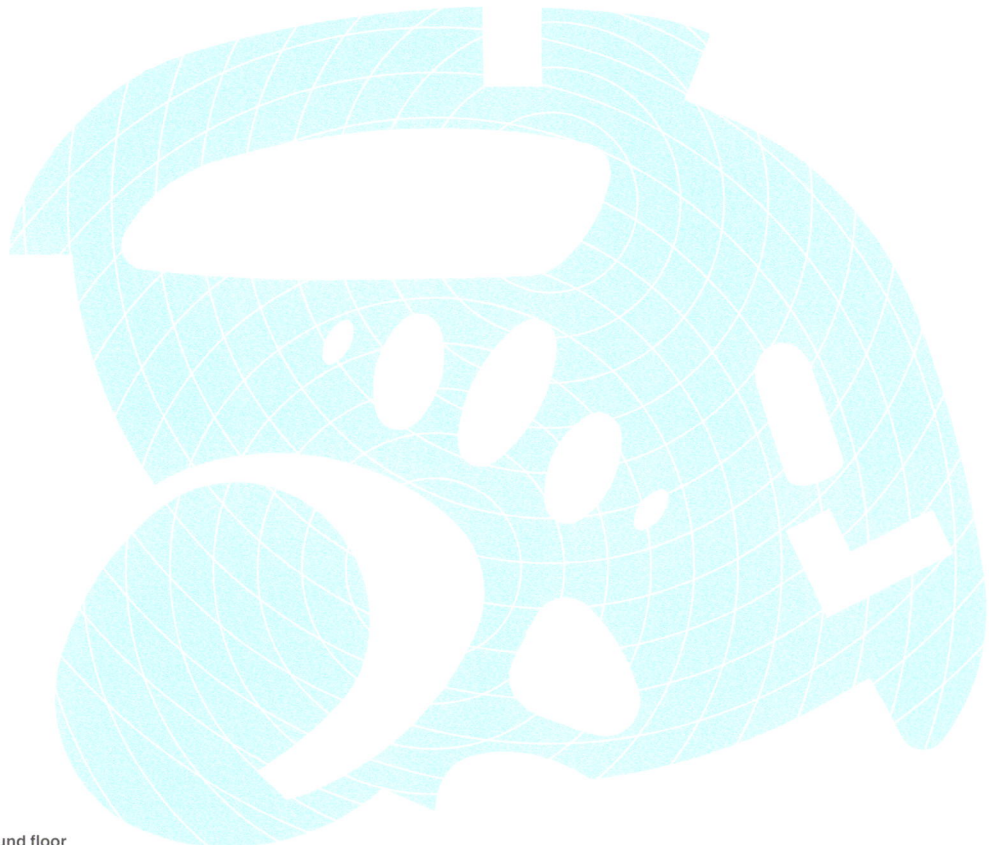

Deckenuntersicht Erdgeschoss

View of the ceiling from below, ground floor

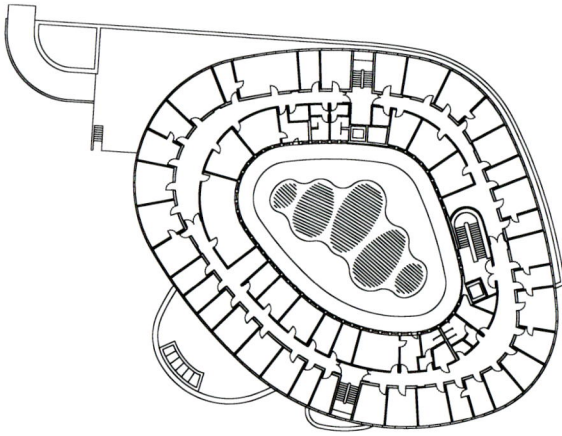

Grundriss Obergeschoss **Upper-floor plan**

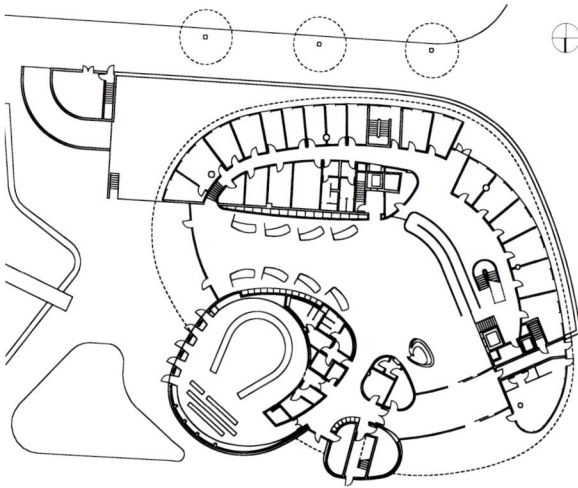

Grundriss Erdgeschoss **Ground-floor plan**

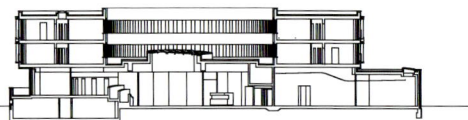

Schnitt **Section**

Innenhof **Courtyard**

Eingangshalle mit Information   **Entrance hall with information desk**

Bürgerforum mit Bürgerbüro und Sozialamt
Citizens' forum with citizens' office and social services office

Zugang Rathaussaal   **Entrance council chamber**

Erweiterung Neue Nikolaischule, Leipzig
Extension of Neue Nikolaischule, Leipzig

schulz & schulz

■ Die bauliche Geste ausgebreiteter Arme findet man in Leipzig in emblematischen Architekturen. Zunächst und stilprägend der ins Völkerschlachtdenkmal eingemeißelte Erzengel Michael mit seinen riesigen Schwingen, die wirken, als wollten sie die Stadt umarmen. Dann als Teil der Ringbebauung, wo die Brigade Rudolf Rohrer ab 1953 einen bis zu zehngeschossigen Arbeiterwohnpalast im Stil der nationalen Bautraditionen realisieren konnte. Nach der Wende dann, als Zeichen eines ökonomischen Neuanfangs, in der Neuen Messe, wobei Volkwin Marg die Topografie ausnutzte und die Figur variierte. Neben diesen drei Prestigeprojekten gibt es ein viertes, nicht ganz so stattlich und doch gewaltig, das die Form der ausgebreiteten Arme aufgreift: Die nun Neue Nikolaischule genannte ehemalige XVII. Bürgerschule im Stil einer spätwilhelminischen Neorenaissance. Otto Wilhelm Scharenberg, dem Stadtbaurat von 1906 bis 1915, hat Leipzig das Krankenhaus St. Georg, ein Stadtbad und ein Leihhaus zu verdanken. Eines seiner letzten Werke war die Anfang 1916 fertig gestellte, heute denkmalgeschützte Bürgerschule in Stötteritz, das 1910 im Zuge der zweiten Eingemeindungswelle städtisch wurde und in dessen nun rasch gebauten Villen ein gehobenes Bürgertum residierte.

Während die Engelsschwingen des nur einen Steinwurf entfernten Völkerschlachtdenkmals nach Nordwesten zeigen, richtete Scharenberg auf einem spitzwinkligen Grundstück die insgesamt fünfteilige, axialsymmetrische Schulanlage in die Gegenrichtung aus. Über den sich senkenden Eingangshof erhebt sich ein fünfstöckiger Mittelrisalit links und rechts daran anschließend, zwei etwas niedrigere Baukörper, welche die beiden mit einem Rundbogenfenster akzentuierten Portale mit den Eingängen für Jungen und Mädchen aufnehmen. An den Enden befanden sich die wiederum geschlechtergetrennten Turnhallen. Die Knabenturnhalle wurde jedoch 1943 durch einen Bombentreffen zerstört. Von 1946 bis 1990 diente das Gebäude als

In Leipzig, the architectural gesture of outstretched arms can be found in the city's emblematic edifices. First and foremost is the figure of the Archangel Michael chiselled into the Völkerschlachtdenkmal that commemorates the Battle of Leipzig in 1813, his vast wings seemingly reaching out to embrace the city. We find this gesture again in the 1953 redevelopment of the city outskirts – known as the Ringbebauung – in which the Rudolf Rohrer Brigade created a "workers' palace" apartment house up to ten storeys high in the traditional national architectural style. After the fall of the Berlin Wall, we find yet another variation on this figure in the Neue Messe trade fair building created to mark the beginning of a new economic era, with architect Volkwin Marg making full use of the topographic situation in his design. Apart from these three prestigious projects, there is a fourth more modest one, impressive in its own right, that adopts the form of outstretched arms: the Neue Nikolaischule. Formerly known as the XVII Bürgerschule, it is built in the style of the late Wilhelmian neo-renaissance. Otto Wilhelm Scharenberg, city architect from 1906 to 1915, gave Leipzig its St. Georg Hospital, a municipal baths and a pawn brokerage. One of his last works was a school – the Bürgerschule in Stötteritz – completed in early 1916 and now a listed building, which was taken over by the municipal authorities in 1910 during the second major expansion of the city boundaries, when the wealthy bourgeoisie rapidly developed the area around it to build their villas.

Whereas the wings of the archangel point north-westwards to the Völkerschlachtdenkmal just a stone's throw away, Scharenberg oriented the five-part axially symmetrical school complex on a sharply angled site in the opposite direction. A five-storey central projection rises above the downward sloping entrance courtyard, on the right of which are two slightly lower structures containing the portals for the girls' and boys' entrances respectively, both accentuated by round-arched windows, with the separate boys' and girls' gyms at either end. The boys' gym was destroyed in a 1943 air raid. From 1946 to 1990 the building was used as a polytechnical college and the remaining walls of the bombed-out gym were the walls of a garden for the students. In 1995, the school was renamed in the tradition of the historic Nikolaischule. An alumni association donated the funds with which the former gym could be reconstructed as a multi-purpose hall. The winning design submitted by architects Ansgar and Benedikt Schulz was approved by architectural conservationists.

The appeal of the new extension lies in its successful balance of innovative intervention and respect for the old building. The reinforced concrete structure is emphatically technical and rational. The new gym is situated in front of the southern gable wall of the school and forms a versatile space between two shear walls with longitudinal roof trusses deflecting the load over the shear walls. The reason for this particular structure becomes evident on the inside: only in this way was it possible to insert a glass joint between

1 Schulhof **Schoolyard**
2 Neue Nikolaischule
  Neue Nikolaischule
3 Erweiterungsbau
  Extension

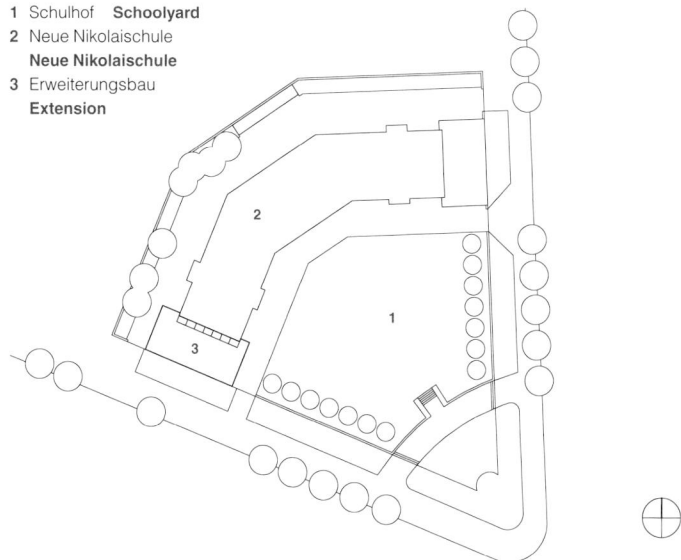

Lageplan **Site plan**

Architekten Architects schulz & schulz, Leipzig, www.schulz-und-schulz.com; Ansgar Schulz, Benedikt Schulz; Team: Matthias Hönig & Dirk Lämmel, Uwe Graalfs
Bauherr Client Stadt Leipzig   **Tragwerk Structural** Dr.-Ing. W. Naumann & Partner Ingenieurgesellschaft mbH, Leipzig   **Fassade Facade** Prof. Michael Lange
Beratender Ingenieur VBI, Berlin   **Wettbewerb Competition** 2000   **Ausführung Construction** 2002/03   **Standort Location** Schönbachstraße 17, Leipzig

polytechnische Oberschule, die Umfassungsmauern der niederge-
brannten Halle umschlossen einen Schülergarten. Seit 1995 nahm
die Schule mit ihrem neuen Namen deutlich Bezug auf die Tradition
der historischen Nikolaischule. Eine Vereinigung ehemaliger Schüler
spendete, um die alte Sportstätte als Multifunktionshalle wieder auf-
zubauen. Beim Wettbewerb setzte sich der Entwurf der Architekten
Ansgar und Benedikt Schulz durch, dem auch die Denkmalschützer
zustimmten.

Seinen Reiz bezieht der Anbau aus der geglückten Balance von
gezieltem Eingriff und Respekt vor dem Alten. Die Stahlbeton-
konstruktion gibt sich betont technisch-rational: Vor der südlichen
Giebelwand der Schule befindet sich die neue Halle, eine vielfältig
nutzbare Fläche zwischen zwei Wandscheiben, wobei die Dach-
träger in die Längsrichtung spannen und die Lasten über die Wandscheiben ableiten. Der Sinn dieser Konstruktion offenbart sich im
Innern der Halle: Nur durch sie wurde es möglich, eine Glasfuge
zwischen Alt- und Neubau einzufügen und damit den Raum natürlich
zu belichten. Darüber hinaus wird die Intervention durch diese Form
der Lastabtragung reversibel. Zusätzliches Licht erhält die Halle
durch ein großzügiges Fensterband, das die Breite der Südwand
einnimmt und mit beweglichen Lamellen verschattet werden kann. In
den Holzschwingboden wurde eine Heizung integriert, die Prall-
wände sind mit weiß beschichteten MDF-Platten verkleidet. Die
Nebenräume für das Lagern der Sportgeräte, die Technikzentrale
und Sanitärräume befinden sich an den Schmalseiten zwischen
Wandscheiben und Fassade.

Mit Letzterer beziehen sich die Architekten explizit auf das domi-
nante Merkmal der unteren beiden Geschosse der Schulhaushülle:
die Bossen, wobei deren Sichtflächen nicht aus bruchrauhen Steinen
bestehen, sondern verputzt sind. Die Notwendigkeit, das Gewicht
der Lamellen zu reduzieren, zwang die Architekten, das Motiv neu
zu interpretieren. Als ›Bossenträger‹ wurden Wabenkernplatten ge-
wählt, die Aluminiumrahmen umfassen. Diese sind vor dem Fensterband durch Gestänge verbunden und werden von Motoren bewegt.
Das vertikale Fassadenraster entspricht dem des Hauptgebäudes,
die Kubatur der neuen Halle spiegelt die der Mädchenturnhalle.
Für den Sockel des Anbaus verwendeten die Architekten jenen
Beuchaer Granit, mit dem bereits der Sockel der alten Knabenturnhalle verblendet worden war. Übrigens der Stein, der auch als Ver-
kleidung des Völkerschlachtdenkmals dient. Mit einer Schattenfuge,
die den Verlauf der ehemaligen Umfassungsmauern zeigt, wird subtil
an den Zustand des Gebäudes zu DDR-Zeiten erinnert. Aus architek-
turhistorischer Perspektive nennt sich Leipzig Hauptstadt des deutschen Historismus. Die Multifunktionshalle der Gebrüder Schulz, die
auch als Theater- und Konzertsaal sowie Ersatzklassenraum genutzt
wird, zeigt, wie das Andenken an dieses bauliche Erbe gewahrt
werden kann, ohne Geschichte zu kopieren oder zu rekonstruieren.
Dass Betrachter nun wieder den Gestus der ausgebreiteten Arme
in all seinen bildungsbürgerlichen Repräsentationsambitionen wahrnehmen, dabei aber das Neue als integralen Bestandteil des Alten
erleben können, lässt auf weitere geglückte Erweiterungsbauten
hoffen.

Enrico Santifaller

the old building and the new extension to allow natural daylight
into the room. Moreover, this load-bearing system means that the
intervention is reversible. The hall gains additional light through a
generously proportioned ribbon of windows along the width of the
south wall that can be shaded by adjustable slats. A heating system
has been integrated into the sprung wooden floors, and the walls
are clad in MDF panels coated in white. The ancillary rooms for
storage of sports equipment, technical services and sanitation are
located on the narrow ends between the shear walls and the facade.

In designing the facade the architects have made explicit reference to the rough-hewn stone that is the predominant feature of the
two lower storeys of the school. However, the surfaces do not con-
sist of quarry-face stone, but are rendered. The need to reduce the
weight of the sun-shading slats meant that the architects were
obliged to reinterpret the motif. They chose to use honeycomb
blocks with aluminium frames. These are linked by rods in front of
the windows and moved by motors. The vertical facade structure
corresponds to that of the main building, while the cuboid structure
of the new gym mirrors the original girls' gym. For the basecourse
of the extension, the architects used the same Beucha granite that
was used to clad the basecourse of the original boys' gym. Inciden-
tally, this is the very same stone that was used for the cladding of
the Völkerschlachtdenkmal. A shadow joint showing the run of the
original outer walls subtly recalls the state of the building as it was
under the communist regime. From the point of view of architectural
history, Leipzig is considered the home of German Historicism. The
Schulz brothers' multi-purpose hall, which can be used as a theatre
and concert hall as well as a classroom, illustrates how a building's
architectural heritage can be retained without simply copying or
reconstructing history. The fact that visitors can now grasp the
"outstretched arms" gesture with all its connotations of bourgeois
educational ambition, while at the same time being able to perceive
the new building as an integral part of the old one, allows us to
look forward with some optimism to seeing more of this kind of
approach to designing extensions for historic buildings.

Enrico Santifaller

Ansicht von Osten **View from the east**

1 Halle **Hall**
2 Cafeteria **Cafeteria**
3 Schülermitverwaltung
  Student administration
4 Umkleideraum
  Changing room

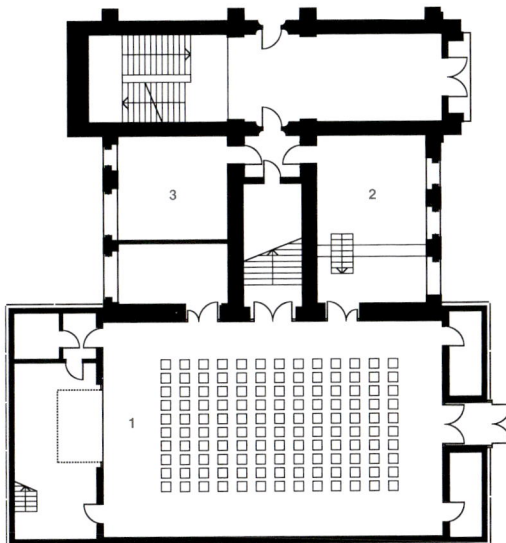

0 1   5   10 m

Grundriss Erdgeschoss **Ground-floor plan**

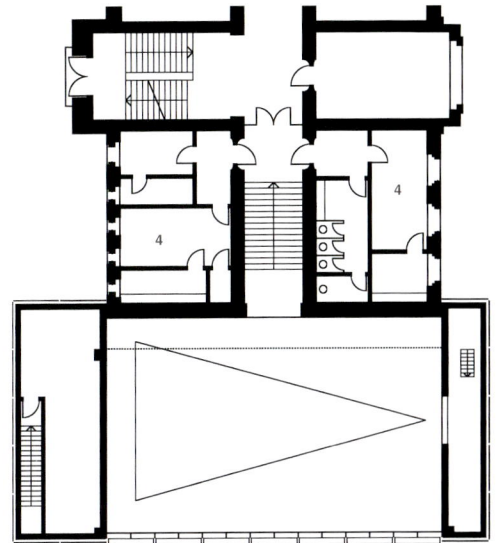

Grundriss Obergeschoss **Upper-floor plan**

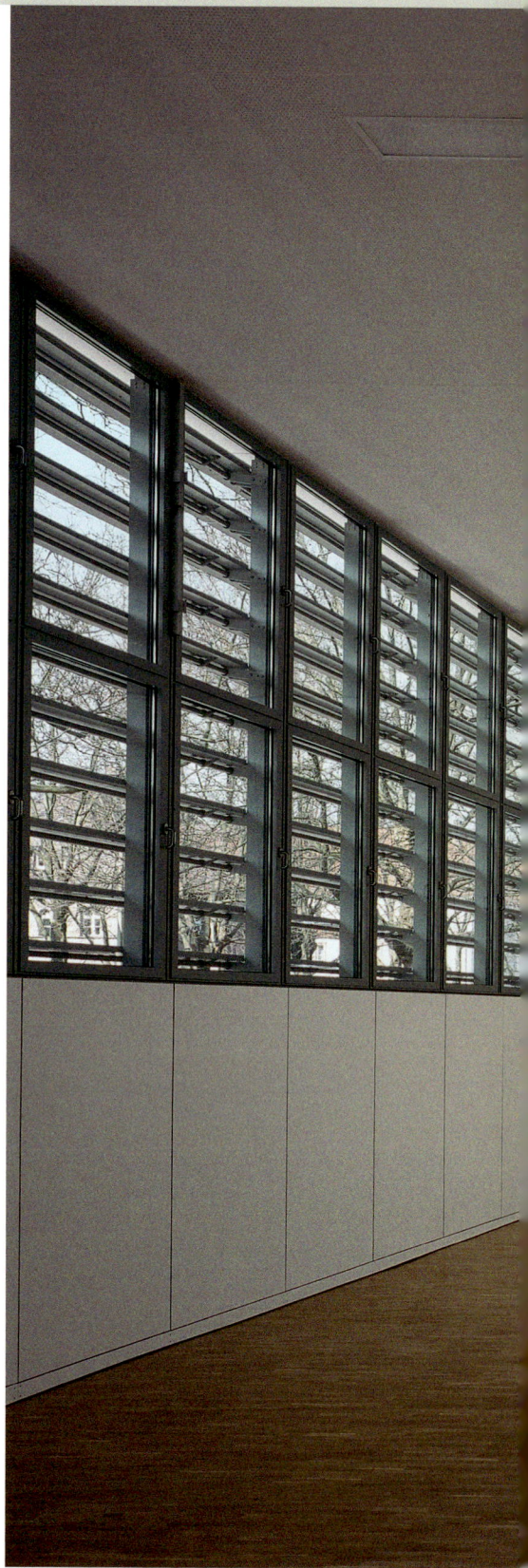

Innenraum **Interior**

Ansicht von Süden mit geschlossenen, halb-
geöffneten und geöffneten Lamellen
**View from the south showing slats closed,
half-open and open**

Poesie und Alltag
Poetry and Ordinariness

Inge Wolf

Bauten und Projekte für den Frankfurter Römerberg

Buildings and Projects for Frankfurt's Römerberg

■ In den Bombennächten von 1944 war die historische Fachwerkalt-stadt von Frankfurt am Main nahezu vollständig zerstört worden. Gleich nach dem Krieg begann der Wiederaufbau, aber es sollte bis in die achtziger Jahre dauern, bis die Lücke zwischen Dom und Römer nach ersten provisorischen und unvollendet gebliebenen Zwischenlösungen wieder geschlossen werden sollte. Rekonstruk-tion des Alten oder modernes Bauen? Man stritt und diskutierte über Jahrzehnte und quer durch alle Parteien. Die Stadt sah mehr als einen Wettbewerb und unterschiedlichste Lösungsansätze.

Das Areal zwischen Römer und Dom war erst Parkplatz, dann kam mit einem Parkhaus und später mit der U-Bahn die Substruktion. An der Oberfläche sah man lange Zeit auf eine Reihe gleichförmiger Würfel, Teil des Stützensystems der unterirdischen Parkebenen, das hier die Abdeckung durchstieß. Es sollte auch als Fundament für die geplante Überbauung nach dem Entwurf des Frankfurter Büros Bartsch, Thürwächter und Weber dienen, der den Römerberg-Wett-bewerb von 1962/63 gewonnen hatte. Nach den Plänen des Büros wurde das Technische Rathaus bis 1972 fertig gestellt. Im selben Jahr wurde auch das Historische Museum im südwestlichen Rand-bereich bezugsfertig. 1978 folgte der Beschluss der Stadtverord-netenversammlung, der die Weichen für die Bebauung in den achtzi-ger Jahren stellte: Ostzeile und Schwarzer Stern nach historischem Vorbild und die moderne Freizeit- und Kulturschirn, die auf die Sub-struktion des Platzes, auf Parkhaus und U-Bahn, Rücksicht nahm. Der Wettbewerb von 1980 wurde zugunsten der Berliner Architekten Dietrich Bangert, Bernd Jansen, Stefan Scholz und Axel Schultes entschieden. 1981 begannen die Bauarbeiten gegenüber dem Rö-mer, in der Saalgasse fanden sie 1988 ihren Abschluss.

Drei Komplexe lassen sich aufführen: der ›historische Block‹ mit den Fachwerkbauten zum Römer hin, die Kulturschirn mit ihrem lang gestreckten Ausstellungstrakt, der nahe an den Dom heranreicht, und die Wohnbebauung der Saalgasse. Die nach historischem Vor-bild rekonstruierte Fachwerkzeile wird durch zwei moderne Parallel-bauten zum Block ergänzt, mit dem man »die Struktur der ehemali-gen Häuserzeilen und Gassen an dieser Stelle wieder aufnehmen« wollte.[1] Das Herzstück des Gesamtplans, die Schirn, flankiert den Platz an der dem Technischen Rathaus gegenüberliegenden Seite mit gleichförmigen Arkaden, die in West-Ost-Richtung einen Verbin-dungsgang zwischen Nikolaikirche und Dom bilden, von den Archi-tekten als Erinnerung an die ehemalige Bendergasse gedacht. Der Quertrakt der Schirn, nach Norden hin mit großer Rotunde und Schirntreff, durchstößt im Süden die Häuserzeile, die sich entlang der Saalgasse erstreckt. Auch der Weg in Nord-Süd-Richtung bleibt offen, Durchgangspassage und Treppenanlage ermöglichen den direkten Abstieg zur Saalgasse. Vor dem Schirntreff steht ›der Tisch‹, Besucherplattform und zugleich eine Art separates Vordach, errichtet

Buildings and Projects for Frankfurt's Römerberg

■ The bombs of 1944 all but obliterated the half-timbered houses that once formed the historic centre of Frankfurt/Main. Although reconstruction began right after the war, it was not until the 1980s that the gap site between the cathedral and the Römer (city hall), with its unfinished and temporary structures, was eventually deve-loped. The question here was: reconstruction of the old or modern architecture? It was a debate that raged for decades right across the political spectrum. The city held competitions and pored over all manner of different solutions.

For a while, the area between the Römer and the cathedral was used as a car park. Then an underground car park was built there. After that, with the metro system, came the substructure. Above ground, the load-bearing system of the subterranean parking levels was visible for a long time where it broke through the surface. It was to be integrated into the projected superstructure designed by Frankfurt-based architects Bartsch, Thürwächter and Weber, who had won the 1962/63 competition to develop the Römerberg square. The Technisches Rathaus was completed by 1972 according to their plans. In the same year, the Historisches Museum at the south-west edge of the site was also completed. Then, in 1978, the municipal council passed a resolution that was to pave the way for the de-velopment of the square in the 1980s: the mediaeval Ostzeile and the house known as Schwarzer Stern were to be reconstructed in their historic form, while the modern complex of the Schirn, with exhibition spaces and cultural facilities, was to be oriented towards the substructure, the car park and the metro. The winners of the 1980 competition were Berlin-based architects Dietrich Bangert, Bernd Jansen, Stefan Scholz and Axel Schultes. Construction work started opposite the Römer in 1981 and ended with the completion of the Saalgasse in 1988.

The complexes involved here are the "historic block" with its row of half-timbered houses facing the Römer city hall, the Schirn cultural centre with its elongated exhibition tract stretching almost up to the cathedral, and the housing development on Saalgasse. The row of half-timbered buildings reconstructed according to historic documents, pictures and photographs has been comple-mented by two modern buildings parallel to the block, intended to "echo the structure of the former rows of houses and alleyways on this site".[1] At the heart of the master plan is the Schirn, which flanks the area opposite the Technisches Rathaus with its uniformly arcaded east-west passageway between the Nikolaikirche and the cathedral – which the architects intended as an echo of the former Bendergasse. The transverse tract of the Schirn, with its huge rotunda housing the Schirntreff cafe-bar at the northern end, pushes through into the row of houses along the Saalgasse to the south. The north-south axis remains open, with a passageway and a

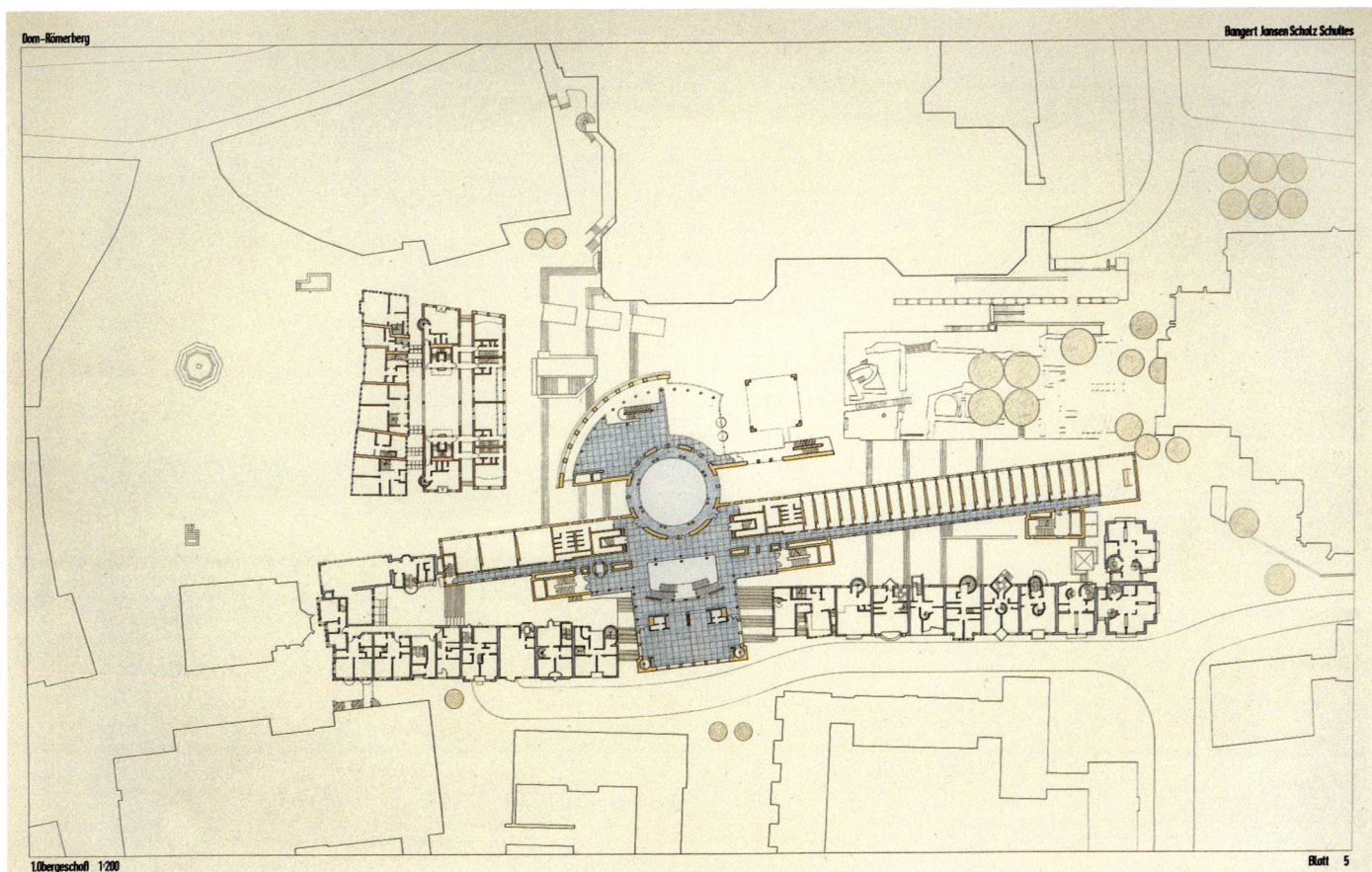

Bangert, Jansen, Scholz und Schultes, Schirn mit ›Historischem Block‹ und Saalgasse, 1. Obergeschoss, Buntstift auf Lichtpause, 1981–1984
Bangert, Jansen, Scholz and Schultes, Schirn with "historic tract" and Saalgasse lane, first floor, coloured pencil on blueprint, 1981–1984

auf vier hohen Stützen. Für die Wohnbauten in der Saalgasse sah man »kleinteilig parzellierte, individuelle Hauseinheiten als Typ des Bürgerhauses in der Stadt, in Korrespondenz zu den rekonstruierten, mittelalterlichen Häusern«[2] vor. Es kam zu der Entscheidung, dass diese Häuser nach Entwürfen verschiedener Architekten ausgeführt werden sollten. Der Auftrag ging an zwölf Büros. Gebunden an strenge Vorgaben mit einheitlicher Höhe und Giebelständigkeit sollte dennoch größtmögliche Vielfalt entstehen.

Das Deutsche Architektur Museum besitzt zu Schirn und Saalgasse eine ganze Reihe von Plänen, Originalskizzen und auch verschiedene Modelle. Neben dem Büro Bangert, Jansen, Scholz und Schultes sind Christoph Mäckler, Eisele und Fritz, Berghof/Landes/Rang, Charles Moore, Natalini/Superstudio, Unglaub und Horvath sowie Jourdan/Müller/Albrecht in der Sammlung vertreten. So unterschiedlich wie die gefundenen Lösungen, so verschieden ist auch das Material, das an das Museum ging. Es reicht von der einfachen Plankopie bis hin zu Zeichnung, Collage und Modell.

Umfangreich und von besonderer Qualität ist der Bestand Adolfo Natalini/Superstudio.[3] Zu seinem Haus in der Saalgasse sind mehr

staircase affording direct access to the Saalgasse. In front of the Schirntreff is a table-like area set on four high supports to create a visitors' platform and separate portico. The apartment buildings on Saalgasse were envisaged as "small-scale individual dwellings as a type of urban bourgeois housing corresponding to the reconstructed mediaeval houses".[2] It was decided that these houses should be built to designs by different architects. Twelve firms were commissioned. They were expected to create the greatest possible range of designs within the strict constraints of uniform height and eaves.

The Deutsches Architektur Museum holds a large number of plans, original sketches and models pertaining to the Schirn and the Saalgasse. Apart from the work of Bangert, Jansen, Scholz and Schultes, the collection also includes designs by Christoph Mäckler, Eisele and Fritz, Berghof/Landes/Rang, Charles Moore, Natalini/Superstudio, Unglaub and Horvath as well as Jourdan/Müller/Albrecht. The material acquired by the museum is as varied as the solutions themselves, ranging from simple plan copies to drawings, collages and models.

Adolfo Natalini/Superstudio, Saalgasse, Haus 4, perspektivische Ansicht, Bleistift, Rötel, Kreide und Farbstift auf Transparentpapier, 1981
Adolfo Natalini/Superstudio, Saalgasse, House 4, perspectival view, pencil, red chalk, chalk and coloured crayon on tracing paper, 1981

als zwanzig Originalzeichnungen und -skizzen und ein ungewöhnliches Bronzemodell, mehr Kunstobjekt als Architektur im Kleinformat, vorhanden. Weitere Zeichnungen enthält der *Codex Klotz,* ein Skizzenbuch, vom Architekten so bezeichnet und mit persönlicher Widmung an den ersten Direktor des Deutschen Architektur Museums, Heinrich Klotz, übergeben. Das Haus von Natalini, Haus 4, ist das letzte im ersten Abschnitt der Häuserzeile, die hier von der Treppe zum Römerberg und dem Schirnflügel unterbrochen wird. Das Gebäude wird damit zum Eckhaus. Die Zeichnungen belegen die Entwicklung von der streng gerasterten Fassade mit geweihartig auskragenden Metallästen hin zum Gebäude aus roten Betonquadern. Die rechte Hausecke, hier verlaufen Lüftungskanäle der unterirdischen Parkdecks, verwandelt sich vom mächtigen Rundpfeiler zum Baum, der mit seiner Krone Fassade und leere Fensterhöhlen durchbricht, und wieder zurück zur schlichten Rundform, die später ausgeführt wird. Die gleichförmigen Fensterreihen werden aufgegeben zugunsten einer großen Vertikalen, die das Haus symmetrisch teilt. Der ursprünglich nach links verschobene Giebel wird in die Mitte gerückt. Von Natalini erfahren wir, dass das Haus mit den Ästen bei der

Adolfo Natalini/Superstudio is particularly well represented with works of exceptional quality.[3] There are more than twenty original drawings and sketches for his house on Saalgasse, as well as an unusual bronze model that is not so much architecture in miniature as a work of art in its own right. Further drawings are included in the *Codex Klotz*, a sketchbook given this title by the architect himself and presented, with a personal dedication, to Heinrich Klotz, founding director of the Deutsches Architektur Museum. The house by Natalini, House 4, is the last one in the first section of the row of houses that is interrupted at this point by the stairs leading to the Römerberg square and the wing of the Schirn. This situation makes it a corner site. The drawings show the development of the stringently structured facade with its antler-like metal branches into a building of red concrete blocks. The right-hand corner, where the ventilation shafts for the underground car park run, changes from a massive round pillar to a tree whose crown breaks through the facade and empty window apertures and then back again to a simple round form that is later built. The uniform rows of windows are replaced by a large vertical that divides the house symmetrically.

57.

SAALGASSE Nr4. " CRESCITA DELL' ALBERO " 7.2.81

Adolfo Natalini/Superstudio, Saalgasse, Haus 4, Perspektive mit Baum, aus dem *Codex Klotz*, Tusche, 1981
Adolfo Natalini/Superstudio, Saalgasse, House 4, perspectival view with tree, from *Codex Klotz*, pen and ink, 1981

Adolfo Natalini/Superstudio, Saalgasse, Haus 4, Italia und Germania, perspektivische Ansicht, Tusche auf Transparentpapier, 1981
Adolfo Natalini/Superstudio, Saalgasse, House 4, Italia and Germania, perspectival view, pen and ink on tracing paper, 1981

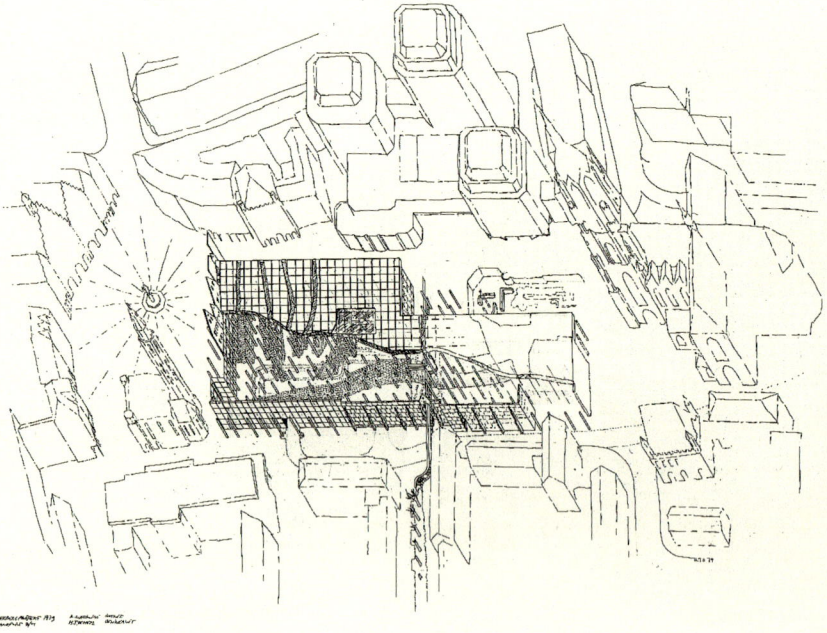

Adolfo Natalini/Superstudio, Saalgasse, Haus 4, Model, Bronze, 1981/82 **Adolfo Natalini/Superstudio, Saalgasse, House 4, model, bronze, 1981–82**

Adolfo Natalini/Superstudio, Projekt für den Römerberg, isometrischer Übersichtsplan, Tusche auf Transparentpapier, 1979
Adolfo Natalini/Superstudio, project for Römerberg square, isometric plan, pen and ink on tracing paper, 1979

Stadt auf wenig Gegenliebe stieß. Man befand es für zu hermetisch und zu wenig modern.[4]

Natalini hatte am offiziellen Römerberg-Wettbewerb nicht teilgenommen. Sein Entwurf war das Ergebnis einer Arbeit mit Studenten im Rahmen eines Seminars der Städelschule. 1979 wurde er zusammen mit anderen Vorschlägen im Frankfurter Steinernen Haus in der Ausstellung *Rekonstruktion des Römerbergs – kritische, ironische, poetische Projekte* präsentiert.[5] Als Beitrag außer Konkurrenz findet man ihn in der Broschüre, mit der das Hochbauamt die Ergebnisse des offiziellen Wettbewerbs veröffentlichte.[6]

Das Römerbergprojekt Natalinis ist mit Skizzen im *Codex Klotz* und vier Einzelblättern in der Sammlung des Deutschen Architektur Museums vertreten. Die aufwendigen Tuschezeichnungen, teilweise koloriert, waren wohl als Präsentationsblätter für die Ausstellung von 1979 gedacht. Ein isometrischer Übersichtsplan zeigt eine riesige Halle, die nahezu das gesamte Areal einnimmt. In der Zeichnung wird das Gebäude mit jenem gleichförmigen Quadratraster überzogen, das schon in den frühen Arbeiten von Superstudio zu sehen ist. Der Entwurf reflektiert die Geschichte des Orts. Das Stützensystem der unterirdischen Parkebenen, das an der Oberfläche als Würfelreihe sichtbar war, war auch Erinnerung an ein unvollendetes Projekt. Bei Natalini wurden Assoziationen an antike Säulenreihen geweckt, er nutzt die Würfel als Sockel für neue Stahlstützen. Es sind 203, schlichte Zylinder, die das Dach des zwölf Meter hohen Gebäudes tragen. Die historische Altstadt spiegelt sich im Entwurf vielfach

The gable, originally set to the left, is shifted to the centre. Natalini explains that the house with the branches found little favour with the council. It was considered too hermetic and not modern enough.[4]

Natalini did not take part in the official Römerberg competition. His design was the result of his work with students in a seminar at the Städel art school. In 1979 it was presented alongside other proposals in an exhibition at the Steinernes House in Frankfurt entitled *Rekonstruktion des Römerbergs – kritische, ironische, poetische Projekte* [Reconstruction of the Römerberg: critical, ironic, poetic projects].[5] It is included as *hors concours* in the brochure in which the city building authority published the results of the official competition.[6]

Natalini's Römerberg project is represented in sketches in the *Codex Klotz* and in four separate works on paper in the collection of the Deutsches Architektur Museum. The finely executed pen and ink drawings, some of them coloured, were probably intended as presentation drawings for the 1979 exhibition. An isometric plan shows a vast hall covering almost the entire area. In the drawing, the building is covered in the uniform pattern of squares that is also to be found in the early works of Superstudio. It is a design that reflects the history of the site. The load-bearing system of the underground car park, visible at the time on the surface as a row of cubes, also recalled an unfinished project. They reminded Natalini of the rows of columns in classical architecture and he used the "cubes" as the

wider. Dort, wo die mittelalterlichen Gassen und Plätze waren, wechselt der Bodenbelag, und die Säulen, die hier stehen, bleiben in voller Höhe sichtbar. Eine gemauerte Steinverkleidung der Säulen, die eine Höhe bis 4,80 Meter erreichen kann, markiert dagegen ehemals bebaute Flächen. Die Außenwände mit Strebepfeilern sind gemauert, roter Naturstein mit Marmorelementen ist hier vorgesehen, die Straßendurchbrüche werden vom Wechsel zu Glasflächen markiert. Ähnlich ist es beim Dach. Auch hier wird der ehemalige Straßenverlauf durch Glas angezeigt, für die übrige Fläche war an eine Bleiabdeckung gedacht. Die Fachwerkzeile zum Römer wandelt sich bei Natalini zur rostigen Stahlwand, die der Halle vorgeblendet wird. In Dimension und Verlauf folgt die Metallwand der historischen Häuserfront. Hinter ihr steigt eine Treppe zu einem hölzernen Steg empor, der die gesamte Halle oberhalb des Dachs diagonal überquert und zur Aussichtsebene des begehbaren Stadtplans wird, den die Blei- und Glasflächen nachzeichnen. Der Blick zum Römer wird aus den Fensteröffnungen von der Treppe aus ermöglicht.

Oswald Mathias Ungers zollte dem italienischen Kollegen hohes Lob. Er sah in Natalinis Beitrag zur Gestaltung des Römerbergs »eines der schönsten ›Architekturgedichte‹, das die jüngste Architekturgeschichte in einer sonst durch die Technokratie hoffnungslos verarmten Welt hervorgebracht hat«.[7] Er empfahl 1980 eine Würdigung durch das damalige Preisgericht und hätte den Alternativ-

bases for new steel pillars. There are 203 of them, plain cylinders supporting the roof of the twelve-metre high building. The historic Old Town is reflected in the design in many ways. Where there were mediaeval lanes and squares, the flooring changes, and the pillars that stand here are visible in full height. Where there were once buildings, the pillars are clad in stone masonry up to a height of as much as 4.80 metres. The outer walls with buttresses are envisaged as being built of red natural stone with marble elements, while the street openings are marked by a change to glass. A similar approach is taken in the design of the roof. Again, the former run of the street is indicated by the use of glass, while the rest is shown as lead-clad. In Natalini's design, the row of half-timbered houses facing the Römer is transformed into a rusty steel wall set in front of the hall. The dimensions and layout of the metal wall echo the historic facades of the former buildings. Behind the wall, a stair leads up to a wooden walkway that crosses the hall diagonally above the roof, creating a viewing platform in the walk-on streetplan mapped out by the areas of lead and glass. From the stairway, the window apertures afford a view towards the Römer.

Oswald Mathias Ungers had high praise for his colleague. He described Natalini's proposal for the Römerberg development project as "one of the most beautiful 'architectural poems' that recent architectural history has produced in a world otherwise hopelessly

Adolfo Natalini/Superstudio, Projekt für den Römerberg, Vogelperspektive/Lageplan, Tusche, Folie, überarbeitete Transparentpause, 1979
Adolfo Natalini/Superstudio, project for Römerberg square, bird's eye view/site plan, pen and ink, film, reworked tracing on tracing paper, 1979

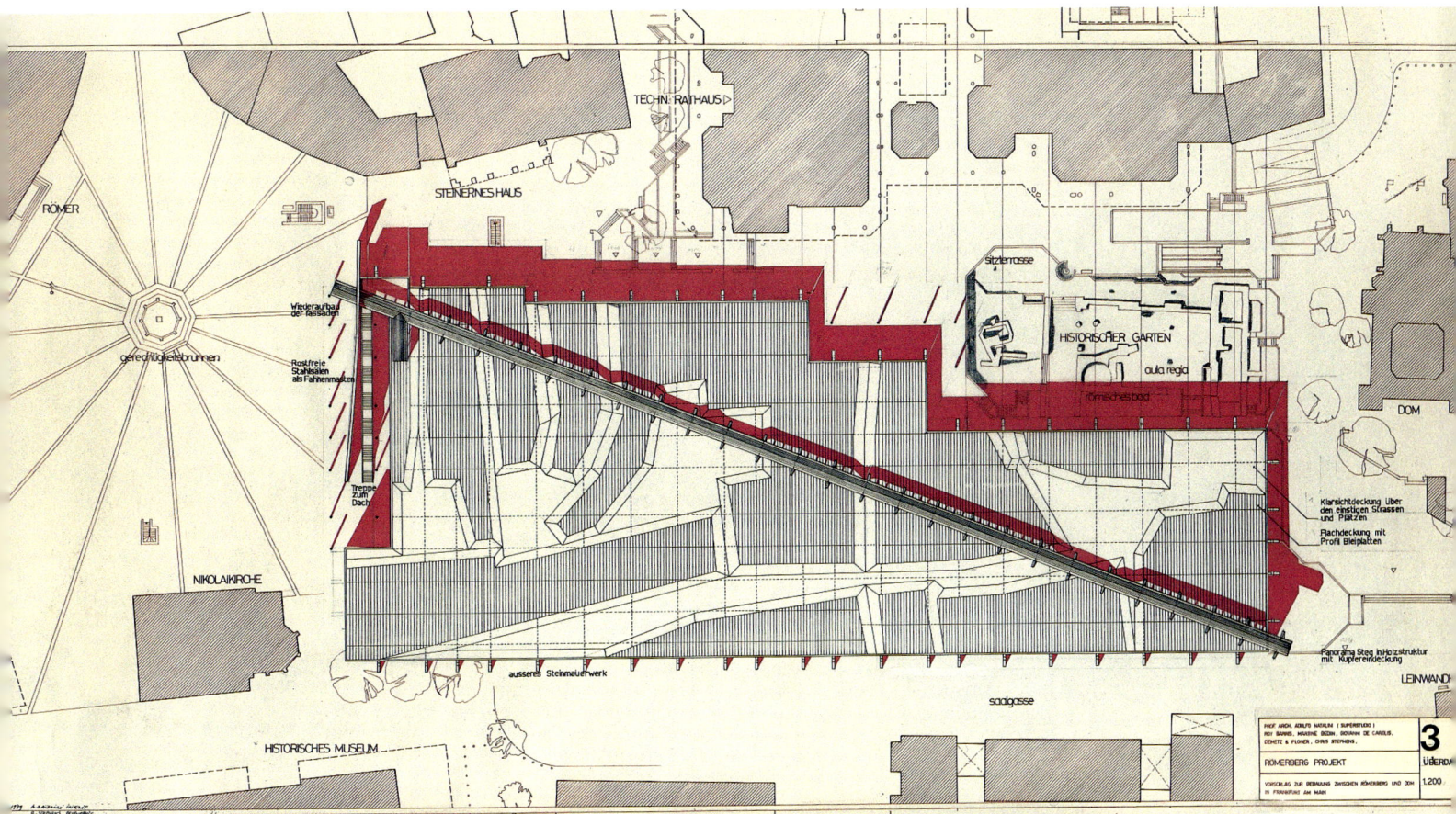

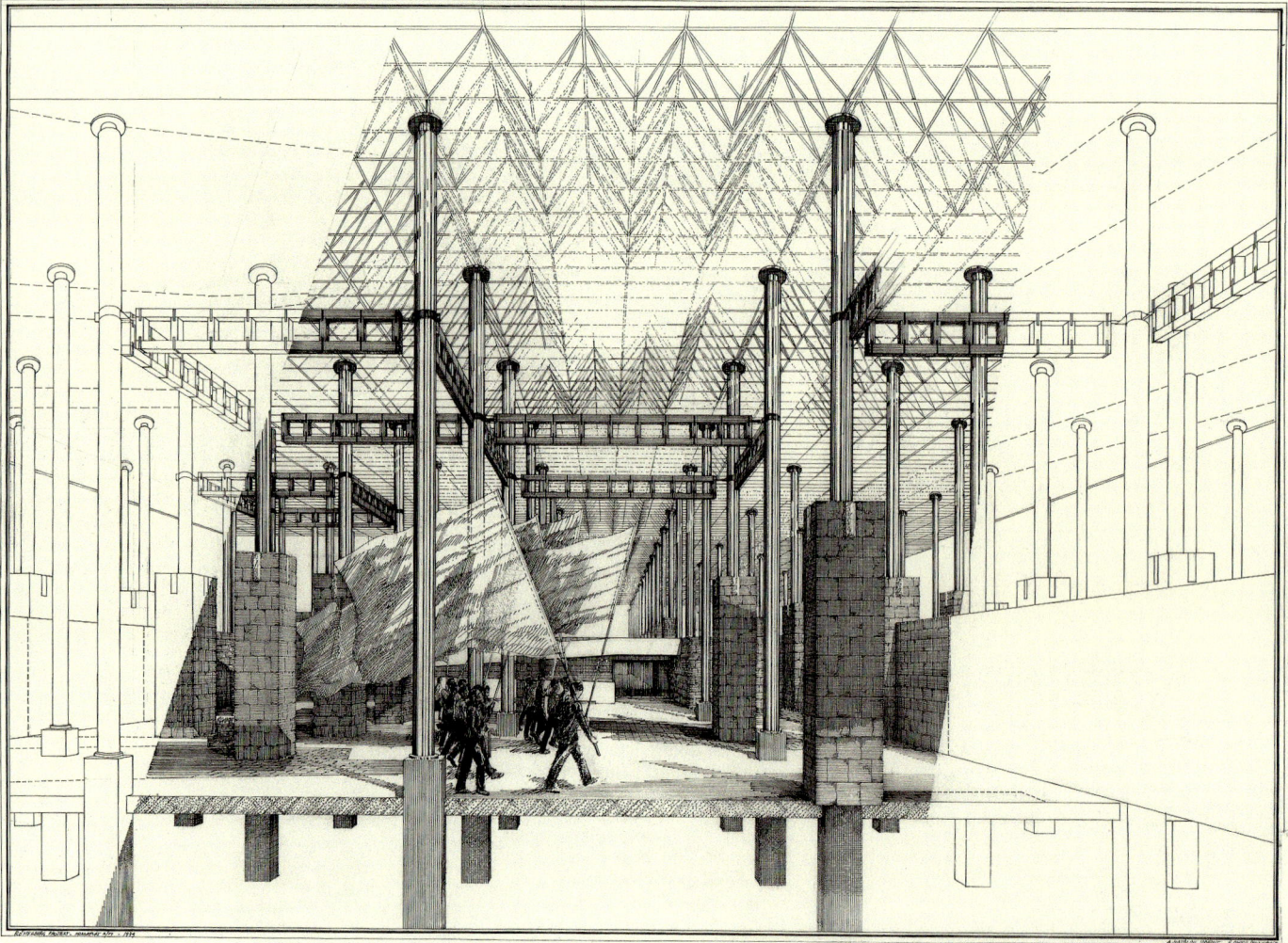

Adolfo Natalini/Superstudio, Projekt für den Römerberg, perspektivische Innenansicht, Tusche auf Transparentpapier, 1979
Adolfo Natalini/Superstudio, project for Römerberg square, perspectival interior view, pen and ink on tracing paper, 1979

entwurf gerne als Anlass zum Nachdenken und Ausgangspunkt für neue Überlegungen gesehen.

Kann man zufrieden sein mit dem, was im Herzen von Frankfurt entstanden ist? Die Passage vom Römer zum Dom wird von den Fußgängern fleißig genutzt, die Schirn hat unter den internationalen Ausstellungshallen ihren festen Platz erobert, die Häuser in der Saalgasse wurden in Besitz genommen. Wenn die Anzahl der Touristenfotos pro Tag ein Gradmesser sein soll, dann kann man mit der historischen Fachwerkzeile auf dem Römerberg mehr als zufrieden sein. Besucher aus aller Welt lassen sich Tag für Tag vor Frankfurts Kulisse Nummer eins ablichten und egal, ob die Häuser zwanzig oder mehrere hundert Jahre alt sind, so will man ein romantisches Stück Good Old Europe mit nach Hause nehmen.

Der große Wurf ist es nicht geworden, was im Herzen von Frankfurt entstanden ist. Ein wenig mehr Poesie hätte es sein dürfen. Die Rekonstruktion des Römers, dazu Wohn- und Geschäftshäuser der fünfziger Jahre, die frühen siebziger mit Historischem Museum und Technischem Rathaus und dann die Wohnhäuser und die Kultur-schirn der achtziger, in all dem spiegelt sich Baugeschichte der

impoverished by technocracy."[7] In 1980 he recommended that this should be acknowledged by the jury, and would gladly have seen the alternative design as the thought-provoking starting point for new deliberations.

Can we be satisfied with what has been built at the heart of Frankfurt? The passage from the Römer to the cathedral is heavily used by pedestrians, the Schirn has established itself as a force to be reckoned with on the international art circuit, the houses on Saal-gasse are in use. If the number of tourist snapshots taken every day is anything to go by, there is every reason to be satisfied with the historic row of half-timbered houses on the Römerberg. Visitors from all over the world have their photos taken in front of Frank-furt's favourite backdrop. No matter whether the buildings are twenty years old or centuries old, people want to take home a romantic souvenir of Good Old Europe.

What has been created at the heart of Frankfurt is hardly a stroke of genius. There could have been a little more poetry in it. The recon-struction of the Römer, the apartment and office buildings of the 1950s, the Historisches Museum and the Technisches Rathaus of

the 1970s, and finally, the 1980s houses and the arts and cultural centre of the Schirn – together, they mirror the architectural history of the post-war era. Added to this is the row of half-timbered houses that stands as a monument to the lost mediaeval city, and the "Historic Garden" excavation that reveals the Roman and Carolingian past. Not much scope for dreams here, and very little poetry – but Frankfurt gets by with it very well.

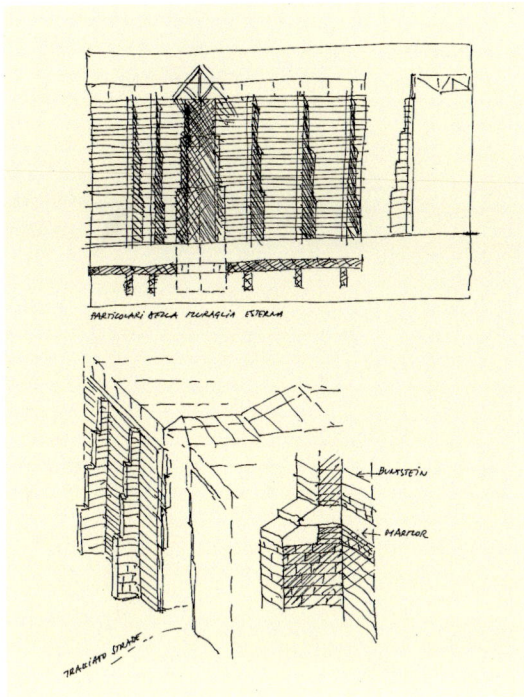

Adolfo Natalini/Superstudio, Projekt für den Römerberg, Skizzen zur Außenwand, aus dem *Codex Klotz*, 1979
Adolfo Natalini/Superstudio, project for Römerberg square, sketches for external wall, from *Codex Klotz*, 1979

1 Bangert, Jansen and Schultes Scholz, "Die Neubauten zwischen Dom und Römer", in *Jahrbuch für Architektur*, edited by Deutsches Architektur Museum, Braunschweig and Wiesbaden 1984, p. 38.
2 Ibid., p. 38.
3 Natalini is one of the founders of the Italian group Superstudio, formed in Florence in 1966. The group came to attention around 1970, above all with its visionary graphic series of megastructures covering the earth. In addition to a large number of drawings for Frankfurt projects, the Deutsches Architektur Museum also has examples of the group's early works, holding more than 80 items spanning the period 1968–1983. A selection can be found in Heinrich Klotz (ed.), *Die Revision der Moderne, Postmoderne Architektur 1960–1980*, exhib. cat. Deutsches Architektur Museum, München 1984, p. 190–205.
4 Adolfo Natalini, "Haus Saalgasse 4", in *Jahrbuch für Architektur*, 1984, p. 47.
5 Adolfo Natalini/Superstudio, *Note in margine al Römerbergprojekt*, 1979, I quaderni bianchi, No. 10, 1979.
6 Stadt Frankfurt am Main, Der Magistrat – Baudezernat (Hrsg.), *Dom-Römerberg-Bereich, Wettbewerb 1980*, Schriftenreihe des Hochbauamtes zu Bauaufgaben der Stadt Frankfurt am Main, Braunschweig 1980.
7 Ibid., p. 118 ff.

Nachkriegszeit wider. Ergänzend dazu findet man als Denkmal für das Untergegangene die Fachwerkzeile, die an das, was hier im Mittelalter stand, erinnert, und den ›Historischen Garten‹, der auf die tiefer liegenden Schichten der römischen und karolingischen Geschichte des Orts verweist. Nicht viel zum Träumen, kaum Poesie – aber Frankfurt kann gut damit leben.

Adolfo Natalini/Superstudio, Projekt für den Römerberg, Skizzen zu Grundriss und Seitenansicht, aus dem *Codex Klotz*, 1979
Adolfo Natalini/Superstudio, project for Römerberg square, sketches for ground plan and side view, from *Codex Klotz*, 1979

1 Bangert, Jansen, Scholz, Schultes, *Die Neubauten zwischen Dom und Römer,* in: *Jahrbuch für Architektur,* hrsg. vom Deutschen Architektur Museum, Braunschweig und Wiesbaden 1984, S. 38.
2 Ebenda, S. 38.
3 Natalini ist einer der Gründer der italienischen Gruppe Superstudio, die sich 1966 in Florenz zusammenfand. Bekannt wurde die Gruppe um 1970 vor allem mit ihren visionären Grafikserien, in denen Megastrukturen die Erde überziehen. Das Deutsche Architektur Museum besitzt neben zahlreichen Zeichnungen für Frankfurter Projekte auch Beispiele der frühen Arbeiten. Der Bestand umfasst mehr als achtzig Objekte aus der Zeit von 1968 bis 1983. Eine Auswahl findet man in: Heinrich Klotz (Hrsg.), *Die Revision der Moderne, Postmoderne Architektur 1960–1980*, Ausst. Kat. Deutsches Architektur Museum, München 1984, S. 190–205.
4 Adolfo Natalini, *Haus Saalgasse 4,* in: *Jahrbuch für Architektur*, wie Anm. 1, S. 47.
5 Adolfo Natalini/Superstudio, *Note in margine al Römerbergprojekt, 1979*, I quaderni bianchi, Nr. 10, 1979.
6 Stadt Frankfurt am Main, Der Magistrat – Baudezernat (Hrsg.), *Dom-Römerberg-Bereich, Wettbewerb 1980,* Schriftenreihe des Hochbauamtes zu Bauaufgaben der Stadt Frankfurt am Main, Braunschweig 1980.
7 Ebenda, S. 118 ff.

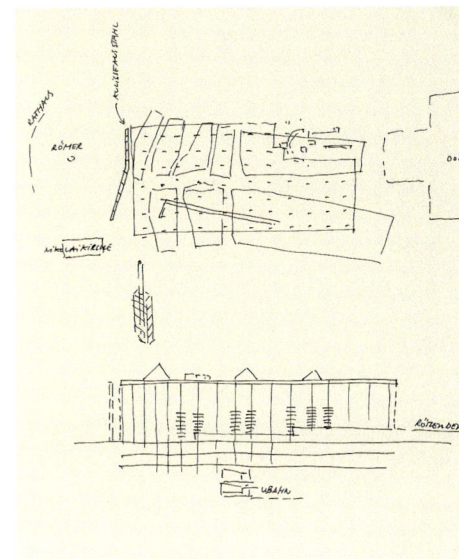

DAM Jahresbericht 2003/04
DAM Annual Report 2003–04

Das Deutsche Architektur Museum (DAM) zeigte 2003/04 folgende
große Ausstellungen:
**In 2003–04 the Deutsches Architektur Museum (DAM) hosted the following
exhibitions:**

■ Bawa – Genius of the place. An Architect of Sri Lanka
Bawa – Genius of the place. An Architect of Sri Lanka
24.07.2004–17.10.2004

■ Stanley Kubrick
Stanley Kubrick
In Kooperation mit dem Deutschen Filmmuseum
In cooperation with the Deutsches Filmmuseum
31.03.2004–04.07.2004

■ Städtebaulicher und architektonischer Realisierungswettbewerb
für den Neubau der Europäischen Zentralbank in Frankfurt am Main
**Urban Planning and Architectural Design Competition for the New
ECB Premises in Frankfurt/Main**
21.02.2004–14.03.2004

■ leicht weit Light Structures. Jörg Schlaich Rudolf Bergermann
leicht weit Light Structures. Jörg Schlaich Rudolf Bergermann
22.11.2003–08.02.2004

In der Aktuellen Galerie des DAM waren folgende Ausstellungen zu sehen:
The following exhibitions were shown at the DAM's Aktuelle Galerie:

■ Internationaler Hochhaus Preis 2004
The International Highrise Award 2004
12.06.2004–11.07.2004

■ Wasa Marjanov. Theater Boxes
Wasa Marjanov. Theater Boxes
28.04.2004–30.05.2004

■ Mies van der Rohe Award 2003.
Der Preis der EU für zeitgenössische Architektur
**Mies van der Rohe Award 2003.
European Union Prize for Contemporary Architecture**
03.03.2004–11.04.2004

■ Günther Domenig. Steinhaus
Günther Domenig. Stone House
14.01.2004–22.02.2004

■ BAUgeSTELLE. Fotografien von Uwe Lohrer
BAUgeSTELLE. Photographs by Uwe Lohrer
26.11.2003–04.01.2004

■ Mach's noch einmal. Was ich schon immer abreißen wollte
Do It again. What I Always Wanted to Have Torn down
15.10.2003–16.11.2003

■ Archigram – Träume vom gebauten Glück
Archigram – Happy Architectural Dreams
03.09.2003–05.10.2003

Dauerausstellung:
Permanent exhibition:

■ Von der Urhütte zum Wolkenkratzer
From Primordial Hut to Skyscraper

Kleinere Ausstellung:
Smaller exhibition:

■ Große Häuser, kleine Häuser.
Ausgezeichnete Architektur in Hessen 1998–2003
**Buildings Small and Large.
Award-Winning Architecture in Hesse 1998–2003**
11.10.2003–09.11.2003

Zahlreiche Vorträge und Symposien widmeten sich aktuellen Fragen
der Architektur:
**Various lectures and symposia devoted to current topics
in architecture:**

■ Große Architekten. Vortragsreihe
Great Architects. Lecture series
Mario Botta: 02.09.2004 Dominique Perrault: 06.05.2004
Álvaro Siza: 04.03.2004 Glenn Murcutt: 13.11.2003

■ Von der Baustelle: Eine Diskussionsreihe vor Ort.
Moderation: Ingeborg Flagge
**From the Building Site: An On-location Discussion Event.
Chaired by Ingeborg Flagge**
Lufthansa Hauptverwaltung Frankfurt am Main **Lufthansa Headquarters
Frankfurt/Main**: 14.05.2004
Mit **with** Klaus Frankenheim, Klaus Dreyer
Ufo Frankfurt: 19.02.2004
Mit **with** Albert Dietz, Ardi Goldmann, Michael Kummer
Waldstadion: 27.11.2003
Mit **with** Volkwin Marg, Klaus Kröll, István Tyukodi
Main Forum: 09.09.2003
Mit **with** Helmut Kleine Kraneburg, Oliver Bäumler, Dieter von Lüpke
Büro- und Wohnbebauung Bockenheimer Landstraße **Office and
Apartment Development Bockenheimer Landstrasse**: 17.07.2003
Mit **with** Jo. Franzke, Gerhard Hilke, Angelika Remmert-Stuckmann

■ Planungen für Olympia Leipzig 2012
Plans for Leipzig's 2012 Olympics Bid
23.06.2004
Vortrag von **lecture by** Friedbert Greif und **and** Engelbert Lütke Daltrup

■ Podiumsdiskussion Europäische Zentralbank
Panel Discussion ECB Premises
05.03.2004
Mit **with** Christoph Mohr, Dieter von Lüpke, Thomas Rinderspacher,
D. W. Dreysse, Moderation **chaired by** Peter Cachola Schmal

■ Konferenz leicht weit Light Structures
Conference leicht weit Light Structures
09.02.2004
Mit **with** Johann Eisele, Burghard Pahl, Jürg Conzett, Jörg Schlaich
Moderation **chaired by** Annette Bögle und **and** Peter Cachola Schmal

■ Architektur als plastisches Gebet –
der mexikanische Künstler Mathias Goeritz
Architecture as Sculptural Prayer –
the Mexican Artist Mathias Goeritz
03.12.2003
Vortrag von **lecture by** Maria Leonor Cuahonte de Rodriguez

■ Mit Bauten Staat machen
Architecture as Statement
29.10.2003
Vortrag von **lecture by** Florian Mausbach

■ 2. Symposium – Marktplätze des Wissens.
Neue Bibliotheksbauten in Europa und den USA
2nd Symposium – Marketplaces of Knowledge.
New Library Buildings in Europe and the United States
08.10.2003
Es wurden vorgestellt die Stadtbibliothek in Ulm durch
Gottfried Böhm und Jürgen Lange sowie die Universitätsbibliothek Bozen
durch Matthias Bischoff, Robert Azzola und Franz Berger, Moderation:
Ursula Kleefisch-Jobst
Presenting: the Ulm Municipal Library by Gottfried Böhm and Jürgen Lange
and the University Library Bolzano by Matthias Bischoff, Robert Azzola
and Franz Berger; Chaired by Ursula Kleefisch-Jobst.

■ Symposium *Neue Kirchen in Deutschland* anlässlich
der Präsentation des *DAM Jahrbuchs 2003*
Symposium *New Churches in Germany*
to coincide with the launch of the *DAM Annual 2003*
26.09.2003
Folgende Projekte wurden vorgestellt: Pfarrkirche St. Theodor, Köln,
von Paul Böhm; Pfarrzentrum St. Franziskus, Regensburg,
von Ulrich Königs; Doppelkirche für zwei Konfessionen, Freiburg,
von Susanne Gross. Moderation: Karin Leydecker
The following projects were presented: Parish Church of St Theodore,
Cologne, by Paul Böhm; Parish Community Centre of St Francis,
Regensburg, by Ulrich Königs; Dual Denominational Church, Freiburg,
by Susanne Gross. Chaired by Karin Leydecker

■ »Die Seele und ihr Zelt« – Über Architektur und Ethik
»The Soul and its Tent« – on Architecture and Ethics
16.09.2003
Vortrag von **lecture by** Jan Teunen

■ Think Design. World Cultural Center New York
Think Design. World Cultural Center New York
12.09.2003
Vortrag von **lecture by** Jörg Schlaich und **and** Rafael Viñoly

■ Bücher ohne Bilder. Symposium zur Ausstellung *City Scape East*
Books without Pictures. Symposium on the *City Scape East* Exhibition
16.07.2003
Mit **with** Jana Hensel und **and** Katja Lange-Müller
Moderation **chaired by** Hanne Kulessa

Folgende Kataloge und Veröffentlichungen wurden erarbeitet:
The following catalogues and publications were produced:

■ *Bawa – Genius of the place. An Architect of Sri Lanka*
Bawa – Genius of the place. An Architekt of Sri Lanka
von David Robson, hrsg. von Ingeborg Flagge, Frankfurt am Main, 2004
By David Robson, edited by Ingeborg Flagge, Frankfurt/Main, 2004

■ *Archigram – Träume vom gebauten Glück*
Archigram – Happy Architectural Dreams
hrsg. vom DAM, Frankfurt am Main 2003
Edited by DAM, Frankfurt/Main 2003

■ *leicht weit Light Structures. Jörg Schlaich Rudolf Bergermann*
leicht weit Light Structures. Jörg Schlaich Rudolf Bergermann
hrsg. von Annette Bögle, Peter Cachola Schmal und
Ingeborg Flagge, München 2003
Edited by Annette Bögle, Peter Cachola Schmal and
Ingeborg Flagge, Munich 2003

■ *DAM Jahrbuch 2003. Architektur in Deutschland*
DAM Annual 2003. Architecture in Germany
hrsg. von Ingeborg Flagge und Annina Götz, München 2003
Edited by Ingeborg Flagge and Annina Götz, Munich 2003

■ *Mach's noch einmal. Was ich schon immer abreißen wollte*
hrsg. vom Lehrstuhl für Gebäudelehre und Entwerfen, Arno Lederer,
Universität Karlsruhe, Frankfurt am Main 2003
Edited by Arno Lederer, Chair of Building Theory and Design,
University of Karlsruhe, Frankfurt/Main 2003

Zu den wichtigsten Neuerwerbungen für das Archiv des DAM zählen:
The most important new acquisitions of the DAM archive include:

Nachlass Dominikus Böhm; Werkarchiv Gottfried Böhm; Werkarchiv Rob
Krier; Nachlass Verena Dietrich; Teilnachlass Günter Bock; Allmann Sattler
Wappner Architekten: Modell und Unterlagen Südwestmetall, Reutlingen;
Nikolaus Bienefeld: Pläne zum Gemeindezentrum Köln-Blumenberg; Erzbi-
schöfliches Bauamt, Freiburg: Modell und Dokumente zum Erzbischöflichen
Archiv, Freiburg; Jauss + Gaupp: Modell Vordach Hauptbahnhof Ulm; Peter
Kulka: zwei Modelle zum Sächsischen Landtag, Dresden (Dauerleihgabe
des Freistaates Sachsen); Schlaich Bergermann und Partner: Modell zum
Seilnetzkühlturm Schmehausen, Modell zur Klappbrücke Kieler Hörn;
Albert Speer & Partner: zwei Modelle, Eiserner Steg und Terminalvorfahrt
Flughafen, Frankfurt am Main; Professor Gerald Staib, Staib Architekten:
Modell zur Gemeindekirche Christus König, Radebeul; Professor Hans
Waechter: Modell zur Autobahnkirche, Medenbach
The estate of Dominikus Böhm; work archives of Gottfried Böhm; work
archives of Rob Krier; the estate of Verena Dietrich; partial estate of Günter Bock;
Allmann Sattler Wappner Architekten: model and documentation of Südwest-
metall Reutlingen; Nikolaus Bienefeld: plans for Community Centre Cologne-
Blumenberg; Erzbischöfliches Bauamt, Freiburg: model and documentation of
Archepiscopal Archives, Freiburg; Jauss + Gaupp: model of cantilevered roof for
Hauptbahnhof Ulm; Peter Kulka: two models of Sächsischer Landtag, Dresden
(on permanent loan from the State of Saxony); Schlaich Bergermann and
Partner: model for Schmehausen network cooling tower, model for Kieler Hörn
bridge; Albert Speer & Partner: two models, Eiserner Steg footbridge and Airport
Terminal approach, both Frankfurt/Main; Professor Gerald Staib, Staib Archi-
tekten: model of Parish Church of Christ the King, Radebeul; Professor Hans
Waechter: model of Highway Chapel, Medenbach

Architekturpreise:
Architecture awards:

Das DAM ist an der Auslobung dreier wichtiger Architekturpreise beteiligt:
an dem alle zwei Jahre auszulobenden ›Licht Architektur Preis‹ und an dem
2002 erstmals von der Messe Frankfurt gestifteten ›Architecture + Technology Award. Europäischer Architekturpreis für Architektur und Technik‹.
Hinzu kam 2003 der von der Stadt Frankfurt am Main ins Leben gerufene
›Internationale Europäische Hochhaus Preis‹, der von der DGZ Deka
Deutsche Kommunalbank finanziert wird. Mit dem Preis werden Hochhäuser
ausgezeichnet, die mindestens 100 Meter hoch sind und bei Redaktions-
schluss der Ausschreibung am 30.11. nicht älter als 24 Monate sind.
The DAM is involved in the presentation of three major architectural awards:
the biannual "Light in Architecture Prize" and the "Architecture + Technology
Award. European Architecture Prize for Architecture and Technology" founded
by Messe Frankfurt in 2002. In 2003 the City of Frankfurt/Main introduced
the "International European Skyscraper Prize", funded by DGZ Deka Deutsche
Kommunalbank, awarded in recognition of high-rises of at least 100 metres
completed no more than 24 months prior to the call for entries on 30.11.

Mäzene und Sponsoren:
Patrons and sponsors:

Alle unsere Aktivitäten im vergangenen Jahr wären ohne die großzügige
Unterstützung zahlreicher Sponsoren nicht möglich gewesen. Seit Anfang
2003 ist Ernst & Young AG Wirtschaftsprüfungsgesellschaft für drei Jahre der
wichtigste Sponsor des DAM. Zu den weiteren Sponsoren, die das Museum
durch Sach- und Geldzuwendungen unterstützt haben, zählen:
None of our activities in the past year would have been possible without
the generous support of our many sponsors. As of the beginning of 2003,
Ernst & Young AG Wirtschaftsprüfungsgesellschaft has become the most
important DAM sponsor, and has committed its support for a period of three
years. Other sponsors who have assisted the museum with professional
and financial assistance include:

ABG Holding; Adler Real Estate Aktiengesellschaft; Akademie der
Architekten- und Stadtplanerkammer Hessen; Amt für Wissenschaft und
Kunst der Stadt Frankfurt am Main; Bilfinger Berger Projektentwicklung
GmbH; Burkhard Leitner Constructiv; Caparol Farben Lacke Bautenschutz
GmbH & Co. Vertriebs KG; DekaBank Deutsche Girozentrale;
Denas Elektrotechnik GmbH; Frankfurter Allgemeine Zeitung; Georg und
Franziska Speyersche Hochschulstiftung; Jo. Franzke Architekten, Frankfurt
am Main; Fraport AG; FSB Franz Schneider Brakel GmbH & Co. KG;
Gesellschaft der Freunde des Deutschen Architektur Museums e.V.; Grohe
Water Technology; Helaba Landesbank Hessen-Thüringen; Hessische
Kulturstiftung; Dieter Köhler, Köhler Architekten, Frankfurt am Main; Alfred
Krupp von Behlen und Halbach Stiftung; Kulturstiftung des Bundes; Kultur-
stiftung der Länder; Messe Frankfurt GmbH; MLP Finanzdienstleistungen AG;
Museumskooperationspool der Stadt Frankfurt am Main; Hilde Riedmüller-
Winzen; Wilhelmi Werke AG; Wilkahn; Ed. Züblin AG; Zumtobel Staff Deutsch-
land Vertriebs-GmbH.

All diesen Förderern, aber auch manchem Mäzen, der ungenannt bleiben
möchte, gilt unser herzlichster Dank.
We owe our heartfelt thanks to all our sponsors as well as to those patrons
who wish to remain anonymous.

Die Autoren
The Authors

Hubertus Adam

*1965. Studium der Kunstgeschichte, Archäologie und Philosophie in Heidelberg. Seit 1992 freiberufliche Tätigkeit als Kunsthistoriker. 1996–1998 Redakteur der Zeitschrift *Bauwelt* in Berlin; seit 1998 Redakteur der Zeitschrift *archithese* in Zürich. Parallel als freier Architekturkritiker tätig, vor allem für die *Neue Zürcher Zeitung*. Zahlreiche Aufsätze und Publikationen zur Architekturgeschichte des 20. Jahrhunderts und zur Architektur der Gegenwart.

Born 1965. Studied art history, archaeology and philosophy at Heidelberg. Freelance art historian since 1992. 1996–1998 editor of the periodical *Bauwelt* in Berlin; since 1998 editor of the periodical *archithese* in Zurich. At the same time freelance architecture critic, mainly for *Neue Zürcher Zeitung*. Has published widely on twentieth-century architectural history and contemporary architecture.

Olaf Bartels

*1959. Studium der Architektur an der Hochschule für bildende Künste, Hamburg; 1987 Diplom. Seit 1984 freiberufliche Tätigkeit als Architekturhistoriker und -journalist. 1989/90 künstlerischer Mitarbeiter an der Hochschule der Künste, Berlin; 1990–1992 wissenschaftlicher Mitarbeiter an der TU Hamburg-Harburg. 1992–1994 Bauleitung eines Wohnungsbauprojekts. 1994–1999 wissenschaftlicher Mitarbeiter an der TU Braunschweig. Tätig als Architekturhistoriker, Architekturjournalist und Hochschullehrer in Hamburg und Berlin.

Born 1959. Studied architecture at the Hochschule für bildende Künste, Hamburg; graduating in 1987. Since 1984 freelance architectural historian and journalist. 1989–90 artistic assistant at the Hochschule der Künste, Berlin; 1990–1992 academic assistant at the TU Hamburg-Harburg. 1992–1994 directed an apartment building project. 1994–1999 academic assistant at the TU Brunswick. Works as an architectural historian, architecture journalist and lecturer in Hamburg and Berlin.

Dieter Bartetzko

*1949. Studium der Kunstgeschichte, Soziologie und Germanistik in Marburg und Berlin; 1984 Promotion über die Theatralik der NS-Architektur. Seit 1994 Redakteur im Feuilleton der *Frankfurter Allgemeinen Zeitung*, Ressort Architektur, Denkmalpflege und Archäologie.

Born 1949. Studied art history, sociology and German literature at Marburg and Berlin; 1984 doctoral thesis on the theatrical aspect of NS architecture. Since 1994 editor of the architecture, conservation and archaeology section of the review pages of *Frankfurter Allgemeine Zeitung*.

Christof Bodenbach

*1960. Schreinerlehre. Studium der Architektur, Germanistik und Innenarchitektur in Darmstadt, Frankfurt am Main, Kassel und Wiesbaden. 1996 Journalistenpreis der Bundesarchitektenkammer und der Zeitschrift *Deutsches Architektenblatt*. Seit 1997 Lehrauftrag an der FH Wiesbaden. 1991–2004 bei der Akademie der Architektenkammer Hessen; seit 2004 Referent für Presse- und Öffentlichkeitsarbeit der Architekten- und Stadtplanerkammer Hessen. Außerordentliches Mitglied im Bund Deutscher Architekten. Regelmäßige Veröffentlichungen zu Architektur und Städtebau. Arbeitet als Journalist in Wiesbaden.

Born 1960. Carpentry apprenticeship. Studied architecture, German literature and interior design in Darmstadt, Frankfurt/Main, Kassel and Wiesbaden. 1996 awarded the journalistic prize of the Bundesarchitektenkammer and of the periodical *Deutsches Architektenblatt*. Since 1997 lectureship at FH Wiesbaden. 1991–2004 at the Akademie der Architektenkammer Hessen; since 2004 press and PR officer for the Architekten- und Stadtplanerkammer Hessen. Extraordinary member of the Bund Deutscher Architekten. Regular publications on architecture and urban planning. Works as a journalist in Wiesbaden.

Harald Bodenschatz

*1946. Studium der Soziologie, Politikwissenschaft, Psychologie und Volkswirtschaftslehre an der LMU München und der FU Berlin; 1978 Promotion; 1986 Habilitation. Seit 1980 planerische Praxis in der Stadterneuerung. Seit 1995 Professur für Planungs- und Architektursoziologie an der TU Berlin. Zahlreiche Veröffentlichungen zur Stadterneuerung, zum postmodernen Stadtumbau, zum suburbanen Städtebau sowie zur Stadtplanungs- und Stadtbaugeschichte. Stadtsoziologe und Stadtplaner in Berlin.

Born 1946. Studied sociology, political science, psychology and economics at LMU Munich and FU Berlin; 1978 doctorate; 1986 habilitation. Since 1980 urban redevelopment planning practice. Since 1995 professorship in the sociology of planning and architecture at TU Berlin. Has published widely on urban regeneration, post-modern urban redevelopment, suburban planning, and the history of town planning and urban development. Urban sociologist and town planner in Berlin.

Hans-Jürgen Breuning

*1963. Studium der Architektur in Karlsruhe, Stuttgart und Florenz; 1992 Diplom; 1999 Promotion. 1992–1999 wissenschaftlicher Mitarbeiter an der Universität Stuttgart, 1999–2001 Assistent am Institut für Baukunst der TU Graz, 2002/03 Lehrtätigkeit an der Universität Karlsruhe. Seit 2000 tätig im Büro Prof. Lederer+Ragnarsdóttir+Oei, Stuttgart. Seit 2001 Kurator in der Architekturgalerie am Weißenhof, Stuttgart. Autor zahlreicher Publikationen zu Architektur und Städtebau.

Born 1963. Studied architecture in Karlsruhe, Stuttgart and Florence; graduated 1992; 1999 doctorate. 1992–1999 academic assistant at the University of Stuttgart, 1999–2001 assistant at the Institut für Baukunst der TU Graz, 2002–03 taught at the University of Karlsruhe. Since 2000 work at the practice of Prof. Lederer+Ragnarsdóttir+Oei, Stuttgart. Since 2001 curator at the Architekturgalerie am Weißenhof, Stuttgart. Author of several publications on architecture and urban planning.

Martina Düttmann

*1938. Studium der Architektur an der TU Berlin; 1968 Diplom. 1966–1970 Redakteurin der Zeitschrift *Bauwelt*, 1972–1975 Curriculumplanung für die FU Berlin, 1975 Gründung des eigenen Architekturbuchverlags Abakon, 1979 in Archibook umbenannt. 1988–1995 Lektorin des Architekturbuchprogramms im Birkhäuser Verlag. 1996–2000 Herausgeberin des *Bauwelt Berlin Annual*. Seither freiberuflich tätig als Autorin und Übersetzerin von Architekturtexten. Lebt in Berlin.

Born 1938. Studied architecture at the TU Berlin; graduated 1968. 1966–1970 editor of the periodical *Bauwelt*, 1972–1975 curricular planning for the FU Berlin; 1975 founded her own architectural publishing house Abakon, renamed Archibook in 1979. 1988–1995 editor of the architecture programme of the publishing house Birkhäuser Verlag. 1996–2000 editor of *Bauwelt Berlin Annual*. Since then, freelance author and translator of texts on architecture. Lives in Berlin.

Ingeborg Flagge

Studium der Philosophie, Geschichte, Archäologie, Ägyptologie, Alten Geschichte und Baugeschichte an der Universität Köln und am University College London; 1971 Promotion. 1978–1983 Bundesgeschäftsführerin des Bundes Deutscher Architekten. 1974–1998 Chefredakteurin der Zeitschrift *Der Architekt*. 1995–2000 Professur für Baugeschichte an der HTWK Leipzig. Seit 2000 Direktorin des Deutschen Architektur Museums in Frankfurt am Main. Tätigkeit als freie Journalistin und Architekturpublizistin.

Studied philosophy, history, archaeology, Egyptology, classical history and history of architecture at the University of Cologne and at University College London; 1971 doctorate. 1978–1983 federal manager of the Bund Deutscher Architekten. 1974–1998 editor-in-chief of the periodical *Der Architekt*.

1995–2000 professor of architectural history at the HTWK Leipzig. Since 2000 Director of the Deutsches Architektur Museum in Frankfurt/Main. Works as a freelance journalist and writer on architecture.

Kaye Geipel

Studium der Architektur und Philosophie in Stuttgart, Paris und Frankfurt am Main. Architekt und Architekturhistoriker mit Schwerpunkt zweite Hälfte 20. Jahrhundert. Redakteur der Zeitschrift *Bauwelt*. Herausgeber und Autor zahlreicher Veröffentlichungen. Lebt in Berlin.
Studied architecture and philosophy in Stuttgart, Paris and Frankfurt/Main. Architect and architectural historian specialising in the second half of the twentieth century. Editor of the periodical *Bauwelt*. Editor and author of many publications. Lives in Berlin.

Annina Götz

*1976. Studium der Architektur an der Universität Stuttgart und der Hochschule der Künste, Berlin; 2001 Diplom in Stuttgart. Seit 2000 freiberufliche Mitarbeiterin des Deutschen Architektur Museums in Frankfurt am Main. Tätig als freie Architekturkritikerin, lebt in Hamburg.
Born 1976. Studied architecture at the University of Stuttgart and Hochschule der Künste, Berlin; graduated 2001 in Stuttgart. Since 2000 freelance work for the Deutsches Architektur Museum in Frankfurt/Main. Works as a freelance architecture critic. Lives in Hamburg.

Oliver G. Hamm

*1963. Studium der Architektur an der FH Darmstadt; 1989 Diplom. 1989–1992 Redakteur der *db – deutsche bauzeitung* und 1992–1998 der Zeitschrift *Bauwelt*. Seit 2000 Chefredakteur der Zeitschrift *Deutsches Architektenblatt*. Deutscher Preis für Denkmalschutz 2003 (Journalistenpreis). Autor zahlreicher Veröffentlichungen zu Architektur-, Stadtplanungs- und Stadterneuerungsthemen. Lebt in Berlin.
Born 1963. Studied architecture at the FH Darmstadt; graduated 1989. 1989–1992 editor of *db – deutsche bauzeitung* and 1992–1998 of the periodical *Bauwelt*. Since 2000 editor-in-chief of the periodical *Deutsches Architektenblatt*. Awarded the Deutscher Preis für Denkmalschutz 2003 (journalistic prize). Has published widely on the subjects of architecture, urban planning and urban regeneration. Lives in Berlin.

Falk Jaeger

*1950. Studium der Architektur und Kunstgeschichte in Braunschweig, Stuttgart und Tübingen; 1977 Diplom an der Universität Stuttgart. 1983–1988 wissenschaftlicher Mitarbeiter am Institut für Architektur- und Stadtgeschichte der TU Berlin. 1993 Promotion. 1993–2000 Hochschuldozent, 2000 apl. Professor für Architekturtheorie und Architekturkritik an der TU Dresden. 1993 Journalistenpreis der Bundesarchitektenkammer und der Zeitschrift *Deutsches Architektenblatt*. 2001 Literaturpreis des Verbands Deutscher Architekten- und Ingenieurvereine. Tätig als freier Autor, Kurator und Architekturkritiker in Berlin.
Born 1950. Studied architecture and art history in Brunswick, Stuttgart and Tübingen; graduated 1977 from the University of Stuttgart. 1983–1988 academic assistant at the Institute for Architecture and Urban History of the TU Berlin. 1993 doctorate. 1993–2000 lectureship, 2000 professorship in architectural theory and architecture criticism at the TU Dresden. 1993 awarded the journalistic prize of the Bundesarchitektenkammer and the periodical *Deutsches Architektenblatt*. 2001 awarded the literature prize of the Verband Deutscher Architekten- and Ingenieurvereine. Works as a freelance author, curator and architecture critic in Berlin.

Gert Kähler

*1942. Studium der Architektur an der TU Berlin; 1969 Diplom. 1969–1976 Mitarbeit in Architekturbüros in Hamburg, Walsrode und Dortmund. 1976–1986 Hochschulassistent an der Universität Hannover. 1981 Promotion; 1985 Habilitation. Gastprofessuren in Braunschweig, Berlin und Aachen. Lehraufträge an der Universität Hannover, Universität Hamburg und der Hochschule für Angewandte Wissenschaften, Hamburg. Seit 1988 freiberuflich als Journalist und Wissenschaftler tätig. Lebt in Hamburg.

Born 1942. Studied architecture at the TU Berlin; graduated 1969. 1969–1976 worked in architectural practices in Hamburg, Walsrode and Dortmund. 1976–1986 assistant at the University of Hanover. 1981 doctorate; 1985 habilitation. Visiting professor at Brunswick, Berlin and Aachen. Lectureships at the Universities of Hanover and Hamburg and at the Hochschule für Angewandte Wissenschaften, Hamburg. Since 1988 freelance journalist and scholar. Lives in Hamburg.

Paul Kahlfeldt

*1956. Lehre als Bau- und Möbeltischler. Studium der Architektur an der TU Berlin; 1984 Diplom. 1987 Gründung eines eigenen Architekturbüros mit Petra Kahlfeldt. 1988–1992 Büroleiter des Berliner Büros von Prof. Josef Paul Kleihues. Seit 1999 Professur für Entwerfen, Baukonstruktion und Gebäudetechnologie an der TU Kaiserslautern. Seit 1999 im Vorstand des Deutschen Werkbunds Berlin; seit 2000 Mitglied der Internationalen Bauakademie Berlin.
Born 1956. Carpentry and cabinet making apprenticeship. Studied architecture at the TU Berlin; graduated 1984. 1987 founded his own architectural practice with Petra Kahlfeldt. 1988–1992 chief of staff of the Berlin office of Prof. Josef Paul Kleihues. Since 1999 professor for Design, Building Construction and Building Technology at the TU Kaiserslautern. Since 1999 member of the board of the Deutscher Werkbund Berlin; since 2000 member of the Internationale Bauakademie Berlin.

Ursula Kleefisch-Jobst

*1956. Studium der Kunstgeschichte, Archäologie und Germanistik in Bonn, München und Rom; 1986 Promotion. 1985–1988 Forschungsprojekt zur italienischen Renaissance-Zeichnung an der Bibliotheca Hertziana, Rom. 1989/90 Mitarbeiterin am Landesamt für Denkmalpflege, Berlin. Seit 1991 freie Architekturkritikerin. Seit 2001 freie Kuratorin am Deutschen Architektur Museum in Frankfurt am Main. Zahlreiche Veröffentlichungen zu Architektur und Städtebau.
Born 1956. Studied art history, archaeology and German literature in Bonn, Munich and Rome; 1986 doctorate. 1985–1988 research project on Italian Renaissance drawing at the Bibliotheca Hertziana, Rome. 1989–90 assistant at the Landesamt für Denkmalpflege, Berlin. Since 1991 freelance architecture critic. Since 2001 freelance curator for the Deutsches Architektur Museum in Frankfurt/Main. Has published widely on architecture and urban planning.

Niklas Maak

*1972. Studium der Kunstgeschichte in Hamburg und Paris; 1998 Promotion. 1999–2001 Redakteur für Architektur im Feuilleton der *Süddeutschen Zeitung*. Seit 2001 Redakteur für den Bereich Kunst im Feuilleton der *Frankfurter Allgemeinen Zeitung*.
Born 1972. Studied art history in Hamburg and Paris; 1998 doctorate. 1999–2001 editor for architecture in the review pages of *Süddeutsche Zeitung*. Since 2001 editor of the art section of the review pages of *Frankfurter Allgemeine Zeitung*.

Wolfgang Pehnt

*1931. Studium der Kunstgeschichte, Germanistik und Philosophie in Marburg, München und Frankfurt am Main; 1957 Promotion. 1957–1963 Lektor im Verlag Gerd Hatje, Stuttgart. 1963–1995 Leiter der Abteilung Literatur und Kunst beim Deutschlandfunk, Köln. Seit 1995 Professor an der Ruhr-Universität Bochum. Mitglied der Akademie der Künste, Berlin, und der Bayerischen Akademie der Schönen Künste, München. Zahlreiche Auszeichnungen. Veröffentlichungen und Buchpublikationen zur Architekturgeschichte des 19. und 20. Jahrhunderts.
Born 1931. Studied art history, German literature and philosophy in Marburg, Munich and Frankfurt/Main; 1957 doctorate. 1957–1963 editor in the publishing house of Gerd Hatje, Stuttgart. 1963–1995 head of the department of literature and art at the broadcasting company Deutschlandfunk, Cologne. Since 1995 professor at the Ruhr University in Bochum. Member of the Akademie der Künste, Berlin, and the Bayerische Akademie der Schönen Künste, Munich. Has won several awards. Publications on the history of nineteenth- and twentieth-century architecture.

Andreas Ruby
*1966. Studium der Kunstgeschichte an der Universität zu Köln sowie der Theorie und Geschichte der Architektur an der Ecole Spéciale d'Architecture Paris bei Paul Virilio und der Columbia University in New York bei Bernard Tschumi. Seit 2003 Gastprofessur für Architekturtheorie und Entwerfen an der Universität Kassel. Gründete 2001 mit Ilka Ruby die Agentur für Architektur-vermittlung textbild und schreibt Essays, publiziert Bücher, kuratiert Ausstellungen, organisiert Symposien und berät Institutionen im Kontext von zeitgenössischer Architektur.
Born 1966. Studied art history at the University of Cologne, theory and history of architecture at the Ecole Spéciale d'Architecture Paris under Paul Virilio, and at Columbia University in New York under Bernard Tschumi. Since 2003 visiting professor for architectural theory and design at the University of Kassel. 2001, together with Ilka Ruby, founded the textbild architectural agency writing essays, publishing books, curating exhibitions, organising symposia and advising institutions in the context of contemporary architecture.

Ilka Ruby
*1969. Studium der Architektur an der RWTH Aachen und TU Wien; 1997 Diplom. Nach der Tätigkeit als Architektin in verschiedenen Architektur-büros arbeitet sie jetzt als Grafikdesignerin, Herausgeberin und Autorin. Gründete 2001 mit Andreas Ruby die Agentur für Architekturvermittlung textbild und schreibt Essays, publiziert Bücher, kuratiert Ausstellungen, organisiert Symposien und berät Institutionen im Kontext von zeitgenössi-scher Architektur.
Born 1969. Studied architecture at RWTH Aachen and TU Vienna; graduated 1997. After working as an architect in various architectural firms, she now works as a graphic designer, editor and author. 2001, together with Andreas Ruby, founded the textbild architectural agency writing essays, publishing books, curating exhibitions, organising symposia and advising institutions in the context of contemporary architecture.

Enrico Santifaller
*1960. Studium der Geschichte und Soziologie in München. Volontariat bei der *Frankfurter Neuen Presse*. 1995 Redakteur der *Offenbach-Post*; 1997–2001 Online-Redakteur der *Deutschen Bauzeitschrift DBZ*. Seit 1994 Architekturjournalist sowie Herausgeber von Monografien zu zeitge-nössischen Architekten. Außerordentliches Mitglied im Bund Deutscher Architekten. Lebt in Frankfurt am Main.
Born 1960. Studied history and sociology in Munich. Internship with *Frank-furter Neue Presse*. 1995 editor of *Offenbach-Post*; 1997–2001 online editor of *Deutsche Bauzeitschrift DBZ*. Since 1994 architectural journalist and editor of monographic studies on contemporary architects. Extraordinary member of the Bund Deutscher Architekten. Lives in Frankfurt/Main.

Axel Simon
*1966. Schriftsetzerlehre. Studium der Architektur an der FH Düsseldorf und der HdK Berlin; 1996 Diplom in Düsseldorf. 1998–2000 Nachdiplomstudium der Geschichte und Theorie der Architektur an der ETH Zürich. 1996–1999 selbstständige und angestellte Tätigkeit als Architekt in Berlin, Düsseldorf, Freiburg und Zürich. Seit 1999 Assistent an der ETH Zürich, seit 2002 am Lehrstuhl für Entwurf und Konstruktion von Peter Märkli und Markus Peter. Seit 2000 Architekturkritiker beim *Tages-Anzeiger*, Zürich.
Born 1966. Typesetting apprenticeship. Studied architecture at the FH Düssel-dorf and the HdK Berlin; graduated 1996 from Düsseldorf. 1998–2000 postgraduate studies in history and theory of architecture at the ETH Zurich. 1996–1999 worked as an architect in Berlin, Düsseldorf, Freiburg and Zurich. Since 1999 assistant at the ETH Zurich; since 2002 assistant to the Chair for Design and Construction held by Peter Märkli and Markus Peter. Since 2000 architecture critic for the *Tages-Anzeiger*, Zurich.

Rudolf Stegers
*1952. Studium der Germanistik und Romanistik in Münster und Berlin. Freier Kritiker und Redakteur in Sachen Architektur. Mitarbeit bei einigen Ausstellungen. Lebt in Berlin.
Born 1952. Studied German and Romance language and literature in Munster and Berlin. Freelance critic and editor in the field of architecture. Has been involved in several exhibitions. Lives in Berlin.

Wolfgang Jean Stock
*1948. Studium der Geschichte, Politischen Wissenschaft und Soziologie in Frankfurt am Main und Erlangen. 1978–1985 Direktor des Kunstvereins München. 1986–1993 Architekturkritiker der *Süddeutschen Zeitung*. 1994–1998 stellvertretender Chefredakteur der Zeitschrift *Baumeister*. Außerordentliches Mitglied im Bund Deutscher Architekten. Arbeitet als freier Journalist und Buchautor in München.
Born 1948. Studied history, political science and sociology in Frankfurt/Main and Erlangen. 1978–1985 director of Kunstverein München. 1986–1993 archi-tecture critic of *Süddeutsche Zeitung*. 1994–1998 deputy editor-in-chief of the periodical *Baumeister*. Extraordinary member of the Bund Deutscher Architekten. Works as a freelance journalist and author in Munich.

Christian Thomas
*1955. Studium der Germanistik, Philosophie und Kunstgeschichte. 1986–1993 freier Journalist. Seit 1993 Redakteur im Feuilleton der *Frankfurter Rundschau*, verantwortlich für Architektur und Städtebau; seit 2003 stell-vertretender Feuilletonleiter. Lebt in Frankfurt am Main.
Born 1955. Studied German literature, philosophy and art history. 1986–1993 freelance journalist. Since 1993 editor of the architecture and town planning section of the *Frankfurter Rundschau* review pages; since 2003 deputy chief editor of the review. Lives in Frankfurt/Main.

Inge Wolf
*1955. Studium der Kunstgeschichte in Frankfurt am Main. Seit 1994 Mit-arbeiterin des Deutschen Architektur Museums in Frankfurt am Main, seit 1996 Betreuung der Plan- und Modellsammlung.
Born 1955. Studied art history in Frankfurt/Main. Since 1994 member of staff at the Deutsches Architektur Museum in Frankfurt/Main, since 1996 in charge of the collection of plans and models.

Abbildungsnachweis
Illustration Credits

- Umschlag **Cover**
Soundchambers, architektonisch-musikalischer Pavillon, Porto, Portugal
Soundchambers, architectural and musical pavilion, Porto, Portugal
Architekten **Architects**: Nikolaus Hirsch/Michel Müller
Fotografie **Photography**: John Lau, Frankfurt am Main

- Frontispiz **Frontispiece**
Umbau und Aufstockung Waterloohain 9, Hamburg
Conversion and extension, Waterloohain 9, Hamburg
Architekt **Architect**: Carsten Roth
Fotografie **Photography**: Klaus Frahm/artur, Köln **Cologne**

- **Essays**
- **Essays**

- Essay Wolfgang Pehnt
8 Celia Körber-Leupold, Erftstadt
9, 12–16 Wolfgang Pehnt, Köln **Cologne**
10 Barbara Burg/Oliver Schuh, Palladium Photodesign, Köln **Cologne**
11 Reinhard Görner/artur, Köln **Cologne**

- Essay Paul Kahlfeldt
19 Hülsdell & Hallegger, Halberstadt
20 Rainer Mader, Schleiden
23 Rainer Viertlböck/artur, Köln **Cologne**
24 Stefan Müller, Berlin

- Essay Harald Bodenschatz
27–29, 31, 32 Harald Bodenschatz, Berlin
30 Thilo Petri, Berlin

- **Rekonstruktion in Deutschland**
- **Reconstruction in Germany**

- Zwischenseiten 34/35 **Opening Pages 34–35**
Wohn- und Geschäftshaus Am Neuen Markt 5, Potsdam
Apartment and office building, Am Neuen Markt 5, Potsdam
Architekt **Architect**: Nicola Fortmann-Drühe
Fotografie **Photography**: Barbara Burg/Oliver Schuh,
Palladium Photodesign, Köln **Cologne**

- Wohn- und Geschäftshaus Am Neuen Markt 5, Potsdam
Apartment and office building, Am Neuen Markt 5, Potsdam
36–41 Barbara Burg/Oliver Schuh, Palladium Photodesign, Köln **Cologne**

- Maximilianhöfe, Neubebauung am Marstallplatz, München
Maximilianhöfe, new development at Marstallplatz, Munich
42–49 Claus Graubner, Berlin

- Firmenrepräsentanz Unter den Linden 1, Berlin
Company representation, Unter den Linden 1, Berlin
50–57 Rainer Mader, Schleiden

- **Architektur in Iaus Deutschland**
- **Architecture in I from Germany**

- Zwischenseiten 58/59 **Opening Pages 58–59**
Institut für Physik der Humboldt-Universität, Berlin
Institute of Physics at Humboldt University, Berlin
Architekten **Architects**: Augustin und Frank
Fotografie **Photography**: Werner Huthmacher/artur, Köln **Cologne**

- Institut für Physik der Humboldt-Universität, Berlin
Institute of Physics at Humboldt University, Berlin
60–67 Werner Huthmacher/artur, Köln **Cologne**

- Vertriebs- und Servicezentrum, Ditzingen
Customer and administration building, Ditzingen
69, 73–75 David Franck, Ostfildern
71, 72 Margherita Spiluttini, Wien **Vienna**, Österreich **Austria**

- Marie-Elisabeth-Lüders-Haus mit Paul-Löbe-Haus,
Deutscher Bundestag, Berlin
Marie-Elisabeth Lüders House with Paul Löbe House,
Deutscher Bundestag, Berlin
77, 80/81 Stefan Müller, Berlin
79, 81–87 Ulrich Schwarz, Berlin

- Wohnhaus im Hinterhof, Düsseldorf
One-family-house in rear courtyard, Düsseldorf
88–93 Michael Reisch, Düsseldorf

- Bender, Wohn- und/oder Geschäftshaus, Berlin
Bender, apartment/office building, Berlin
94–101 Klemens Ortmeyer, Braunschweig **Brunswick**

Die Rechte für Zeichnungen liegen bei den jeweiligen Architekten.
The copyright holders as regards drawings are the respective architects.

Die Herausgeber und der Verlag danken den Inhabern von Bildrechten,
die freundlicherweise ihre Erlaubnis zur Veröffentlichung gegeben
haben. Etwaige weitere Inhaber von Bildrechten bitten wir, sich mit den
Herausgebern in Verbindung zu setzen.
**The editors and the publisher would like to thank those copyright
owners who have kindly given their permission for material to be
published in this volume. The editors would be pleased to hear from
any copyright holder who could not be traced.**

Impressum
Imprint

Herausgegeben von **Edited by**
Ingeborg Flagge und **and** Annina Götz
im Auftrag des **on behalf of** Dezernats für Kultur und Freizeit,
Amt für Wissenschaft und Kunst
der Stadt Frankfurt am Main

Redaktion **Editing** Annina Götz

© Prestel Verlag, München · Berlin · London · New York, 2004
© Deutsches Architektur Museum, Frankfurt am Main, 2004
© Für die abgebildeten Werke bei den Architekten und Künstlern,
ihren Erben oder Rechtsnachfolgern
For the artworks with the architects and artists, their heirs or assigns

Urhebernennungen stammen von den beteiligten Architekten selbst.
Für die Richtigkeit dieser Angaben übernehmen das
Deutsche Architektur Museum
und der Prestel Verlag keine Gewähr.
**Names of copyright holders of the material used have been
supplied by the architects themselves. Neither the Deutsches Architektur Museum nor Prestel Verlag shall be held responsible for any
omissions or inaccurancies.**

Die Deutsche Bibliothek verzeichnet diese Publikation in
Die Deutsche Nationalbibliografie; detaillierte bibliografische Daten
sind im Internet über http://dnb.ddb.de abrufbar.
**The Deutsche Bibliothek holds a record of this publication in the
Deutsche Nationalbibliografie; detailed bibliographical data can
be found under http://dnb.ddb.de**

Library of Congress Control Number is available.

Prestel Verlag
Königinstraße 9
D-80539 München
Telefon +49 (0) 89/38 17 09 0
Telefax +49 (0) 89/38 17 09 35
info@prestel.de
www.prestel.de

Prestel Publishing Ltd.
4 Bloomsbury Place
London, WC1A 2QA
Telefon +44 (0) 20/73 23 50 04
Telefax +44 (0) 20/76 36 80 04

Prestel Publishing
900 Broadway, Suite 603
New York, N.Y. 10003
Telefon +1/212/9 95 27 20
Telefax +1/212/9 95 27 33

www.prestel.com

Deutsches Architektur Museum
Schaumainkai 43
D-60596 Frankfurt am Main
Telefon +49 (0) 69/2 12 3 63 13
Telefax +49 (0) 69/2 12 3 63 86
info.DAM@stadt-frankfurt.de
www.DAM-online.de

Übersetzungen **Translations** Ishbel Flett
(deutsch-englisch **German-English**)

Koordination **Coordination** Ruth Klumpp, Darmstadt
Lektorat **Copyediting** Ruth Klumpp, Darmstadt (deutsch **German**),
Cynthia Hall, Rosenheim (englisch **English**)
Gestaltung und Herstellung **Design and production** Cilly Klotz
Reproduktion **Lithography** Ludwig, Zell am See
Druck und Bindung **Printing and binding** Appl, Wemding

Gedruckt auf chlorfrei gebleichtem Papier
Printed on acid-free paper

Printed in Germany

ISSN 1611-1370
ISBN 3-7913-3172-8